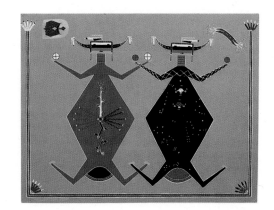

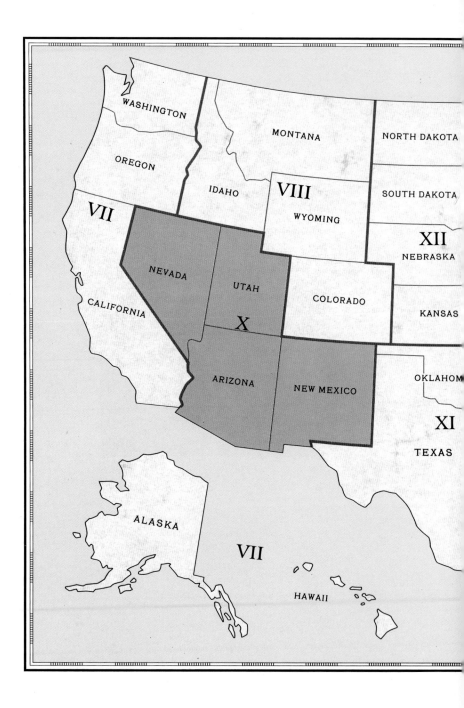

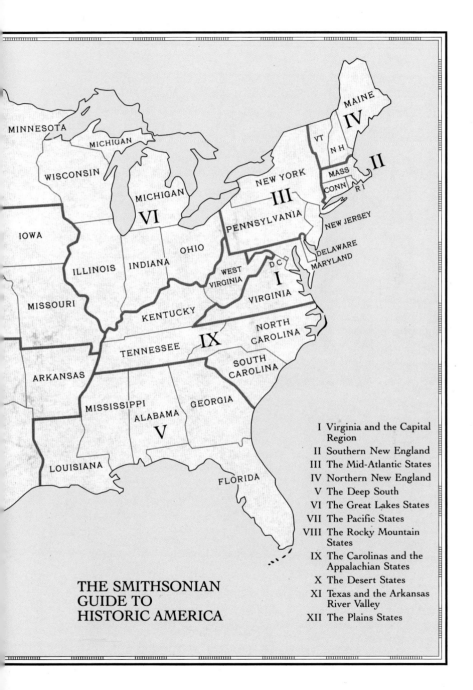

MINNESOTA

MICHIGAN

WISCONSIN

MICHIGAN

VI

IOWA

ILLINOIS INDIANA OHIO

MISSOURI

KENTUCKY

ARKANSAS

TENNESSEE **IX**

MISSISSIPPI ALABAMA GEORGIA

V

LOUISIANA

FLORIDA

MAINE **IV**

VT N H

NEW YORK MASS **II**

CONN R I

III

PENNSYLVANIA NEW JERSEY

DELAWARE
MARYLAND

WEST
VIRGINIA D C **I**

VIRGINIA

NORTH
CAROLINA

SOUTH
CAROLINA

I Virginia and the Capital
 Region
II Southern New England
III The Mid-Atlantic States
IV Northern New England
V The Deep South
VI The Great Lakes States
VII The Pacific States
VIII The Rocky Mountain
 States
IX The Carolinas and the
 Appalachian States
X The Desert States
XI Texas and the Arkansas
 River Valley
XII The Plains States

THE SMITHSONIAN
GUIDE TO
HISTORIC AMERICA

THE
SMITHSONIAN
——— GUIDE TO ———
HISTORIC AMERICA

THE DESERT STATES

TEXT BY
MICHAEL S. DURHAM

EDITORIAL DIRECTOR
ROGER G. KENNEDY
DIRECTOR OF THE NATIONAL MUSEUM
OF AMERICAN HISTORY
OF THE SMITHSONIAN INSTITUTION

Stewart, Tabori & Chang
NEW YORK

All information is accurate as of publication. We suggest contacting the sites prior to a visit to confirm hours of operation.

Published in 1990 by Stewart, Tabori & Chang, Inc., 740 Broadway, New York, NY 10003.

FRONT COVER: Canyon de Chelly, AZ.
HALF-TITLE PAGE: Mother Earth and Father Sky sand painting, Wheelwright Museum of the American Indian, NM.
FRONTISPIECE: Cathedral of Saint Augustine, AZ.
BACK COVER: Piper's Opera House, NV.

SERIES EDITOR: HENRY WIENCEK
EDITOR: MARY LUDERS
PHOTO EDITOR: MARY Z. JENKINS
ART DIRECTOR: DIANA M. JONES
ASSISTANT PHOTO EDITORS: BARBARA J. SEYDA, REBECCA WILLIAMS
EDITORIAL ASSISTANT: MONINA MEDY
DESIGN ASSISTANT: KATHI R. PORTER
CARTOGRAPHIC DESIGN AND PRODUCTION: GUENTER VOLLATH
CARTOGRAPHIC COMPILATION: GEORGE COLBERT
DATA ENTRY: SUSAN KIRBY

LIBRARY OF CONGRESS CATALOGING-IN-PUBLICATION DATA

Durham, Michael, 1935-
    The Desert States / text by Michael S. Durham; special photography by Chuck Place; editorial director, Roger G. Kennedy,
    — 1st ed.
        p. cm. — (The Smithsonian guide to historic America)
    Includes index.
    ISBN 1-55670-105-5: $24.95 — ISBN 1-55670-109-8 (pbk.): $17.95
    1. Southwest, New—Description and travel—1981—Guide-books.
2. Deserts—Southwest, New—Guide-books. 3. Historic sites—
Southwest, New—Guide-books. I. Place, Chuck. II. Kennedy, Roger G.
III. Title. IV. Series.
F787.D87 1990   89-4599
917.90—dc20   CIP

Distributed by Workman Publishing, 708 Broadway, New York, NY 10003

Printed in Japan

10 9 8 7 6 5 4 3 2 1
First Edition

C O N T E N T S

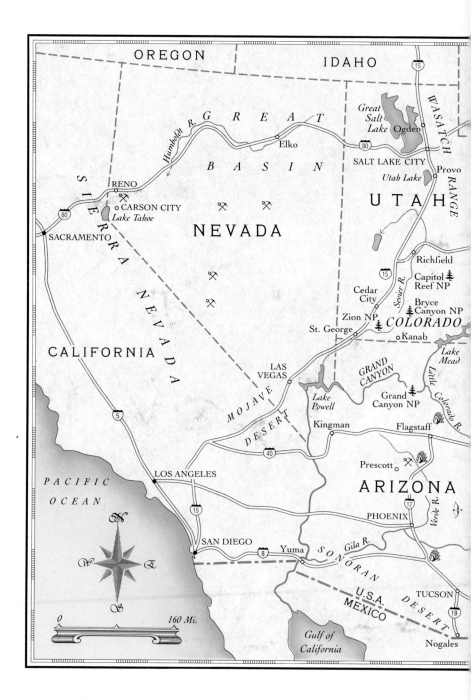

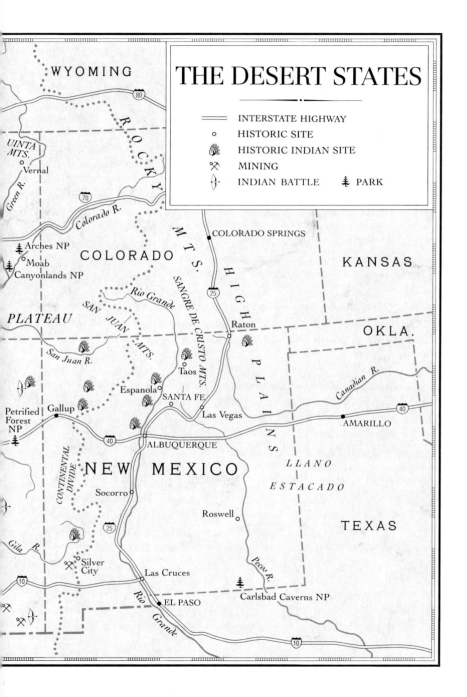

THE DESERT STATES

═══	INTERSTATE HIGHWAY
○	HISTORIC SITE
🪶	HISTORIC INDIAN SITE
✗	MINING
⚔	INDIAN BATTLE ⚜ PARK

WYOMING

ROCKY

80

UINTA MTS.
Vernal

Green R.

70

Colorado R.

MTS.

COLORADO SPRINGS

⚜ Arches NP
⚜ ○ Moab
⚜ Canyonlands NP

COLORADO

HIGH

25

SANGRE DE CRISTO MTS.

Rio Grande

SAN JUAN MTS.

PLATEAU

San Juan R.

Raton 🪶

KANSAS

OKLA.

PLAINS

Canadian R.

🪶 Taos ○

Espanola ○ 🪶
🪶 SANTA FE ○
Las Vegas ○

40

AMARILLO ●

Petrified Forest NP 🪶 Gallup ● 🪶

⚜

40 ALBUQUERQUE ●

NEW MEXICO

CONTINENTAL DIVIDE

🪶

Socorro ○

LLANO ESTACADO

Roswell ○

TEXAS

Gila R.

25

✗ ○ Silver City

Las Cruces ●

Pecos R.

10

✗ ⚜

Rio

EL PASO ●

Grande

Carlsbad Caverns NP ⚜

10

I N T R O D U C T I O N

ROGER G. KENNEDY

S itting at the close of day upon a rock in Arizona, watching the shadows move out from the walls of a very old adobe building. They turn the gray-brown earth darker until it is almost blue. Things do not seem the same as they did in a garden on the Potomac. Nostrils and mouth very much in need of another run on the canteen. Hands are gritty. Has it ever rained here? I don't recall a blade of grass, much less a tendril of vine, in the last five miles. Later, the moon crawls up the bowl of an indigo sky uncomplicated by clouds but punctured by the dry light of the desert stars.

Dry. This climate preserves ruins very neatly. We know that civilization is especially old in places such as Arizona, the Nile Delta, or Mesopotamia because architecture survived so long there. But maybe civilization is older in the Amazon or the Congo or the lower Mississippi Valley; in those rainy places, the evidence would have been decomposed by quick-growing vegetation that enshrouded, split, crumbled, and finally dissolved it; cities and strongholds, gardens and fortresses may now be reduced to mud, downstream in a delta. Not here.

Dry. The delta of the Colorado has no water in it much of the time, unlike the Nile's. That is our fault; we have so overgrazed and overbuilt in the valley of the Colorado that what rain there is sluices, and then the puddles burn out. We have given our great river flash floods and have presented to Mexico, into which it occasionally flows, cracked and baked-out plains. Somehow, the desolation we have wrought has diminished our esteem for the people who preceded us and who made a civilization upon this ground before we laid it waste. It is as if, by devaluing the achievements of the ancient peoples of the Southwest, we could lighten our burden of responsibility for what we have done and are doing to their land. This was once a vast grassland, a dry, but not a desert, prairie, feeding herds of animals and providing sustenance to many villages. In some places were larger communities, some on hills and mesas, some along slow-moving streams—where there were fish to catch and nutritious plants to harvest—that are now dry. During the last half

OPPOSITE:*The Acoma pueblo, also known as Sky City, may be the oldest continuously occupied site in the Western Hemisphere. It has an elevation of 6,600 feet.*

of the nineteenth century, we turned this into a desert. The enormous aqueducts that bring water here cannot repair that damage, though they slake the thirst of a million or more new inhabitants who might otherwise be drinking water in California. Modern Arizona is an artifice, probably the world's largest demonstration of aquaculture. This is a civilizing—city-making—achievement in the literal sense, and the cities of the Southwest have achieved miracles of civilizing in larger and subtler ways as well. The fresh-fledged cities of the plain—Phoenix, Sun City, and Scottsdale—dazzle us. This essay, however, is devoted to a closer look at what lies beyond that manifest achievement, and before it.

There are buildings here as old as those of the pharaohs, but we do not approach them as we do the ancient objects of the Mediterranean. Our education is classical, which is to say, rooted in Greece and Rome. The Renaissance taught Europeans to revere the Greeks and Romans, to live in awe of their predecessors. We do not.

A *hopi woman grinding corn, photographed in 1901.*

We are, so to speak, cut off from our own antiquity and our own Middle Ages by a European Renaissance. So it is little wonder that we come to Canyon de Chelly expecting less than we do at Persepolis or the Acropolis or the Coliseum. There are, of course, more columns to be found, upright or prone, in European than in American ruins, but there is as much architecture remaining aboveground from the ancient past in Arizona and New Mexico as there is in Syria and Iran. The most staggering accomplishment of the Anasazi, of the Hohokam of the Gila Valley, and of the Salado of the upper Salt River valley was not *on* the ground but *in* it: their irrigated agriculture. Remnants of their canal systems still carry water in Arizona.

The dry Southwest has presented us with an astonishing profusion of ruined villages, watchtowers atop mesas, cliffside sanctuaries and fortresses, and the markings of an extensive medieval road system. But our admiration for the achievements of the Old World stands between us and the architectural legacy of our own country. It is as if we were dyslexic to its masonry literature. We reject the immense presence of the hill towns of the Anasazi, though we travel into the vastnesses of central Asia for a few tumbled towers, fervently delve through the coastal towns of Turkey seeking relics of Ulysses, and some of us, even now, travel into the hostile valleys of Syria for the sight of a red-rock carving. It remains difficult for minds schooled in Old World history to register that our Southwestern marvels were built long before the births of Columbus, Cortéz, and certainly Captain John Smith. Our culture has found few opportunities to celebrate the accomplishments of an architecturally sophisticated medieval people within our own borders. We still do not know what to make of the grandeur they left behind.

Our history books celebrate certain milestones of settlement— Saint Augustine, Santa Fe, Jamestown, Plymouth, Boston—places that were founded in the era we consider the American genesis, the 1500s and 1600s. Perhaps there should be other names at the top of that list, such as Keet Seel, east of Lake Powell in Arizona, where the Anasazi lived for 2,000 years, developing an ever more complex culture and architecture. But a name that should be lodged in the memory of every student of our history is Acoma. It is possible that Acoma is the oldest continuously occupied town in the United States, with a thousand years of history. Perhaps Oraibi is even older. We cannot know for certain; there are no records.

Continuously occupied—that bland phrase does not adequately convey the startling fact that masonry dwellings atop the mesas at Acoma and Oraibi are still occupied by the descendants of those who built them and are full of life today. Equally startling is the fact that the religions of the Native Americans are not, as many assume, extinct. Native American religious rituals are still performed, although not always in public. One does not make the steep ascent to Acoma uninvited without quickly learning how private the Southwest can be. Visitors are welcome at certain times, but only with an explicit invitation from the elders. The people of the pueblos and the Hopi of the mesas guard their traditions from profanation, courteously but firmly turning away the idly curious.

Native American history in the Southwest and elsewhere presents us with a grandeur of achievement that we cannot quite comprehend, with mysteries that we have not yet solved and may never solve. For example, the Navajo who are farming today near Keet Seel, in Canyon del Muerto, arrived there three centuries ago from whence we know not, to replace Anasazi who had departed, we know not why or whither, three centuries earlier. In the nineteenth century, people wondered and permitted their historic imagination to run beyond the documentary evidence to try to understand these events. Those who had read the Bible and *La Morte d'Arthur,* and the Chronicles of Charlemagne and the Norse Eddas naturally thought of great battles as explanations for the disappearance of peoples. Did some ancient American Armageddon account for the abandonment of this set of buildings or another? How do we account for a whole valley full of buildings, such as the Ohio or the Colorado or the Salt? Tiresome twentieth-century pedantry, nourished not in the library but in the data bank, speaking in unrhymed and unmetered bytes, has belittled such grand explanations, yet it has offered nothing satisfactory in its stead.

Religion has always responded to mystery, because it is about mystery. In the 1830s the Mormon religion was founded by a man, Joseph Smith, who offered an explanation for the abandonment of Native American habitations: an ancient battle between the forces of good and evil during which whole populations were annihilated. Smith had grown to manhood amid the ruins and remnants of prehistoric civilization around Palmyra, New York, and there he was called to prophesy. As a result, the Book of Mormon is the only major religious tract of the European tradition to place Native

Americans at the center of its story. It is unique in requiring Euro-Americans to consider soberly their relationship with those who preceded them upon this continent.

"Mormon," according to Joseph Smith, was the name of a non-Indian who died in the ancient battle, leaving behind a record of the early history of his people committed to his son Moroni, who set down the rest to be found by Smith. Was Smith correct in his history? The remains of fortresses and mounds and the density of arrow and spear points around Palmyra may, indeed, indicate that great contests were fought among Indian nations there about the time of the possibly historic King Arthur of Britain. Skeptics cannot prove the contrary, and, as Winston Churchill said of Arthur, "It is all true, or it ought to be; and more and better besides." The Mormons do not expect Gentiles (non-Mormons) to agree with them about the historical aspects of their faith, and they guard the privacy of certain religious matters as tenaciously as the Native Americans guard some of their rituals. It is not wise to blunder into a Mormon temple—tabernacles, yes, but temples are not for Gentiles.

We can see what the Mormons learned from the Native Americans if we turn to the landscape these people have created. In many places Mormon and Pueblo landscapes are directly juxtaposed or superimposed. One thing that is revealed is that these were the two most proficient irrigators in our history. After the Pueblo, no one managed this so well until the Mormons, who were the first Euro-Americans to use irrigation for farming.

Sixty miles beyond the Arizona border, in the Mexican state of Chihuahua, is a remarkably intact pueblo complex, known as Casas Grandes, within sight of the thriving Mormon town of Nuevo Casas Grandes. Blue-eyed, blond-haired people, speaking Spanish or English, often with Scandinavian accents, can be found here. The "new town" of Casas Grandes lies in an irrigated oasis first created by the canal system of the departed people of the pueblo. The Mormon community is laid out in the manner of their other villages throughout the Great Basin, set in wide-open configurations quite unlike the villages of the Midwest. White-painted houses are set back twenty-five feet from streets that seem as wide as the boulevards of

OVERLEAF: *Ship Rock, a basalt monolith in the New Mexico section of the Navajo Reservation, is twenty stories taller than the Empire State Building.*

Paris, allowing for irrigation ditches alongside. There is more space around the dwellings than is customary among the Gentiles, space that is much needed, for behind the houses in the center of town are farm buildings and farm machinery. Mormons have a saying that nothing should be thrown away; they are remarkable for their abhorrence of waste.

There are other Mormon signs and symbols: Against the sky is the spindly crotchet known as the Mormon hay derrick, like the skeleton of a windmill without blades. It is wooden where wood can be found; where a little more wood was found and saved, it was often used to make a "Mormon fence" of vertical slats. Along the fence, if there is water enough, one sees a few "Mormon poplars," though insects and drought have done in most of them.

Early on, Mormon settlers also learned from their Pueblo neighbors how to use adobe—the people of Casas Grandes, for example, baked their building materials in units three feet long and twenty inches wide. Much Mormon adobe is still to be found as far north as Idaho, along with stonework almost as fine as the Anasazi construction on Pueblo Bonito in Canyon de Chelly, about 800 years older. Mormon teaching and practice emphasized masonry construction; they recruited masons and deployed them to sustain until the end of the nineteenth century building patterns largely abandoned elsewhere in the United States. Mormon villages with a high percentage of masonry—such as Willard, in the Cache Valley; Alpine or Spring City, Utah; or Snowflake, Arizona—also have many houses with four rooms over four, under gable roofs, like those of New England towns of the 1750s; and fine adobe center-hall houses distinguish Saint George and Santa Clara, in the Virgin River country of Southwest Utah. When one approaches a white-frame meetinghouse such as that in Pine Valley, only the tiny brackets under the eaves and hillsides beyond, blue-green with sage and juniper, tell us that we are not in some New Hampshire dale.

The Mormon landscape, so peaceful today, tells of a past that was violent: Their architecture traces the history of their persecution from east to west. Joseph Smith and his family were driven out of New York to Kirtland, Ohio, in 1831–1836. There he devised the first of the curious admixtures of traditional New England meetinghouse forms with Carpenter Gothic elements, which reappeared to the end of the century in Utah. Another curious admixture, developed in Kirtland and extended to Utah, was the United Order of

Enoch, an egalitarian social and economic system that adapted the communitarian ideals of several sects (such as the Rappites, Shakers, and Fourierists) and helped the Mormons to draw poor converts into the church. Kirtland was no more secure than New York had been. Smith was tarred and feathered by a lynch mob. He took his flock west to Missouri, where an advance guard of Mormons had settled in 1831, and a second temple was commenced at Independence. It was never completed; mutual hostility, murder, barn burnings, and harassment recurred between Mormons and their neighbors, Moving from county to county, Smith responded to attacks by threatening vengeance.

The Mormons consistently strove to convert the Indians to join with them; that is one reason why they were so unpopular with the frontiersmen of Missouri. There was ample reason to fear a Mormon alliance with the Sac and Fox, who had been herded into the neighborhood after Black Hawk's War and had shown how effective they were in battle. For consorting with the Indians as well as other misdemeanors, eighteen Mormons were killed and fifteen wounded at Haun's Mill in September 1838; a surrender to the militia barely prevented a much larger massacre. The First Mormon War set neighbor against neighbor in Missouri and trained many in guerrilla warfare (this training was later put to use in Bloody Kansas, where pro- and antislavery forces turned the landscape red). Smith was taken hostage, and his people retreated eastward out of Missouri, retracing their steps to establish themselves in Illinois.

Fifteen thousand strong, they became a political force welcomed by Abraham Lincoln; their neat masonry town of Nauvoo became the largest in the state. To this day people in Utah, Arizona, New Mexico, and Idaho apply the architectural lessons of the 1840s learned there; those center-hall, four-over-four dwellings are their "Nauvoo houses." Once again, however, there was no peace. Smith and his brother were killed by a lynch mob with the complicity of jailers in Carthage, Illinois. The Mormons commenced another long march, now under the leadership of Brigham Young, this time across Iowa and the Great Plains to Utah, following advice from John C. Frémont. Frémont had published a report on Utah's Bear River valley and the eastern shores of Great Salt Lake: "water excellent, timber sufficient, soil good and well adapted to grains and grasses . . . will sustain any amount of cattle." The missionaries and trappers interviewed by Young confirmed Frémont's description, as

did the evidence before the Mormons' delighted eyes when they gazed upon their new Zion in the summer of 1847.

Utah was Indian territory, only nominally governed by Mexico; Young continued to be solicitous of Indian welfare, recruiting tribesmen to fight battles with those who threatened his flock. Mormons and non-Mormons deployed Indians against each other. One hundred twenty men, women, and children making for California across Mormon territory were massacred in September 1857 in Mountain Meadows, in southern Utah. By a miracle of last-minute negotiation and by a tacit agreement to narrow responsibility for the Mountain Meadows massacre to the Mormon leader actually on the scene, a Second Mormon War was averted. The Buchanan administration had that as its only remarkable diplomatic triumph as it blundered into the Civil War. In the midst of that war, Abraham Lincoln spoke to an emissary from Utah: "When I was a boy . . . in Illinois there was a great deal of timber on the farms which we had to clear away. Occasionally we would come to a log . . . too hard to split, too wet to burn, and too heavy to move, so we plowed around it. That's what I intend to do with the Mormons. You go back and tell Brigham Young that if he will leave me alone, I will let him alone."

In the west the Mormons renewed the architecture of lost Zions: Palmyra, Kirtland, Independence, and Nauvoo. The ordered, hierarchical landscape they imposed upon the western land is the direct projection of the persistence of a patriarchy that commenced with their prophet, Joseph Smith, and their Moses, Brigham Young. These were builders in the precise, vocational sense; one was a glazier-carpenter, the other a carpenter-builder by trade. Perhaps that is why they were such effective builders in the metaphorical and institutional realms. They had a full consciousness of the interaction of buildings and people, of how the constructed environment shapes behavior.

They envisaged an agricultural community, a holy experiment not unlike that of the Pilgrim fathers. Young made the necessary adjustments to the desert West, but he could not anticipate the harsher adjustments his rural society would have to make to the rush of mining and industrialization that overwhelmed the Mormon heartland in the twentieth century. That rush came so quickly that the older West continued to persist side by side with the new. Here

OPPOSITE: *The Bonneville Salt Flats, a large expanse of salt and alkali deposits, and the adjacent Great Salt Lake, are both remnants of an enormous prehistoric body of water called Lake Bonneville.*

are three examples drawn from the year 1923, within many living memories. The U.S. Smelting and Refining Company's copper-smelting plant was under construction in Midvale, on the east bank of the Jordan River, on the outskirts of Salt Lake City. Here was the consummate expression of the homogenized American of the corporation. Samuel Untermyer, the company's lawyer, removed the irritations of competition in the production of copper and received the largest legal fee paid to that date, $750,000—about $8 million in 1990 purchasing power.

The land around the smelter was once a mountain, part of a blue-green, sage-covered range the Paiute called *Oquirrh,* or "shining mountains." Mining has "brought low" the mountain near Midvale; it is now a colossal crater, striated in red, gray, and brown, crawling with huge, snarling machines, producing gold, silver, copper, lead, and zinc. The *WPA Guide to Utah,* written in 1940, predicted the state would "have enough ore bodies to last until 1990."

Almost. People packing up in the little towns along what was once Bingham Canyon, amid exhausted earth and abandoned smelters, may quote to each other the words of Brigham Young in 1848, rebuking Sanford and Thomas Bingham for prospecting: "Instead of hunting gold, let every man go to work at raising wheat, oats, barley, corn and vegetables and fruit in abundance that there may be plenty in the land." The same WPA guide (the most idiosyncratic, poetic, and uninhibited of the series) remarks upon the older, sweeter sounds that could be heard on the slopes of those hills until, in 1923, they were drowned out by the roar and snarl of the machines. The Shoshoni and the Paiute were a very musical people, and so were the Mormons. The Indians put a high premium upon "the man with a sweet voice," and the Mormons have always been famous for their choruses. Brigham Young was a musical man as well as a master carpenter; the Salt Lake Tabernacle Choir and the extraordinary acoustics of its tabernacle both manifest his devotion to "sweet voices." It happens that it was in 1923 that the Mormons around Salt Lake produced their first operas under the Lucy Gates Grand Opera Company, under the aegis of Madame Gates, a coloratura soprano and granddaughter of Young, and her brother, B. Cecil Gates, a composer. The new West was crystalized in the presence of the most complex of Euro-American art forms upon the stage in Salt Lake City.

The old West, the less harmonious West, the West of hatred and violence, had one last gunfight left in it during the summer of 1923. Toward the end of the summer, "Old Posey," chief of the dispossessed Paiute of the San Juan Valley, made his last raid on the colonists near the town of Bluff, broke two of his tribesmen out of jail, fought a running two-day battle with a posse, and at the end, was mortally wounded in Comb Wash. He took shelter in a cave, propped himself up in its mouth, managed to stuff medicinal weeds into his wounds, but died—facing his enemies. His kind of death was one answer to a world that had no place for him, as it had no place for the mountain that became a pit by order of the U.S. Smelting and Refining Company. Radical alterations like these, however, are not the common means by which the people of the desert Southwest have adjusted to the industrial, urban, corporate world of large units and exploded communities. Life has proceeded in innumerable minute adaptations, only discernible when assessment is made at the end or beginning of things, at funerals and weddings, plant closings and grand openings, at the boarding up of exhausted houses and at an open house.

The desert Southwest has new ruins every day, and new starts as well. It presents its accumulated ugliness, mercilessly preserved by the dryness of the desert, without the underbrush and vines that disguise the worst of mankind's wastes in other parts of the country, while not very far away are gardens and buildings of a beauty so direct and spare as to make the opulence of other places seem anxious and fussy. It is not true that all human interventions in the landscape make it worse; the intentional creation of comeliness thrives in this dry climate amid the natural drama of the region. Painters have congregated around Taos; architects, visionary and otherwise, around Scottsdale; and, more recently, filmmakers and writers at Sundance. And there is probably no other part of America where so much good music is made per capita; after the Lucy Gates Opera Company came another, at Santa Fe, and smaller ones elsewhere. Choruses and quartets, country fiddlers and pickers abound.

And on the horizon there remain those meticulously joined walls of the Anasazi, as finished as a page of Mozart's, the highest achievement in the use of the materials at hand. When the Mormon Tabernacle Choir is singing what it most fervently believes, it reaches the level of the work at Chaco Canyon.

SANTA FE
AND
NORTHERN
NEW MEXICO

OPPOSITE: *San José de Gracia, one of the best preserved of the surviving New Mexican adobe churches, was completed about 1776. The wooden towers are later additions.*

In 1908 a roving cowboy named George McJunkin found an elegantly crafted arrowhead embedded in a bison skeleton near Folsom, New Mexico. The discovery, once accurately dated, was evidence that the human species had been in northern New Mexico for at least 10,000 years, much longer than believed possible before. Since then, similar discoveries at Sandia and Clovis have proven that the Folsom man had cousins several thousand years older. These people hunted giant mammoths driven south by the Ice Age.

By about the dawn of the Christian Era, groups of Anasazi began gathering in communities as they drifted from the Four Corners region where present-day Colorado, Utah, Arizona, and New Mexico meet. These settlements may have begun as cliff dwellings—such as those preserved at Bandelier National Monument—and developed into pueblo-style structures four or five stories high. The New Mexican center of Anasazi civilization was at Chaco Canyon, today a national historical park. The Chacoans had neither the wheel nor beasts of burden, but they managed to build roads, wide and straight, to satellite communities that modern archaeologists call outliers. One road, remnants of which are still visible, stretched sixty miles north from Chaco Canyon to the outlier at Aztec.

We do not know why the Anasazi deserted their settlements or where they went, but the Pueblo living in New Mexico today consider them their ancestors and regard many Anasazi sites as sacred. When the Spanish explorer Francisco Vásquez de Coronado crossed New Mexico in 1540, he found Indian pueblos, not the cities of immense wealth he had hoped for. Vásquez de Coronado had been sent on his journey of exploration by Viceroy Antonio de Mendoza of Mexico, who named the area New Mexico in the expectation that it would prove to be as richly endowed with gold and silver as Aztec Mexico was.

The first Spanish colonizer of New Mexico, Juan de Oñate, led a party of 130 families to the Rio Grande Valley. Oñate's successor as governor, Pedro de Peralta, founded Santa Fe on a tributary of the Rio Grande in 1610. Construction, using Indian labor, began immediately on the Palace of the Governors, a municipal hall, and a church. The Indian servants the colonizers brought from Mexico lived across the river in the Barrio de Analco; and the Chapel of San

OPPOSITE: *A 1901 photograph of a young Hopi maiden, wearing the traditional "squash blossom" hairstyle, which was worn only by unmarried women who had reached puberty.*

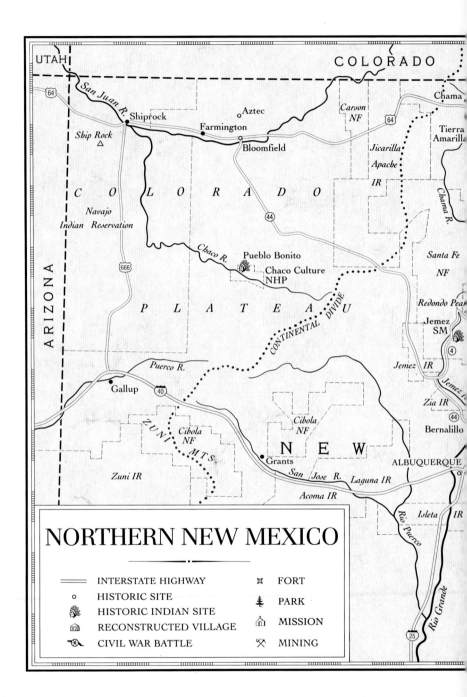

NORTHERN NEW MEXICO

═══ INTERSTATE HIGHWAY		⌂ FORT	
○ HISTORIC SITE		🌲 PARK	
🪶 HISTORIC INDIAN SITE		🏛 MISSION	
🏠 RECONSTRUCTED VILLAGE			
🪓 CIVIL WAR BATTLE		⚒ MINING	

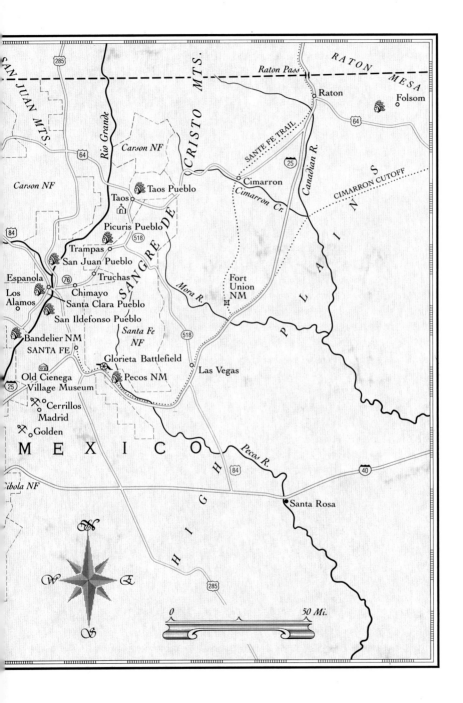

Miguel, often called the oldest church in the United States, was built for their use. At this early stage, Santa Fe was a small and isolated frontier outpost resupplied by wagon train every three months. By 1630 its population numbered only 250.

The first seventy years of Spanish rule were marked by conflict between civil and ecclesiastical officials, Apache attacks, drought, and smallpox epidemics. Conversion of the Indians to Christianity took place as much by force as by persuasion. In 1598 Oñate told tribal chiefs from thirty pueblos that they would suffer "cruel and everlasting torment" unless they allowed themselves to be baptized immediately. In 1675 forty-seven tribal religious leaders were seized for "practicing witchcraft"; most were flogged, three hanged. One of the survivors, a medicine man named Popé from the pueblo of San Juan, went to the pueblo of Taos to plot his revenge.

The result was the well-organized Pueblo Revolt of 1680. Beginning on August 10, angry Indians destroyed mission churches and massacred priests in pueblos across New Mexico. The friar at the pueblo of Jemez was slain at the altar; one of the few missionaries who escaped death, at the pueblo of Cóchiti, disguised himself as an Indian and slipped away in the darkness. By August 15 Santa Fe was under siege with 1,000 Spanish men, women, and children barricaded in the Palace of the Governors. The attackers sent two crosses —one red, one white—to Governor Antonio de Otermín. If the governor returned the white cross, it would indicate surrender, and the Spanish could leave unharmed. Instead, he returned the red cross, a sign they would fight on. Faced with starvation, the Spanish counterattacked on August 20; the next day they escaped from Santa Fe and headed south. The Indians celebrated their departure by tearing down churches, converting the governor's palace into a pueblo, and washing baptized Indians with soapweed to purify them. The province was reconquered in 1692 by General Diego de Vargas with an army of 300 men. Santa Fe was taken peacefully, and the people of some pueblos submitted to Spanish rule once again. Many did not—the pueblos of Santo Domingo and Jemez were abandoned, and their people were pursued into the hills by Vargas's troops.

Santa Fe grew rapidly in the next century: It had a population of 2,500 by 1800. In July 1776 the Franciscan fathers Francisco Silvestre Vélez de Escalante and Francisco Atanasio Domínguez left Santa Fe to establish a route that would link the town with the Spanish missions in California. They reached Lake Sevier (in present-day Utah) before winter forced them to return to Santa Fe in January 1777. Their route was later called the Old Spanish Trail. In 1792 a French pathfinder named Pedro Vial, who earlier had established a route from San Antonio to Santa Fe, was sent to Santa Fe to blaze a trail to Saint Louis. His path became known as the Santa Fe Trail.

After the Louisiana Purchase in 1803, the Spanish were unable to keep Americans out of their territory. In 1807 Lieutenant Zebulon Pike, probing this frontier under orders from the U.S. government, was arrested and brought to Santa Fe after he strayed—perhaps intentionally—into New Mexican territory. After his release Pike published an account of his adventure, which increased American interest in New Mexico. With Mexican independence in 1821, New Mexican borders were opened, and the next year wagonloads of goods from Missouri entered Santa Fe.

On August 15, 1846, the commander of the United States Army of the West, General Stephen Watts Kearny, claimed New Mexico for the United States in the town plaza in Las Vegas, New Mexico. The Mexican governor fled before Kearny reached Santa Fe, where Kearny immediately began building Fort Marcy behind the Palace of the Governors. Five months later, Charles Bent, the prominent frontier trader Kearny had appointed governor, was assassinated during an uprising in Taos. The revolt ended when U.S. troops fired upon those who had sought refuge in the Taos Pueblo church. U.S. authority was not challenged thereafter. Most of New Mexico officially became part of the United States with the Treaty of Guadalupe Hidalgo in February 1848.

As the Civil War approached, many military men stationed in Southern New Mexico joined the Confederacy, although the civilian population tended to side with the Union. After defeating Union forces at the Battle of Valverde in southern New Mexico, the Confederate army of General Henry Hopkins Sibley headed north: Sibley planned to capture Fort Union in northwestern New Mexico, then continue on to take Denver and finally San Francisco. After briefly occupying Santa Fe, the Confederate forces met the enemy at Glorieta Pass on the Santa Fe Trail on March 28, 1862. Although the rebels won the day, they lost their supply train during the fighting. Without supplies the Confederate forces had no choice but to

OVERLEAF: *The mesa near Glorieta Pass, the site of a decisive Confederate defeat in 1862.*

retreat south, leaving Santa Fe, New Mexico, and the West as part of the Union.

In 1879 the Atchison, Topeka & Santa Fe Railroad came to New Mexico: south from Colorado through Raton to Las Vegas, then through the 7,453-foot Glorieta Pass, dropping more than 2,000 feet in forty miles to Albuquerque. The line actually bypassed Santa Fe, but an eighteen-mile spur connecting the capital city with Lamy was completed in 1881. New Mexico's best-known territorial governor, Lew Wallace, author of *Ben Hur*, drove in the last spike. That same year Wallace resigned his post in frustration. He had tried and failed to break the Santa Fe Ring, a group of corrupt and politically powerful investors who schemed, cheated, and murdered to gain control over the 2 million acres in northern New Mexico and southern Colorado known as the Maxwell Land Grant.

New Mexico had a military government from 1846 to 1850, when it applied for statehood at the instigation of President Zachary Taylor and other anti-slavery politicians, eager to increase the number of abolitionist votes in Congress. Slavery, which had been forbidden under Mexican rule, did not exist in New Mexico. Pro-slavery Texans, who maintained that New Mexico was part of Texas, prepared to invade the region; in response, President Taylor sent orders to the federal troops in Santa Fe to repel any incursion. As part of the Compromise of 1850 between the pro- and anti-slavery factions, New Mexico and Arizona were organized into a single territory (as a territory it had no votes in Congress), with the proviso that the territory would decide to permit or forbid slavery within its borders when it became a state. That day did not come until six decades had passed—New Mexico was admitted as the forty-seventh state on January 6, 1912.

In recent history, Santa Fe and northern New Mexico have undergone tremendous changes. During World War II, an isolated boys' boarding school in the mountains northwest of Santa Fe was chosen as the site for the top secret Manhattan Project, which developed the atomic bomb. Los Alamos continues to be a center for nuclear research. But the pervading atmosphere of the region is one of a more distant history: prehistoric ruins of vanished peoples, ancient pueblos still functioning as villages, a famous art colony remembered in Taos, frontier architecture preserved in once-rowdy towns such as Cimarron and Las Vegas, and historic sites such as Santa Fe's Palace of the Governors, the oldest seat of government in the European tradition in what is now the United States.

After describing Santa Fe, this chapter covers northern New Mexico by making two partial loops through the northwestern and northeastern parts of the state. The historic sites are arranged to take the traveler from Santa Fe to Los Alamos, west past the Jemez State Monument, and north past Chaco Canyon to Aztec. The northwestern part of the tour concludes by following Route 64 through Chama and across the Rio Grande Gorge to Taos. From Taos, the loop travels through northeastern New Mexico via Cimarron and Raton, on the old Santa Fe Trail close to the Colorado border. Routes I-25 and 84/85 follow the trail past Fort Union, Las Vegas, and Glorieta Pass, where an important Civil War battle was fought.

S   A   N   T   A   F   E

The historic sites of Santa Fe are clustered in the downtown area, many of them on or near the historic **Plaza,** a logical starting place for a tour. Across the river from the Plaza is Guadalupe Street and the old residential quarter known as Barrio de Analco. Canyon

The Oldest House in Santa Fe has foundations that may have been built by Pueblo Indians, although the adobe walls and vigas are much later.

Road, with its array of galleries and old buildings, can also be explored. A bit farther is the Camino Lejo Museum Complex, where two branches of the Museum of New Mexico—one devoted to international folk art, the other to Indian arts and culture—and the Wheelwright Museum of the American Indian are located.

The Plaza has been at the center of Santa Fe life for almost four centuries. After Mexican independence was achieved in 1821, the square, once much larger than it is today, was proclaimed the Plaza de la Constitución. It became the terminus of the Santa Fe Trail. William Becknell, "Father of the Santa Fe Trail," brought the first wagonload of goods here from Missouri on November 6, 1822. In an 1844 account about the trail, Josiah Gregg wrote: "The arrival of the caravan always was productive of great excitement among the natives. 'Los Americanos! Los Carros! La entrada de la caravana!' were to be heard in every direction." After the United States took over New Mexico in 1846, the Plaza was made smaller when adobe buildings fronted by *portales*, or porches, were constructed on the side of the governor's palace. The Plaza was surrounded with a picket fence, and the open space was once used to grow alfalfa. From 1846 on the one-story adobe hotel near the southeast corner of the plaza called the **Exchange Hotel** was the center of Santa Fe society. Here Kearny held the victory ball celebrating U.S. occupation. The building was demolished in 1919, and a new hotel was erected in 1925. Today the pueblo-style building at 100 East San Francisco Street is a busy commercial hotel filled with Spanish Colonial furniture, fireplaces, and southwestern art and artifacts.

MUSEUM OF FINE ARTS

This 1917 building, designed by the Colorado firm of Rapp and Rapp, is a replica of the New Mexico building at the 1915 Panama-California International Exposition in San Diego. Its tower was based on the mission at Acoma, and additional details were inspired by other Spanish missions around the state. The museum is a good example of the pueblo or Santa Fe style.

When new, the museum was unique in several respects. The core of its collection was contemporary works donated by local

OPPOSITE: *The Santa Fe Museum of Fine Arts, designed by Rapp and Rapp in 1917, was the first Pueblo Revival style building constructed in Santa Fe.*

artists. The museum also provided exhibit space for all Santa Fe artists, regardless of reputation or talent. This open-door policy, which has since ended, was adopted on the advice of the well-known artists Robert Henri and John Sloan, who had been in New Mexico since the early 1910s. The collection contains works by Ernest L. Blumenschein, a leader of the art colony in Taos, and Bert Geer Phillips, who came to New Mexico with Blumenschein by wagon in 1898. It also contains paintings by the Cinco Pintores (the Five Painters): Fremont F. Ellis, Jozef Bakos, Willard Nash, Will Shuster, and Walter Mruk. This group formed in the 1920s to support artists in Santa Fe, bring art to the people, and to resist commercialism. The museum's permanent collection includes art of the Southwest, both contemporary and historic, as well as American art from other regions. The **Saint Francis Auditorium** is designed in the style of a mission chapel. Six murals depicting the life of Saint Francis were designed by the artist Donald Beauregard and completed by Kenneth Chapman and Carlos Vierra after his death.

LOCATION: 107 West Palace, on the Plaza. HOURS: March through December: 10–5 Daily; January through February: 10–5 Tuesday–Sunday. FEE: Yes. TELEPHONE: 505–827–4452.

Construction on the **Cathedral of Saint Francis** (one block east of the Plaza at San Francisco Street and Cathedral Place) lasted from 1869 to 1886. The first church on this site was destroyed in the Pueblo Revolt of 1680. The cathedral was built under the direction of Archbishop Jean-Baptiste Lamy, a French cleric who was the model for Bishop Latour in Willa Cather's novel *Death Comes for the Archbishop.* As he attempted to reform the clergy, Lamy made many political enemies. The cathedral was built out of limestone blocks around a 1713 parish church, or *parroquia,* so that services could continue during construction. Part of the parroquia is incorporated in the construction of the cathedral's **Chapel of Our Lady of the Rosary,** which displays a small wooden madonna brought to Santa Fe from Mexico about 1625. There is a bronze statue of Archbishop Lamy by the entrance outside.

North of the cathedral, **Sena Plaza** (125 East Palace Avenue, 505–988–5792), built in the 1840s, was the thirty-three-room adobe house of Major José de Sena. When the capitol burned in 1892, the state legislature met in Sena's second-floor ballroom. The rooms of the refurbished building now contain shops, which completely enclose the open-air courtyard. During World War II, the smaller **Trujillo Plaza** (109 East Palace Avenue) was the Santa Fe office of the top secret Manhattan Project in Los Alamos, where the atomic bomb was developed.

When the **Loretto Chapel** (Old Santa Fe Trail near Water Street) was completed in the 1870s, the religious order that ran the girls' school discovered there was no way for their charges to reach the choir loft. According to legend, their prayers to Saint Joseph, the patron saint of carpenters, were answered when a nameless carpenter appeared, built a spiral staircase without nails or supports, and disappeared when the job was finished without waiting to receive thanks or payment. The Gothic chapel, drawn very generally from the shape of Sainte Chapelle in Paris, was designed by a French architect working simultaneously on the cathedral. He was shot and killed by a nephew of Bishop Lamy, John Lamy, who accused the architect of seducing his wife.

From Guadalupe Street on the west and Paseo de Peralta on the east, the area around the meandering creek known as the Santa Fe

Santa Fe's Cathedral of Saint Francis was constructed by the French bishop Jean Baptiste Lamy, who chose the Romanesque style of his native France instead of the traditional Hispanic styles.

River holds many buildings of historical and architectural significance. The old buildings in the district around the railroad depot
have been restored and house a variety of businesses, although the
area is not as fashionable as others in the city. The railroad depot
only serviced a small spur line; the main line of the Atchison,
Topeka & Santa Fe Railroad never went directly to Santa Fe.

PALACE OF THE GOVERNORS

Now a history museum, the palace, which has been in continuous
use since 1610, is the oldest government building in the European
tradition in the United States. When it was built by Pedro de Peralta,
the second Spanish governor of New Mexico, it extended several
hundred feet farther to the north and west. After driving the Spanish
out of the city during the bloody Pueblo Revolt of 1680, the Indians
converted the palace into a pueblo village by blocking the doors and
windows and entering the rooms on ladders from the roof.

The Palace of the Governors remained the seat of power from
the Spanish reconquest in 1692 until around the turn of the century.
One of the U.S. territorial governors who lived in the palace after
Kearny occupied the city in 1846, was Lew Wallace, author of *Ben
Hur.* Wallace did not find the quarters congenial; he wrote of the
"grimy" walls, the "undressed boards of the floor," and "the tons and
tons of mud composing the roof [that] had the threatening down-
ward curvature of a shipmate's cutlass." After the federal government
gave the building to the territory of New Mexico—an unwanted
gift—the territorial legislature voted in 1909 to restore it as the
Museum of New Mexico. There are now ten permanent exhibits in
the palace. One honors Jesse L. Nusbaum, a documentary photographer and archaeologist who restored the palace in 1909. Among
other accomplishments, he excavated 1,315 sites along more than
6,000 miles of pipeline laid by the El Paso Natural Gas Company in
1950. An exhibit of pottery from the Pío Puerco and Moqui regions
is displayed as it was in 1909. A re-creation of the **Reception Room of
Governor L. Bradford Prince, 1893,** contains hide paintings, *retablos,
bultos,* rugs, and pottery. Other rooms include the **Mexican
Governor's Office,** a restoration of the room that governors used
during the period of Mexican rule, 1821 to 1846.

The **New Mexico Chapel** (1821–80) has an altarpiece of hand-
hewn timbers covered with gesso and painted with homemade,
water-soluble pigments. Another room devoted to the history of the

palace displays the original wood flooring, the oldest chess pieces found in the United States, wallpaper, pottery, and other utensils discovered during the restoration. Until the Museum of Fine Arts was built nearby in 1917, local artists used the north side of the patio as studios. The space now houses the museum's **Print Shop and Bindery.** There are four horse-drawn vehicles in the patio, including an ornately carved wooden hearse used between 1910 and 1919 in Santa Rita, New Mexico.

LOCATION: North side of the Plaza (Palace Avenue). HOURS: March through December: 10–5 Daily; January through February: 10–5 Tuesday–Sunday. FEE: Yes. TELEPHONE: 505–827–6474.

SANTUARIO DE GUADALUPE

Built by Franciscan missionaries between 1776 and 1795, the santuario functioned as the mission church at the end of El Camino Real, (Royal Road), from Mexico City to Santa Fe. The church, which has adobe walls three feet thick, has been restored and remodeled several times: once in 1882, again after a serious fire in 1922, and finally for the nation's bicentennial in 1976, after which it opened as a history museum, art gallery, and performing arts center. A 1783 oil painting of Our Lady of Guadalupe by the Colonial artist José de Alzibar hangs in the sanctuary. One sacristy is now a meditation chapel adorned with native New Mexican *santos.*

LOCATION: 100 Guadalupe Street at Agua Fria. HOURS: May through October: 9–4 Monday–Saturday, 12–4 Sunday; November through April: 9–4 Monday–Friday. FEE: Yes. TELEPHONE: 505–988–2027.

In Spanish colonial times, the Spanish soldiers, priests, and other colonists lived on the north side of the river while their Indian servants from Mexico lived on the south side in a section called Barrio de Analco, meaning Other Side of the River. Approaching this section from the west—from Don Gaspar—there are two historic adobe houses on either side of De Vargas Street. The **Roque Tudesqui House** (129–135 East De Vargas Street, private) was probably built in the mid-eighteenth century. Tudesqui, an Italian trader on the Santa Fe Trail, purchased the house in 1841. The **Gregorio Crespin House** (132 East De Vargas Street, private) was built in the first half of the eighteenth century on land that

The chapel at San Miguel, rebuilt in 1710 after the original structure was nearly destroyed in the Pueblo Revolt of 1680. OPPOSITE: *Inside the San Miguel Chapel are many eighteenth-century decorations in both Old- and New-World styles.*

General Vargas granted to Juan de León Brito in return for his services in the Spanish reconquest of the city.

The Oldest House (215 East De Vargas Street, private), named for its unsubstantiated claim to being the oldest house in the United States, is a good example of old adobe construction with walls of poured mud instead of bricks. The foundations may have been built by Pueblo Indians in the thirteenth century; the present *vigas,* or roof beams, however, only date to about 1750. Another old adobe house, the privately owned **Boyle House** (327 East De Vargas Street), was probably built in the mid-eighteenth century. At the east end of the barrio, the **Adolph Bandelier House** (352 East De Vargas Street, private) was rented by the Swiss-born anthropologist Adolph Bandelier in the 1880s. Bandelier was one of the first scholars to recognize the historical importance of the Pueblo culture.

The **Chapel at San Miguel** (401 Old Santa Fe Trail) was built about 1636 for the use of the Tlaxcalan servants of Spanish colonists

and may be the oldest Christian church in continuous use in the country. Only the walls of the building are original; the church was almost completely destroyed in the Pueblo Revolt of 1680. After the Spanish reconquest, the original walls were made thicker to fortify the building. The church's square tower was built in the 1870s. The reredos, or altar screen, was made in 1798 as a backdrop for the small gilded statue of Saint Michael, probably sculpted in 1709. There are also several paintings on animal skins done by the missionaries to teach Bible stories to the Indians. The Christian Brothers, brought to Santa Fe by Bishop Lamy, have operated the church since the mid-nineteenth century. The bell displayed in the gift shop was probably cast by an itinerant bell maker in 1856.

Before the Spanish began building here in the early eighteenth century, **El Camino del Cañon** was an Indian trail leading from Santa Fe to Pecos. The adobe houses along the route today often have plain facades and are built around elaborate courtyards. The Santa Fe art colony settled here in the early twentieth century. Today high real estate prices have driven out most artists, and the old houses have been converted into art, antiques, and crafts galleries.

The **Juan José Prada House** (519 Canyon Road, private) probably dates from the latter half of the eighteenth century. Prada, who purchased the house in the 1860s, divided it into two sections separated by a corridor. In the 1930s the house was purchased by Mrs. Charles Dietrich, who restored it and joined the two sections. Mrs. Dietrich, an early Santa Fe preservationist, also restored the **Borrego House** (724 Canyon Road, private) in the 1930s. According to deeds of sale, the house existed as early as 1753. The **Olive Rush Studio** (630 Canyon Road) is now a Quaker meetinghouse. Rush, who moved to Santa Fe in 1920, was the first woman artist in the city's growing art colony. She purchased and preserved the old adobe house, which probably dates from the first half of the nineteenth century. The **Cristo Rey Church** (1107 Cristo Rey Street) is believed to be the largest adobe church in the world. It was built using almost 200,000 adobe bricks in 1940 on the 400th anniversary of Coronado's expedition. The church houses an ornate stone reredos carved in 1760 for the military chapel on the Plaza. When the chapel was torn down, Archbishop Lamy hid the reredos in Saint Francis Cathedral.

OPPOSITE: *A collection of* bultos *and* santos, *carved wooden saints, from the collecion of the Museum of International Folk Art.*

CAMINO LEJO MUSEUM COMPLEX

Museum of International Folk Art

The acquisition of the collection of Alexander and Susan Girard (106,000 objects from 100 countries) in 1978 and the construction of the museum's Girard Wing in 1982 put the Museum of International Folk Art at the forefront of the world's folk-art museums. Florence Dibell Bartlett founded the museum in 1953 with a gift of 4,000 objects. The Bartlett Wing is used to house changing exhibits of an international scope. A permanent display of material from the Spanish Colonial collection of religious and household folk art from New Mexico and from Spanish colonies around the world is housed in the new Hispanic Heritage Wing. The permanent exhibit in the Girard Wing—"Multiple Visions: A Common Bond"—was designed by Girard, an architect and designer with an international practice. He groups items from different cultures together to create dioramas with such titles as "Heaven and Hell," "Dolls' Christmas Lunch," and "Pueblo Feast Day." The other exhibits include collections of Navajo flag rugs, folk costumes and textiles, religious and ceremonial art, ceramics, silver, and toys, including a tin band of musical mice made by Louis Marx & Co. in 1930.

LOCATION: Camino Lejo Museum Complex. HOURS: March through December: 10–5 Daily; January through February: 10–5 Tuesday–Sunday. FEE: Yes. TELEPHONE: 505–827–8350.

Museum of Indian Arts and Culture

This museum opened in 1986 to house the considerable collection of the Laboratory of Anthropology, which was founded in 1923—with a collection of southwestern Indian pottery—to study the development of Indian art from prehistoric times to the present. The laboratory's building, adjacent to the new museum, was completed in 1931. The laboratory continues to excavate building sites throughout the state before they are developed. The new building, the first passive-solar museum structure in the country, has 10,000 square feet to exhibit art, crafts, and other artifacts. The resource center has displays of pottery, ancient tools, and other artifacts that can be handled; soundproof booths for listening to recordings of

A Navajo rug featuring five yei figures woven in the 1890s, probably for a white trader, and now in the collection of the Museum of Indian Arts and Culture in the Camino Lejo Museum complex.

Indian music and recitations of folk history; a small research library; and a multimedia theater.

> LOCATION: Camino Lejo Museum Complex. HOURS: March through December: 10–5 Daily; January through February: 10–5 Tuesday–Sunday. FEE: Yes. TELEPHONE: 505–827–8941.

Wheelwright Museum of the American Indian

Founded in 1937 to study and preserve aspects of Navajo culture, the museum building was designed to resemble and capture the spirit of a Navajo hogan. Many of the Navajo ceremonial objects from the original collection of the Bostonian Mary Cabot Wheelwright have been returned to the tribe. However, the museum now owns a wide range of items from the Apache, Pueblo, Plains, California, and Athapaskan, including sand painting rendered in tapestries and watercolors by the Navajo medicine man Hastiin

Klah. (Sand paintings were created during rituals and immediately destroyed—it was very unusual to preserve their sacred designs in other media.) Wheelwright met Klah through traders in western New Mexico and later dedicated herself to preserving his work and a large collection of ceremonial objects. There is a working trading post in the building and a library that includes early recordings of Navajo songs.

> LOCATION: Camino Lejo Museum Complex. HOURS: 10–5 Monday–Saturday, 1–5 Sunday; closed Monday in December, January, and February. FEE: None. TELEPHONE: 505–982–4636.

NORTHERN NEW MEXICO

OLD CIENEGA VILLAGE MUSEUM

A combination of original ranch buildings, re-creations of early New Mexican buildings, and historic structures moved here from elsewhere, this outdoor museum is located on **El Rancho de las Golondrinas** (Ranch of the Swallows), a few miles south of Santa Fe city limits. The historic ranch was the last stopping place, or *paraje,* on El Camino Real from Santa Fe to Mexico City. In 1932 the ranch was acquired by the Curtin-Paloheimo family, who created the living museum of Spanish colonial heritage. Today the many buildings include an eighteenth-century *placita* house with a *torreón defensivo,* or defensive tower, a nineteenth-century home with outbuildings, a molasses mill, several waterwheels, and a re-created Spanish mountain village complete with *trochil y gallinero* (pigsty and chicken house) and *casa de la abuelita* (grandmother's house). Another section contains a cemetery, a Calvary cross, and a *morada,* or chapel, used by *penitentes* in their religious ceremonies.

> LOCATION: Exit 271 off Route I-25 south of Santa Fe. HOURS: Open on selected weekends and by appointment; call for information. FEE: Yes. TELEPHONE: 505–471–2261.

Known for the locally grown chilies, **Espanola** was a terminus for the Chili Line that the Denver & Rio Grande Railroad built to Antonito,

OPPOSITE: *The Chapel at El Rancho de las Golondrinas is a converted eighteenth-century adobe farm building.*

The Las Golondrinas morada *is a replica of the churches built by the* penitentes, *a southwestern mystic Catholic sect.*

Colorado, in the late 1870s. With the exception of the rambling **Bond House** (316 Onata, 505–753–2377) of 1877, which a local entrepreneur gave to the town as its city hall, Espanola has little of historical or architectural interest. It is, however, a convenient starting point for several pueblos in the area.

SAN ILDEFONSO PUEBLO

Juan de Oñate named San Ildefonso in honor of a seventeenth-century archbishop of Toledo, Spain. A mission church was built here in 1617. In 1676 the Spanish executed four Indians for practicing their religion and sold fifty others into slavery. Four years later the two missionaries at the pueblo were killed in the Pueblo Revolt. The Spanish reconquered the village in 1694, but two years later the Indians burned the church and joined other Pueblo tribes on the top of Black Mesa, which is within view north of the pueblo. They were finally starved into submission.

Today the pueblo consists of over 200 buildings around a large central plaza. The church, built in 1968, is intended to be a replica of the first seventeenth-century mission. There is a small museum in the building housing the governor's office. In 1919 the celebrated potter Maria Martinez and her husband, Julian, developed the technique for crafting the now world-famous black-on-black pottery with a highly polished finish and black matte design. The technique has been carried on by potters working in this pueblo and elsewhere.

LOCATION: Route 502, 13 miles south of Espanola. HOURS: 8–5 Daily. FEE: Yes. TELEPHONE: 505–455–2273.

SANTA CLARA PUEBLO

Originally called K'hapoo (Where the Wild Roses Grow), the Tewa pueblo of Santa Clara was probably settled in the early 1500s by Anasazi from the Four Corners region. (According to legend, the Tewa people emerged from a lake in Colorado.) Completed in 1629, the first Spanish mission at Santa Clara was destroyed in the Pueblo Revolt of 1680. The Santa Clarans revolted again in 1694—two years after the Spanish reconquest of New Mexico—and banded together with other Tewa tribes at nearby Black Mesa. The

Side and overhead views of a ca. 1925 polychrome pot made by Maria Martinez, a master potter from Pueblo San Ildefonso.

pueblo is noted for its fine polychrome and black-on-black pottery; the colorful, detailed paintings of Pablita Velarde and her daughter, Helen Hardin, are also widely known.

LOCATION: Route 5, 1.3 miles west of Espanola. HOURS: 8–5 Daily. FEE: None. TELEPHONE: 505–753–7326.

The Santa Clara Pueblo also owns the **Puye Cliff Dwellings** (505–753–7326), located off Route 30 about eleven miles west of Espanola at the top of the Pajarito Plateau. Here the cliff dwellings extend for more than a mile along the base of a precipice. These dwellings, both along the cliff and on the mesa top, were constructed between A.D. 600 and approximately 1580, when the settlement was abandoned. Dwellings hollowed out of the cliffs range to three stories in height.

SAN JUAN PUEBLO

The first European to visit this pueblo wrote in 1591: "The very sight of us frightened the inhabitants, especially the women, who wept a great deal." In July 1598 Juan de Oñate proclaimed the pueblo the capital of the province and renamed it San Juan de los Caballeros (Saint John of the Gentlemen). He then proceeded to oust the inhabitants and confiscate their belongings. One month later he moved to a nearby pueblo he had renamed San Gabriel (only the ruins of the San Gabriel mission church remain), and the residents of San Juan returned. In 1675 a San Juan medicine man named Popé was publicly flogged for practicing his religion, which the Spanish called "witchcraft." Soon thereafter he began organizing the overthrow of Spanish rule, culminating in the successful Pueblo Revolt of 1680. Today many craftspeople work out of San Juan Pueblo, where the Artisans Guild sells work from all eight northern pueblos. About 100 of the buildings in the pueblo date back 700 years, and many are restored.

LOCATION: 4 miles northeast of Espanola. HOURS: 8–5 Monday–Saturday. FEE: None. TELEPHONE: 505–852–4400.

OPPOSITE: *The ruins of an Anasazi village dating from ca. 1400 at Puye Cliffs, part of the Santa Clara Pueblo.*

The twin-towers of the Santuario del Señor de Esquipulas at Chimayo, an early nineteenth-century church that is believed to be the site of miraculous cures.

CHIMAYO

For a century after it was settled around 1740, Chimayo, the easternmost outpost of the province of New Mexico, was the place of banishment for serious offenders. The town is noted for the quality of its weaving and for the twin-towered adobe church known as **Santuario del Señor de Esquipulas,** built around 1814. There is a walled cemetery, or *campo santo,* in front. One of the legends about its origins says that the builder, Don Bernado Abeyta, found a crucifix—and recovered from a serious illness—after he was told in a vision to dig in the earth at a certain spot. Many hold that the earth from a pit in the chapel floor has curative powers, and the sanctuary is lined with crutches and offerings of thanks from the cured. The weaving tradition in Chimayo dates from 1805, when the Spanish government brought two Spanish weavers to Santa Fe in an attempt to revive the weaving tradition there. The weavers disliked Santa Fe and moved to Chimayo, where the activity took hold.

From Chimayo, the High Road to Taos—as Route 76 is called—winds its scenic way through the mountains to the eighteenth-century Spanish town of **Truchas** (Trout) and to **Trampas** (Traps), the site of the exceptionally large, eighteenth-century church **San José de Gracia.** The church, which has twin bell towers, also has an exterior choir loft, so the singers can accompany processions inside and outside the church.

West of where Route 76 joins Route 75, Tribal Route 120 leads to **Picurís Pueblo** (505–587–2519), a large and militant village during the days of Spanish colonization. Today there are only about 200 Tiwa-speaking residents in the village. Its white-fronted church, the **Mission of San Lorenzo** (505–587–2519), was built about 1775; the original church was destroyed in the Pueblo Revolt of 1680 in which the Tiwa killed at least twenty Spanish settlers before joining the march on Santa Fe. There are guided tours of the ruins of the original pueblo; a small tribal museum exhibits prehistoric artifacts

The interior of the Santuario at Chimayo features an altarpiece by the great early nineteenth-century santero, *or religious artist, Mollero.*

excavated from the pueblo, which, archaeologists say, was first occupied in the mid-thirteenth century.

LOS ALAMOS

Prior to World War II, the site of present-day Los Alamos was inhabited by the Los Alamos Ranch School and homesteaders. Before 1917
Los Alamos Ranch was the largest homesteading enterprise in the
Pajarito Plateau. Ashley Pond bought it in 1917 and established the
Los Alamos Ranch School in 1918. The boarding school that special-
ized in providing a rigorous outdoor life for wealthy students from
the East closed for good when its facilities were taken over during
World War II by the Manhattan Project, the top secret effort to develop and test an atomic bomb. General Leslie Groves, chief of the
Manhattan Project, and J. Robert Oppenheimer, its scientific head,
together selected the site on the Pajarito Plateau in the Jemez
Mountains for both its access to a major city—Santa Fe—and its isolation. Oppenheimer recruited such scientists as Enrico Fermi, Edward
Teller, George Kistiakowsky, Hans Bethe, and Isidor I. Rabi to develop the weapon. The need for a large team and facilities in which it
could work and live precipitated a building boom on the mesa.
Despite the feverish activity, work continued in secret. Personnel
assigned to the project were told no more than to report to 109
Palace Avenue in Santa Fe. Once they were at the laboratory, calls and
mail were censored and movement restricted. The project would cost
$2.2 billion and involve more than 125,000 people at 37 facilities.

The first atomic bomb was successfully detonated—flashing with
"the brightness of several suns at midday"—on July 16, 1945, at the
remote Trinity Site sixty miles from Alamogordo, New Mexico, in
the desert. After being told of the successful test, President Truman
wrote in his diary, "We have discovered the most terrible bomb in
the history of the world. It may be the fire destruction prophesied
[in the Bible]." Just three weeks after the test—on August 6—an
atomic bomb was dropped on Hiroshima, Japan. Another bomb was
dropped on Nagasaki on August 9. The devastating results hastened
Japan's surrender. Soon thereafter Oppenheimer and those scientists who believed that nuclear weapons development should cease
in the interest of humanity left the project; others stayed on at Los
Alamos to develop the vastly more destructive hydrogen bomb.

OPPOSITE: *J. Robert Oppenheimer and General Leslie Groves stand over the remains
of the steel detonating tower, at ground zero of the Trinity Site, September 1945.
Cloth shoe coverings were worn against radiation.*

Today nuclear research continues in this government town. Its makeshift wartime buildings have long since been replaced by more permanent structures. The Los Alamos Scientific Laboratory, now under the jurisdiction of the Department of Energy, is operated by the University of California.

Exhibits on the Los Alamos Ranch School and the early days of the Manhattan Project are featured among the displays at the **Los Alamos County Historical Museum** (1921 Juniper Street, off Central Avenue, 505–662–6272). The museum is housed in a log cabin that was once the infirmary for the school. Another log building, **Fuller Lodge** (Central Avenue), completed in 1928, served as the dining and recreational hall for scientists in the early days of the Manhattan Project. It now houses the **Fuller Lodge Art Center,** which exhibits the work of northern New Mexico artists.

Bradbury Science Museum

Although they receive no special prominence among the many high-tech exhibits explaining current atomic research, the obvious highlights of this museum are two casings made for atomic bombs during World War II. They are displayed to provide an idea of the size and shape of the two bombs that were used against Japan: "Little Boy," dropped on Hiroshima, and "Fat Man," the implosion-type plutonium bomb dropped on Nagasaki. The unimpressive size of the casings (one of them is 120 inches long and 28 inches in diameter) belies the enormous destructive power of the World War II bombs—"Little Boy" detonated over Hiroshima with a force equivalent to that of 16,000 tons of TNT. Other exhibits trace the history of nuclear research from the initial splitting of the uranium atom in 1938 and the attempt to explain how nuclear weapons derive their explosive force from fission to other technical matters relating to atomic energy and weaponry.

LOCATION: Diamond Drive. HOURS: 9–5 Tuesday–Friday, 1–5 Saturday–Monday. FEE: None. TELEPHONE: 505–667–4444.

BANDELIER NATIONAL MONUMENT

When this fifty-square-mile area of scenic wilderness, volcanic rock formations, and prehistoric dwellings—often carved out of the soft volcanic tuff—was made a national monument in 1916, it was named for the Swiss-born anthropologist Adolph F. Bandelier, who first came to New Mexico in 1880. Bandelier, who grew up in Illinois, was 40 years old when he gave up international banking to pursue his lifelong interest in natural history and prehistoric societies. He and his Cóchiti guides descended into Frijoles Canyon in October 1880: "The grandest thing I ever saw," he wrote after viewing the cliff dwellings and caves. The region became the setting for a novel about prehistoric pueblo life, *The Delight Makers,* which Bandelier published in 1890.

Prehistoric life within the monument and on the surrounding Pajarito Plateau thrived for about 400 years, from 1150 to 1550. As the population increased with the migration of Anasazi from the Four Corners region, the original small, family-sized pueblos were consolidated into larger villages ranging in size from 100 to 1,000 rooms. The structures of soft volcanic stone were built at the foot of

A ceremonial cave, part of the extensive Anasazi ruins in Bandelier National Monument.

Within the Bandelier National Monument Wilderness Area, known as the Back Country, is the Shrine of the Stone Lions, still a place of worship for Pueblo Indians.

cliffs. Additional rooms were carved out of the rock base. Frijoles Canyon, where the **Visitor Center** is located, was first excavated by Edgar Lee Hewett in 1907. Hewett, who was the first director of the School of American Research and the Museum of New Mexico, tried to have the entire Pajarito Plateau declared a "National Park of the Cliff Cities"; instead, a forty-two-square-mile area was designated the Bandelier National Monument in 1916. A trail leads from the visitor center to the canyon's cliff dwellings and kivas. Hewett and his students also excavated the ruins at **Tyuonyi,** the large, oval-shaped pueblo built of volcanic tuff that might have had as many as 300 rooms and may have stood three stories high. At **Ceremonial Cave,** Hewett discovered a large, well-preserved kiva, or ceremonial chamber. The cave is located about 150 feet above the canyon floor and is entered by climbing a series of long ladders.

The monument also has approximately seventy miles of hiking trails, some leading to the more distant sites such as the intriguing **Shrine of the Stone Lions,** where two felinelike stone animals are surrounded by rocks, a thirteen-mile round-trip from Frijoles Creek. **Frijolito Ruin** is a half mile off the main road, while the site known as **Painted Cave** is a twenty-mile round-trip. A detached section of the monument, **Tsankawi,** is located about eleven miles north of Bandelier's main entrance. A trail leads to the mesa-top location of an unexcavated prehistoric village; the remains of pueblo dwellings can be seen at the base of the cliff. The ancient trail has been worn deep into the volcanic rock in places. The top of the mesa, with a magnificent view of the Los Alamos area, is reached by a ladder. There are also petroglyphs—rock carvings of human figures, birds, four-pointed stars, and other images—on the cliffs.

LOCATION: Route 4, 46 miles northwest of Santa Fe. HOURS: September through May: 8–5 Daily; June through August: 8–6 Daily. FEE: Yes. TELEPHONE: 505–672–3861.

From Bandelier, Route 4 proceeds west through the beautiful **Valle Grande,** a broad expanse of open country ringed by mountaintops. Once thought to be the largest volcanic formation in the world, it is actually a portion of the Jemez Caldera, 14 miles wide, which was formed by volcanic eruptions 1.4 million and 1.1 million years ago. These eruptions created 450 cubic miles of fantastic pink rock formations surrounding Los Alamos called the Pajarito ("Little Bird") Plateau. The route makes a sharp turn south to the ruins at Jemez State Monument, located in a picturesque, piñon- and juniper-covered valley in the foothills of the Jemez Mountains.

JEMEZ STATE MONUMENT

The ruins of the pueblo of Giusewa, which the Jemez abandoned after the Pueblo Revolt of 1680, and the ruins of San José de los Jemez, the mission church, are the attractions at this state monument. Even in its deteriorated state, the church is an impressive structure: 111 feet long and 34 feet wide. The walls, designed for fortification, are from 6 to 8 feet thick. The 40-foot tower above the altar is also fortresslike in appearance. There is an adjacent monastery with small cubicles and the remains of a chapel. The church, destroyed by Navajo soon after it was completed in 1622,

The ruins of Mission San José de los Jemez and its adjacent monastery, which were burned during the Pueblo Revolt of 1680.

was rebuilt five years later. It lasted until it was burned during the Pueblo Revolt. A small museum at the visitor center exhibits a reproduction of the frescoes archaeologists discovered on the church walls in the 1920s.

> LOCATION: Route 4, just north of Jemez Springs. HOURS: May through September: 9–6 Daily; October through April: 8–5 Daily. FEE: Yes. TELEPHONE: 505–829–3530.

South of Jemez State Monument (and four miles north of San Ysidro), a side road leads to **Jemez Pueblo,** home of the Jemez tribe, which spread over a vast area at the time of the Spanish appearance in New Mexico. In 1540 one of Coronado's captains counted seven villages in this area alone. The Jemez fiercely resisted Spanish rule; however, after an unsuccessful revolt in 1696, they fled west to Navajo country. They returned several years later and settled here.

CHACO CULTURE
NATIONAL HISTORICAL PARK

One of the most important archaeological sites in North America, Chaco Canyon preserves a complex of ruins that give some idea of the remarkable social and architectural sophistication of the Anasazi. Construction of the pueblos did not start in earnest until about 1030, although the canyon had been inhabited a century earlier. The advanced construction of the architecture, the wide, straight roads that led to outlying settlements, and the intricate irrigation system for diverting runoff water represent a peak of Anasazi civilization. In and near this arid, fifteen-mile-long rift known as Chaco Canyon, there are more than 2,000 prehistoric ruins in a thirty-two-square-mile area. Within the monument itself, there are eleven major pueblos and some 400 smaller archaeological sites. Perhaps as many as 5,000 Anasazi inhabited the canyon—a flourishing center of agriculture and trade. The inhabitants imported

The ruins of Pueblo Alto, atop the mesa at the convergence of several prehistoric roads, is one of several pueblos in Chaco Canyon. OVERLEAF: *Pueblo Bonito, centerpiece to the Chaco Culture National Historical Park, is a manifestation of the dense urban culture of the Anasazi.*

turquoise and worked it into beads, and engaged in commerce with
people in what is now Mexico.

The size of the settlement only intensifies the mystery that surrounds every Anasazi site: Why did they settle here? Without horse or
wheel, how did they manage to build so extensively? How did they
learn to survive in such inhospitable terrain and climate? Why did
they leave so suddenly? Where did they go? In 1849 Lieutenant James
H. Simpson, a scientist accompanying the U.S. Army in actions
against the Navajo, was the first to report on, measure, record, and
name the sites at Chaco Canyon. In May 1877 the photographer
William Henry Jackson spent five days mapping, sketching, and
reconnoitering the canyon (but his photographs did not come out).
In 1896 the pioneering guide and archaeologist Richard Wetherill
led the Hyde Exploring Expedition to Chaco Canyon, where it spent
four years excavating the canyon's principal ruin, **Pueblo Bonito.**

In 1907 President Theodore Roosevelt proclaimed Chaco
Canyon a national monument. Archaeologists finished excavating
Pueblo Bonito and uncovered about fifty rooms in **Pueblo del
Arroyo** in 1921. A 1929 Smithsonian expedition unearthed remnants of a late Basket Maker settlement called Shabik´eshchee that
predates the pueblos. Edgar Lee Hewett of the University of New
Mexico excavated Chetro Ketl just east of Pueblo Bonito in the
1930s. In the 1970s the National Park Service and the university
established a modern research facility called Chaco Center to use
such techniques as remote sensing—an advanced form of aerial
photography—to study the site. In December 1980 the monument
was enlarged and its name changed to Chaco Culture National
Historical Park. Recent research has detected the remains of a very
straight and wide highway linking the canyon settlements with satellite communities called outliers. One such thoroughfare, the Great
North Road, runs from **Pueblo Alto** to Aztec National Monument
near the Colorado border.

The 800-room Pueblo Bonito, the canyon's most important community, is the park's centerpiece. One theory holds that it was built
to house people from the outliers who came to the canyon for religious ceremonies. Much of the complex is surrounded by an 800-
foot-long wall faced on both sides with small, intricately fitted stones
and filled with rubble, a technique found in ancient Roman and
Greek architecture. There are also thirty-two small clan kivas and two
great kivas, one fifty-two feet in diameter. The great kiva at **Casa**

Rinconada is one of the largest ever discovered: sixty-two and a half feet in diameter. Painted plaster probably once covered its beautiful stonework. A film and exhibits on the different cultures inhabiting the canyon await travelers at the **Visitor Center** off Route 57, one and a half miles from the south entrance of the park.

> LOCATION: Route 57, 60 miles north of Thoreau. HOURS: *Visitor Center:* 8–6 Daily. FEE: Yes. TELEPHONE: 505–988–6727.

AZTEC

This small, attractive town is little changed from when it was settled in 1890. A number of original adobe and frame buildings still stand, and the **Aztec Museum** (125 North Main Street, 505–334–9829) has an outstanding collection of artifacts and memorabilia from the

The Great Kiva at Aztec Ruins National Monument, reconstructed in the 1930s, was originally built by the Chacoans toward the end of their occupation of the site, and then remodeled by the later Mesa Verdeans.

A metate *and* mano—*the Anasazi mortar and pestle, used for grinding corn—at the Aztec Ruins National Monument.*

town: Included are an early barbershop and telephone exchange; oil-drilling equipment such as a 1920 engine and wooden rig; and exhibits on the oil and gas industry in the San Juan Basin. The town takes its name from the nearby prehistoric ruin that early settlers mistakenly thought had been built by the Aztecs.

Aztec Ruins National Monument

In addition to being one of the largest and best-preserved Anasazi ruins in the Southwest, Aztec has the only restored great kiva in existence. Aztec probably had cultural and economic ties with the two major Anasazi centers: Chaco Canyon about sixty miles south and Mesa Verde forty miles northwest, in what is now Colorado. At different times, Aztec was an offshoot community or outlier of either or both of these places. Archaeological evidence unearthed by Earl Morris of the American Museum of Natural History between 1916 and 1923 showed that Indians from Chaco Canyon began building Aztec about 1110. They lived here until the turn of the century. The pueblo was abandoned for about twenty-five years until Mesa Verdeans rebuilt it and lived here for the rest of the century. The

Anasazi were probably drawn here by the availability of water from the Animas River, but why the settlement was abandoned twice remains a mystery. At its height, the settlement probably had about 220 ground-floor rooms, 119 second-story rooms, and 12 or more third-story rooms. Estimates of the population range from 500 to 700. The **West Wing** of the pueblo has been almost completely excavated, and the boundaries of the central **Plaza,** where most of the daily activities took place, can be clearly seen. In the northeast corner, at the **Hubbard Site,** named for an early owner of the property, there is an unusual tri-walled structure sixty-four feet in diameter, which probably was used for religious ceremonies. There were small rooms between the outer walls and the kiva, or ceremonial chamber, in the center.

Earl Morris excavated the ruin's **Great Kiva** in 1921 and rebuilt it in 1934. With an interior diameter of forty-eight feet, the Great Kiva is smaller than those at other prehistoric sites, but this is the only one that has been reconstructed. Great kivas, which probably spread into Anasazi settlements from the south, might have been used for administrative and social purposes as well as religious ceremonies. The ceiling beams are supported by four massive pillars and held up a roof that archaeologists estimate weighed ninety-five tons.

LOCATION: Off Route 550. HOURS: September through May: 8–5 Daily; June through August: 8–6:30 Daily. FEE: Yes. TELEPHONE: 505–334–6174.

BLOOMFIELD

This oil, gas, and agricultural town was once the home of the notorious outlaw Port Stockton, a veteran of the Lincoln County Wars in southern New Mexico and a leader of a gang of cattle rustlers. In a desperate attempt to convert him to the side of law and order, the town briefly made Stockton sheriff but found this only made matters worse. Stockton was shot to death in 1881 while trying to protect another outlaw from peace officers. Bloomfield is also the site of a notable county-owned prehistoric site: the **Salmon Ruin** (Route 64, 505–632–2013). Like Aztec just to the north, Salmon was built by Anasazi from Chaco Canyon as an outlier toward the end of the eleventh century. This two-story, 250-room, C-shaped pueblo had been abandoned for almost a century when Anasazi from Mesa Verde to the north occupied it between 1225 and 1240. A feature of

this ruin is a tower kiva built on a twenty-foot-high platform. Salmon Ruin is named for the farmer who owned it and helped protect it from vandals and pothunters. Today the San Juan County Archaeological Research Center administers the site and a small museum two miles west of town.

CHAMA

As the southern terminus of the **Cumbres & Toltec Scenic Railroad** (505–756–2151)—a sixty-four-mile, narrow-gauge, steam-driven line to Antonito, Colorado—the mountain town of Chama keeps its railroad past alive. The line was built in the 1880s as the San Juan extension of the Denver & Rio Grande Railroad to service mining camps in the San Juan Mountains. After climbing the 10,015-foot Cumbres Pass, it descends a precipitous 4 percent grade into Chama. Lucius Beebe, a writer and railroad buff, called it "the most awesomely spectacular example of mountain railroading in North America." After the D & RGW abandoned the line, Colorado and New Mexico purchased it jointly in 1970.

TAOS

Taos derives its reputation from the blend of cultures that gives the town its cosmopolitan air. Taos Pueblo, properly known as San Gerónimo de Taos, is one of the oldest, most traditional, and picturesque of all of New Mexico's nineteen Indian pueblos. Ranchos de Taos, a Spanish farming community, was originally settled by Indians from Taos Pueblo. The official name of the third and central community, Taos proper, is Don Fernando de Taos, after a leading citizen of the seventeenth century. The town is in a spectacular setting on the broad Taos Plateau at the foot of the high peaks of the Sangre de Cristo Mountains to the northeast.

A Spanish priest, Friar Pedro de Miranda, the first European to settle in Taos, located his mission outpost close to the pueblo; it was moved to what is now the town plaza after Indians killed a priest and two soldiers in 1631. The Pueblo Revolt of 1680, which drove the Spanish from New Mexico, was led from Taos Pueblo, and the Indians there proved particularly difficult for the Spanish to sub-

OPPOSITE: *Ladders are used to reach upper-story rooms in the Taos pueblo, where the dwellings do not have interior stairs.* OVERLEAF: *The turtle dance in Taos Pueblo.*

due after 1692. In the next century, settlers and Indians joined forces to protect themselves from the raids of the Ute, Comanche, and Navajo; after these Indians made away with fifty women and children in 1760, pursuing Spanish soldiers massacred 400 Indians in retaliation.

After Mexican independence in 1821 opened New Mexico's border to Americans, Taos became an important fur-trading center and rendezvous for the free-spirited American mountainmen. The most famous of these was Kit Carson, who arrived in Taos as a teenager in 1826. Although he married a local woman and called Taos home, he spent most of the next thirty years on the trails, trapping, fighting Indians, and guiding John C. Frémont's western expeditions. In 1853 he settled in Taos as an Indian agent until the outbreak of the Civil War, when he organized a company of New Mexican volunteers. Another Taos-based trader, Charles Bent, went on to become the first U.S. governor of New Mexico after the United States seized the territory in 1846.

The influx of artists into Taos began with Joseph Henry Sharp, who first visited in the 1880s. In 1895 he told two young New York illustrators, Bert Geer Phillips and Ernest Blumenschein, about the charms of the Southwest, and in 1898 the pair set off to see for themselves. The men were heading for Mexico when a broken wagon wheel forced them to detour to Taos, and there they stayed. All three—Phillips, Blumenschein, and Sharp—eventually settled in Taos, where they later formed the Taos Society of Artists with several other artists. Five other painters—Oscar Berninghaus, Irving Couse, W. Herbert "Buck" Dunton, Victor Higgins, and Walter Ufer—at first were summer residents who returned East to work as illustrators in the winter. But all eventually settled permanently in Taos. Blumenschein dominated the Taos colony during what has been called its formative years from 1900 to 1920. From 1920 to 1942, the so-called Golden Era, Taos's leading artist was Andrew Dasberg, noted for his Cézannesque scenes of the Southwest. Other artists of this era included Howard Norman Cook, Catherine Critcher, Nicolai Fechin, and Georgia O'Keeffe, who spent time in Taos before settling in Abiquiu. Like so many of the leading artists, writers, musicians, and other creative individuals of the day, O'Keeffe had been at one time the guest of Mabel Dodge, a restless heiress, writer, patroness of the arts, and "collector of people," who arrived in Santa Fe in 1917 with her third husband, the artist

Georgia O'Keeffe, seen here in a 1937 photograph by Ansel Adams, found inspiration in the New Mexican landscape for many of her paintings. OVERLEAF: Red Hills and Pedernal, *painted by O'Keeffe in 1936 (detail).*

Maurice Sterne. She caused something of a local scandal when she divorced Sterne and married an Indian from Taos Pueblo, Antonio Luhan. Not all of the artists who arrived in Taos stayed on, but even the transients were charmed by the isolation, the dramatic setting, the clear quality of the light, and the unique cultural mix. An early visitor, Frederic Remington, wrote of Taos: "Americans have gashed this country up so horribly with their axes, hammers, scrapers, and plows that I always like to see a place that they have overlooked; some place before they arrive with their heavy-handed God of Progress."

Today Taos is a popular tourist town and ski center spread out along a commercial highway developed without much consideration for the town's history or character. Still, the town plaza remains, along with a number of historic buildings. The **Plaza,** which was fortified against attack after the Pueblo Revolt of 1680, is still the town's focal point. Ever since Kit Carson and other citizens raised the Union flag during the Civil War and protected Taos from south-

ern sympathizers, a flag has flown day and night from the pole in the center of the Plaza. The original copper-covered bandstand was a gift of Mabel Dodge Luhan. On the south side of the Plaza, **La Fonda Hotel** is built on the site of the Bent-Saint Vrain Store, the family enterprise of Governor Charles Bent. Inside the hotel is an exhibit of the paintings of D. H. Lawrence, who came to live and work in Taos at the urging of his hostess, Mable Dodge Luhan: She hoped he would write about what she called "this mysterious land."

The work of many Taos artists is on display at the **Harwood Foundation** (238 Ledoux Street, 505–758–3063), a gallery, library, and auditorium owned by the University of New Mexico. The core of the landmark building was built in 1860. Displays include the Mabel Dodge Luhan New Mexico Santo Collections, wood carvings of Patrocino Barela, who died in Taos in 1964, and the works of such painters as Berninghaus and Lady Dorothy Brett, an English artist

The kitchen of Kit Carson' adobe in Taos has been furnished in a manner appropriate to the years Carson lived there, from the 1840s to the 1860s.

who came to Taos with the D. H. Lawrences in 1924 and stayed to dedicate herself to painting the American Indian "as he sees himself rather than the way we see him." The Harwood Foundation was the home of the artists Bert and Elizabeth Harwood, who came to Taos in 1918. It also houses the Taos public library, which has a collection of works and papers of D. H. Lawrence. A half block east of the Plaza is the **Kit Carson Home and Museum** (Kit Carson Road/Route 64, 505–758–0505), located in the 1825 adobe building Carson purchased in 1843 when he married Josefa Jaramillo, the daughter of a prominent local family. The museum is crowded with art and artifacts from early New Mexican history and includes mountainmen exhibits, a gun room, and an Indian archaeology room. The living room, bedroom, and kitchen are all furnished as period rooms. Carson, his wife, Antonio Martínez (the priest who married them), and Mabel Dodge Luhan are buried in the cemetery in **Kit Carson Memorial State Park,** two blocks north.

Ernest L. Blumenschein Home

Although portions of this rambling adobe home date to the 1790s, most of it was built as additions by Ernest Blumenschein and his wife, the artist Mary Shepard Greene. The couple purchased the home in 1919 from Herbert "Buck" Denton, friend and fellow member of the Taos Society of Artists, which Blumenschein had helped found in 1912 to promote the work of Taos artists. Rooms are furnished with many of the Spanish Colonial and Mexican pieces the couple collected, and the walls display their work and that of their daughter, the artist Helen Blumenschein, who gave the house to the Kit Carson Foundation in 1962. Two bedrooms and a linen storage room are now an art gallery for changing exhibits of arts and crafts.

LOCATION: 13 Ledoux Street. HOURS: 9–5 Daily. FEE: Yes. TELEPHONE: 505–758–0505.

La Hacienda de Don Antonio Severino Martínez

This massive, fortresslike adobe building had only four rooms when Don Antonio Severino Martínez purchased it in 1804. At his death in 1827, there were twenty-one rooms built around two *placitas,* or courtyards. Don Antonio, an important trader on the Chihuahua Trail that connected Santa Fe and northern Mexico, was mayor of

Taos. His son, Antonio José Martínez, was an influential Catholic priest, the first president of the territorial legislature, and an opponent of Bishop Lamy, who eventually excommunicated him. The family lived in larger rooms around the larger *placita* in the front, while the servants' quarters and storage rooms were in the rear. The thick, windowless, exterior walls were for protection against occasional Indian raids. This house is one of the few restored haciendas in existence from Spanish colonial times. Inside are period furnishings and exhibits on Spanish culture and on the Chihuahua Trail, and archival photographs of Taos.

> LOCATION: 2 miles west of Taos on Ranchitos Road and Route 240.
> HOURS: 9–5 Daily. FEE: Yes. TELEPHONE: 505–758–0505.

Mission San Francisco de Asís

The elements of many mission churches in the Southwest—thick adobe walls, twin towers, and massive buttresses—come together here in an unusually harmonious way. The church, built by the

The abstract forms of the eighteenth-century mission church of San Fransicso de Asís in Ranchos de Taos have attracted many artists, including Georgia O'Keeffe.

The cemetery used for those who converted to Christianity surrounds the ruins of the old mission church at the Taos Pueblo. OVERLEAF: *The Taos Pueblo.*

Franciscans in the late 1700s, was a favorite subject of many Taos artists including Georgia O'Keeffe and is frequently photographed. The courtyard and the 120-foot-long church are surrounded by an adobe wall; each of the two bell towers supports a cross. The exterior is replastered yearly with a mixture of mud and straw. Inside large *vigas,* or roof beams, support the ceiling. In the rectory, the so-called Mystery Painting, "The Shadow of the Cross," is the subject of a special exhibit. When the portrait of Christ is shown in the dark, a cross not visible in daylight appears over the right shoulder, and the sea and sky take on a luminescent glow. The painting was exhibited at the Saint Louis World's Fair of 1904 and given to the parish in 1948.

LOCATION: Route 68, Ranchos de Taos, 3 miles west of Taos. HOURS: 9–4 Monday–Saturday. FEE: None. TELEPHONE: 505–758–2754.

Taos Pueblo

The multistoried pueblo at Taos is the most northern of New Mexico's nineteen pueblos. Most of the adobe buildings can now be

The "new" adobe church of San Geronimo at the Taos pueblo, built after the earlier structure was destroyed by the U.S. Army during the Taos Revolt in 1847.

entered through doors, even those on the upper stories. The pueblo, which has refused to permit electricity or telephones in the old buildings, is dramatically situated at the foot of the 13,160-foot Wheeler Peak, the highest mountain in New Mexico and part of the Sangre de Cristo range.

There have been Indians in the Taos region since about A.D. 900. Tiwa were living in a village close to the present settlement when Captain Hernando de Alvarado from the Coronado expedition came upon it in 1540. Alvarado was cordially received, but in the years that followed, relations with the Spanish were marked by discord and bloodshed. In 1598 Juan de Oñate ordered the Mission of San Gerónimo de Taos built, and although all Pueblo were converted to Christianity, most were unhappy with Spanish rule. In 1639 they abandoned the pueblo and fled east. Two years later Spanish soldiers rounded them up and forced them to return. The persuasive medicine man Popé, from San Juan Pueblo, lived at Taos while he was planning the Pueblo Revolt of 1680. During the revolt, the Taos Indians redressed their many grievances by killing two priests and a few settlers in the vicinity. The Spanish burned the pueblo to the ground during the reconquest in 1692, but the Taos people revolted again in 1695. Diego de Vargas forced them to surrender once again, and by 1700 a new pueblo and church were under construction. The final revolt occurred in 1847, this time against the United States, which had taken possession of New Mexico the previous year. Governor Charles Bent, who had a home in Taos, was killed in the uprising led by the Pueblo leader Tomasita and the Mexican Pablo Montoya. When American troops arrived at the pueblo, nearly seven hundred Indians took refuge in the San Gerónimo mission. One hundred and fifty of them died during the attack in which the mission church was destroyed by artillery. The ruins of the church and its Christian cemetery can be visited.

The pueblo is divided by the Taos River into a northern section and a southern section, and visitors are restricted mostly to the large plaza on either side. Taos Pueblo artisans produce drums, woven textiles, and an unadorned pottery with a glittering mica finish.

LOCATION: Off Route 68, 2 miles north of Taos. HOURS: June through August: 8–6 Daily; September through May: 9–5 Daily. FEE: Yes. TELEPHONE: 505–758–8626.

Millicent Rogers Museum

During the time that Millicent Rogers, a Standard Oil heiress, lived in Taos—from 1947 until her death in 1953—she amassed a noteworthy collection of Hispanic and Indian art and crafts with an emphasis on northern New Mexico. To keep the collection in Taos, her family founded the museum in 1956; it moved into its present building in 1968. Mrs. Rogers's collection is the core of the museum, which continues to make acquisitions such as religious articles of Hispanic New Mexico and the black-on-black pottery of Maria Martinez. The American Indian collection also includes Navajo and Pueblo jewelry, Navajo textiles, Hopi and Zuni kachina dolls, and a variety of baskets. There is also a replica of a Navajo silversmith's shop from about 1940. The Hispanic collection includes an extensive display of wool-on-wool *colcha* embroidery from the northern Rio

Grande valley. *Colchas* mean coverlets or bed coverings in Spanish, but they were also used as curtains and altar carpets in churches.

> LOCATION: Off Route 3, 4 miles north of Taos. HOURS: May through October: 9–5 Daily; November through April: 9–5 Tuesday–Sunday. FEE: Yes. TELEPHONE: 505–758–2462.

Eight miles northwest of Taos, Route 64 crosses the **Rio Grande Gorge Bridge,** one of the highest spans in the country, 650 feet above the river. Fifteen miles north of Taos on Route 3, signposts point to the **D. H. Lawrence Ranch** (505–776–2245). The property, which Lawrence called Kiowa Ranch, was a gift from Mabel Dodge Luhan to Lawrence's wife, Frieda, who gave her a manuscript of Lawrence's *Sons and Lovers* in return. Lawrence lived in Taos for three six-month periods between 1922 and 1925. After he died in France in 1930, his ashes were buried in a chapel at the ranch. The ranch is now owned by the University of New Mexico; only the chapel is open to the public.

Several routes wend from Taos to Cimarron. The southernmost, Route 64, passes the **Vietnam Veterans Memorial** of the Disabled American Veterans, about thirty miles east of Taos. The curvilinear chapel with superb views of the Sangre de Cristo Mountains was built by hand by members of the Westphall family, whose son was killed in Vietnam.

CIMARRON

Cimarron was a stop on the mountain branch of the Santa Fe Trail and also headquarters for the Maxwell Land Grant, an enormous, almost-2-million-acre spread controlled by Lucien Bonaparte Maxwell, who inherited it from his father-in-law. Maxwell, a former mountainman who was once a scout for John C. Frémont, sold the grant in 1870 to an English land company. After several years, the land was purchased by a Dutch-based company that eventually sold it in tracts for farms and ranches. William "Buffalo Bill" Cody organized his Wild West Show here in the latter half of the nineteenth century. The town was also a haven for outlaws such as Clay Allison and "Black Jack" Ketchum. The Las Vegas *Gazette* once wrote:

OPPOSITE: *A Navajo chief's blanket, ca. 1880, in the collection of the Millicent Rogers Museum in Taos (detail).*

"Things are quiet in Cimarron; nobody has been killed in three days." Maxwell's 1864 gristmill is now the **Old Mill Museum** (one block north of Route 21, 505–376–2913), which houses an extensive collection of artifacts from the area. Still in operation, the 1872 **Saint James Hotel** (off Route 1, 505–376–2664) was where Cody worked on his Wild West extravaganza. He returned on Christmas to put on a show for the local children. The hotel was built by Henry Lambert, a chef for President Abraham Lincoln.

Four miles south of town on Route 21, the **Philmont Scout Ranch** (505–376–2281) was owned by Oklahoma oilman Waite Phillips, who donated it to the Boy Scouts of America as a national camping area in 1941. It comprises 137,493 acres and hosts more than 15,000 scouts on backpacking expeditions annually. The **Philmont Museum** contains displays of southwestern art and history. The adjacent **Seton Memorial Library** contains the private library and artworks of Ernest Thompson Seton, writer, naturalist, illustrator, and first chief scout of the Boy Scouts.

RATON

In 1866 a frontier character known as "Uncle Dick" Wooton constructed a road over the Raton Pass, a difficult twenty-seven-mile stretch of the Santa Fe Trail, and charged a toll of $1.50. Wooten's enterprise was said to be so lucrative that he took his profits to the bank in kegs filled with silver dollars. Willow Springs, where Wooten took in travelers, was renamed Raton after the pass. Among other exploits, Wooten and a corps of volunteers put down the Taos Pueblo Revolt of 1847 in which Governor Charles Bent was killed. Many of the buildings along 1st, 2d, and 3d streets, comprising the **Raton Downtown Historical District,** date from the arrival of the railroad in 1879, including the 1896 **Palace Hotel** (Cook and 1st streets), now a restaurant. The **Raton Museum** (216 South 1st Street, 505–445–8979) has collections on Indians, ranching, and railroad history.

East of Raton in the town of **Folsom,** the **Folsom Museum** (off Route 72, 505–278–2122) has displays relating to the discovery by a cowhand of a 10,000-year-old arrowhead embedded in a bison skeleton, including the chipped stone darts known as Folsom points. The discovery, which was followed by an extensive archaeological dig in

Melted adobe walls and brick chimneys are all that remain of Fort Union, which in the nineteenth century was the largest U.S. military post in the southwest. The stabilized ruins comprise Fort Union National Monument.

1926, led anthropologists to revise their estimates of the duration of a human presence in North America. There is a historical marker at the **Folsom Archaeological Site** west of town.

FORT UNION NATIONAL MONUMENT

Fort Union was established in 1851 near the fork where two branches of the Santa Fe Trail converged. In addition to being the main quartermaster depot for military posts in the Southwest, the fort was also the staging area for operations against the Ute, Jicarilla Apache, Comanche, and Kiowa. In 1854, after the Apache defeated a cavalry unit, the fort commander, Philip Saint George Cooke, launched a campaign against the Apache and inflicted a serious defeat on them. Cooke was aided by a volunteer force of Taos Pueblo led by Kit Carson. During the Civil War, the fort was the objective of its former commander, Confederate general Henry H. Sibley, and his army marching north from El Paso. Sibley's troops were turned back at the Battle of Glorieta Pass on March 28, 1862. Fort Union was closed in 1891. By then, the Indian threat had ended and the railroad had replaced the Santa Fe Trail. Only the stabilized ruins of this important fort on the Santa Fe Trail remain today. There is a self-guiding trail through 100 acres of the ruins of the fort; a museum, featuring exhibits on the fort's history and demonstrations led by guides in military costume, is located at the visitor center.

LOCATION: Route 161, 8 miles northwest of Watrous. HOURS: 8–6 Daily. FEE: Yes. TELEPHONE: 505–425–8025.

LAS VEGAS

Settled in 1835 in lush meadows, Las Vegas (The Meadows) was originally known as Nuestra Señora de los Dolores de Las Vegas. Although it was the Santa Fe Trail's point of entry into Mexico, the town grew slowly. According to one traveler, Las Vegas was a place of "one hundred odd houses and poor dirty-looking inhabitants" in 1846, the year General Stephen Watts Kearny proclaimed New Mexico part of the United States, in the town plaza. Thereafter Las Vegas became an important military post—with the greatest arsenal and supply of material and men to the western third of the country—until operations shifted to newly built Fort Union in 1851.

The coming of the railroad in 1879 precipitated a building boom; it also attracted a number of gunmen and outlaws who gave Las Vegas the reputation of being one of the toughest towns in the West. One chronicler reported that twenty-nine men died violently in one month in 1880. To curb the lawlessness, vigilantes took to hanging outlaws regularly from the windmill derrick in the town plaza, while the Women's Christian Temperance Union erected a public drinking fountain topped by a stone lion in hopes that the availability of water would diminish the consumption of alcohol. The fountain still stands in **Lion Park,** at the corner of Lincoln Street and Grand Avenue. One of the stipulations of the original Las Vegas land grant was that the settlers build a town plaza. Today the **Old Town Plaza** is a historic district where many of the adobe buildings that predate the arrival of the railroad are located. The **Plaza Hotel** (230 Old Town Plaza) was built in 1880–81 as a retreat for consumptives. Nearby are the sandstone **First National Bank** building constructed in 1888 and the redbrick **Louis C. Ilfeld Law Office** (220 North Plaza), built in 1921.

By the turn of the century, Las Vegas was the largest town in New Mexico. The town's **Roughriders Memorial and City Museum** (725 Grand Avenue, 505–425–8726) commemorates the Roughriders' New Mexican headquarters. Forty percent of the unit was from New Mexico; in 1899 Theodore Roosevelt came here for a Roughrider reunion. The museum also has early items from the pioneer days. The **Masonic Temple** (6th Street) is an exceptionally good example of the Richardsonian Romanesque style, with a tower entrance. It was built in 1894–95 from purplish, locally quarried sandstone. The **Bank of Las Vegas** (622 Douglas Street), a 1921 Classic Revival Missouri sandstone building with fluted columns, and the **Crockett Block,** an 1898 building with a Neoclassical entrance on 6th Street, were both designed by the architects Rapp and Rapp, brothers from Trinidad, Colorado, who designed structures throughout the Southwest.

In 1898 the railroad hotel magnate Fred Harvey built **La Castaneda Hotel** (525 Railroad Avenue), a Mission Revival–style building that was one of the showplaces of the Harvey chain. La Castaneda's facade and courtyard face the railroad tracks. The Harvey Girls, who worked in the hotel's dining room, lived across Railroad Avenue in the 1899 **Rawlins Building**, a now-deteriorating landmark building with one of the few pressed-metal fronts in New Mexico. In 1917 the Santa Fe Railroad built the still-standing **Roundhouse** near the Gallinas River at the end of Railroad Avenue. The roundhouse had thirty-four stalls and employed 380 mechanics working three shifts around the clock. From Old Town Plaza, Hot Springs Boulevard (Route 65) runs northwest for five miles to the old **Montezuma Hotel.** This grand, 343-room castle was built in 1888 by the Santa Fe Railroad to take advantage of the thermal baths known as the Las Vegas Hot Springs. The hotel, which had the first electric lights in the state, was the railroad's grandest until the railroad closed it in 1903. In 1981 the Armand Hammer Foundation restored it for the United World College.

PECOS NATIONAL MONUMENT

This extensive Anasazi pueblo was founded about 1300 by groups of Pueblo Indians displaced by population shifts in the Rio Grande valley. The pueblo at Pecos thrived because of its location. It served as a center for trade between the Plains and Pueblo peoples. When the Spanish settled the area, they saw Pecos as a rich source of tribute and as fertile ground for religious conversion. In 1540 Coronado had heard reports of a fabulously rich city called Quivira to the northeast. He set off to find it in 1541 under the lying guidance of a local Indian known as the Turk, but discovered only a few poor Indian villages. The Pueblos hoped he would die or become hopelessly lost on the plains.

By 1620 the Franciscans had established a mission at Pecos. The mission church, completed in 1625 with walls 8 to 20 feet thick and a nave measuring 40 by 133 feet, was destroyed during the Pueblo Revolt of 1680. After the Spanish reconquest of 1692, another church was built on the foundations of the first. Finished in 1717, its ruins are visible today. Despite Comanche raids in the mid-1700s, a smallpox epidemic in 1788, and the growth of nearby towns, the pueblo survived until 1838, when its last seventeen residents joined the Jemez Pueblo. At its height between 1450 and 1600, the fortresslike pueblo had 700 rooms built in a quadrangle around an interior plaza. The buildings rose "four and five stories," according to the Spanish explorer Castaño de Sosa, who occupied the pueblo with his small force in 1591. For ten summers between 1915 and 1929, Alfred V. Kidder excavated the pueblo at Pecos in expeditions sponsored by the Phillips Academy of Andover, Massachusetts. In his work at Pecos, Kidder helped shift the emphasis in archaeology from the accumulation of objects for museum display to the systematic interpretation of a site.

A one-mile self-guiding trail travels through the monument, and exhibits on the history of the pueblo and artifacts from the excavations are on display at the visitor center.

LOCATION: Route 63 off Route I-25, 2 miles south of Pecos. HOURS: Labor Day through Memorial Day: 8–5 Daily; Memorial Day through Labor Day: 8–6 Daily. FEE: Yes. TELEPHONE: 505–757–6414.

GLORIETA BATTLEFIELD

Although the Civil War battle fought at this site is often called "the Gettysburg of the West," only a historical marker indicates the six-mile stretch over which hundreds of Union and Confederate troops

OPPOSITE: *Ruins of the eighteenth-century mission church at Pecos, built on the foundations of the original mission, which was destroyed in the Pueblo Revolt of 1680.*

Abandoned miners' dwellings in Madrid, once a prosperous coal-mining center. In 1954, the Albuquerque & Cerrillos Coal Company placed this advertisement in the Wall Street Journal *: "For Sale: Entire Town."*

fought in March 1862. The battle thwarted the grand plans of Brigadier General Henry H. Sibley to conquer the West for the Confederacy. After capturing Fort Union, Sibley planned to take Denver and the gold fields of Colorado before heading west to capture the gold fields of California and the city of San Francisco. Sibley's advance force, commanded by Major Charles Pyron, occupied an undefended Santa Fe early in March 1862. When Pyron learned the Union army was marching on Santa Fe from Fort Union, he moved his 300-man force out to meet them and camped at what is now the town of Canoncito. The next day, on March 26, Union major John M. Chivington attacked Pyron's forces near Pigeon's Ranch in the Glorieta Pass. Chivington forced Pyron to withdraw with a flanking maneuver and a cavalry charge.

After this initial skirmish, both sides were reinforced: the Confederates by 800 men commanded by Lieutenant Colonel William R. Scurry, the Union side by Colonel John P. Slough with

900 men. The battle began at approximately 10:30 on the morning of March 28 when Slough's force met Scurry's about a mile west of Pigeon's Ranch. The Confederates charged five times; all their field officers were either killed or wounded, and they finally broke under the fire of Slough's artillery. Later, however, they retook their lines under a barrage of rifle fire from Texas sharpshooters and forced the Union troops to withdraw. When the battle ended at approximately 5 P.M., the Confederates appeared to be the victors. It was then learned that Chivington and his men had slipped around the pass and destroyed the Confederate supplies, which Scurry had left lightly defended. With nothing left to sustain them, the Confederates withdrew to Texas.

Only an old adobe building on Route 50 remains of Pigeon's Ranch, once an important way station on the Santa Fe Trail. In June 1987 the skeletons of thirty-three Confederate soldiers were uncovered at a building site nearby.

MADRID

During their long stretch of productivity—from 1869 to the closing of the mines in 1959—Madrid's coal mines yielded up to 100,000 tons annually. Once owned entirely by the Albuquerque & Cerillos Coal Company, Madrid (pronounced MAD-rid) has now been taken over by artists and craftsmen, who have converted the old frame buildings into residences, galleries, shops, and studios. A view down into an actual mine shaft is one of the attractions of the **Old Coal Mine Museum** (Turquoise Trail and Route 14, 505–473–0743), which also displays mining equipment, mining cars, and a restored locomotive. Before World War II, Madrid was known for its display of Christmas lights; planes would detour over the town so that passengers could enjoy the sight.

Route 14, linking Madrid with Santa Fe to the north and Albuquerque to the south, is called the Turquoise Trail by local promoters, a reference to the high-quality turquoise that was once taken from the mines at **Cerrillos** (Little Hills), another mining ghost town a few miles north of Madrid also in the process of a crafts and tourist revival. In its heyday in the 1880s, Cerrillos had twenty-one saloons and four hotels. In 1825 the town of **Golden** south of Madrid was the site of the first gold rush west of the Mississippi.

ALBUQUERQUE
AND
SOUTHERN
NEW MEXICO

OPPOSITE: *The ruins of the Mission de la Purísima Concepción de Cuarac, in the Salinas National Monument. Hispanic missionaries were attracted to the region because of its abundant salt.*

J ust south of Santa Fe, the Santa Fe Plateau drops off sharply at a point known as La Bajada, or The Descent. The steep and dangerous grade was a challenge for wagon trains in the territory's early days, and even today it can be hazardous for automobiles in bad weather. La Bajada, the result of volcanic activity some seventy million years ago, divides the state north and south—divisions that are called Río Arriba, or Upper River, and Río Abajo, or Lower River (the river referred to is the Rio Grande). The city of Albuquerque, a relative newcomer among New Mexico's settlements, is the undisputed capital of Río Abajo as well as the state's largest and most modern city. Geographically, Albuquerque is still well within the northern half of the state: The actual midway point is farther south, near where the 1908 railroad line known as the Belen Cutoff makes its way from Clovis to the Rio Grande. Of the two families driven off this land by the Pueblo Revolt of 1680, only one, the Trujillos, returned after General Diego de Vargas reconquered the province in 1692. In 1706 thirty families from Bernalillo settled here and began farming the fertile bottomland. It is from their arrival that the city of Albuquerque dates. The settlers called their settlement San Francisco de Alburquerque in honor of the duke of Alburquerque, the viceroy of New Spain. The duke in turn changed the name to San Felipe de Alburquerque after King Philip of Spain. (Eventually the first r was dropped and the name shortened to Albuquerque.) The new center grew quickly: By the end of the century it was New Mexico's largest town, with over 6,000 residents. It has retained that distinction, except for a brief period in the 1880s when Socorro, swelled in size by a silver boom, surpassed it.

Southern New Mexico had been well traveled by Indians and Europeans long before Albuquerque was settled. The prehistoric Mogollon (pronounced Muggy-own) Indians inhabited pithouses in the mountains of southwestern New Mexico as early as A.D. 500. After they came into contact with Anasazi drifting down from the north, they built the more elaborate habitations now preserved as the Gila Cliff Dwellings National Monument. The mesa-top pueblo of Acoma was in existence as early as the late twelfth century and is one of the oldest continuously inhabited towns in the country.

OPPOSITE: *General Diego de Vargas, the Spanish leader who led the reconquest of New Mexico in 1692, and achieved this, as a seventeenth-century Spanish scholar noted, "without wasting an ounce of powder, unsheathing a sword, or (what is most worthy of emphasis and appreciation) without costing the Royal Treasury a single copper."*

El señor D.ᵃ Diego de
Barvas Zapata Lufan Pon
ze de León, Marques de la Na
ba de Barcinas del Orden de
S.ᵗᵎ Tiago, Governador, Conquis
tador, Pacificador, y Capitan
General del Nuebo Mejico,
perdio la Vida en Canpaña
Rasa por libertar las Va
sos Salvados en el Sitio
de Bernalilla año
de MDCCIV

Este cuadro que el Instituto de Cultura Hispánica ofrece al Museo de Nuebo Mejico, es có
pia del verdadero retrato de D. Diego Barvas Zapata "de la Casa de los Vargas" cuyo original se
conserva en la capilla de San Isidro sita en el Pardil de Santisteban de Madrid.

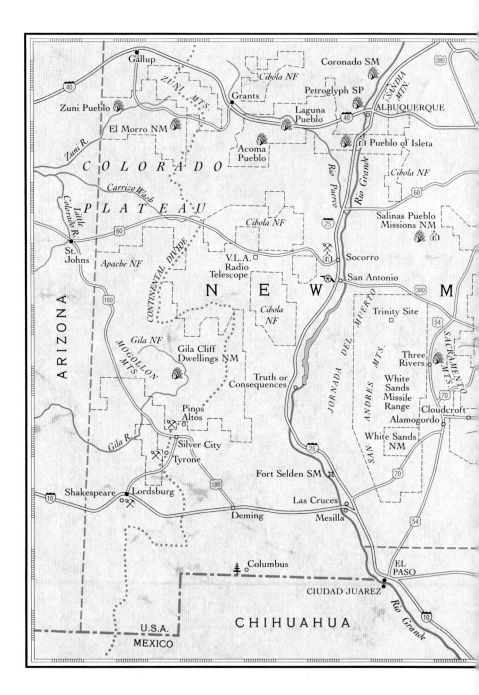

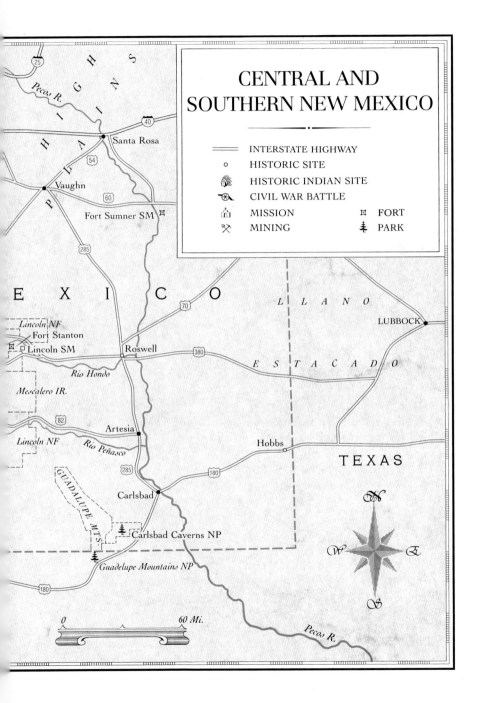

CENTRAL AND SOUTHERN NEW MEXICO

═══════ INTERSTATE HIGHWAY
○ HISTORIC SITE
  HISTORIC INDIAN SITE
  CIVIL WAR BATTLE
  MISSION   FORT
✕ MINING   PARK

25

Pecos R.

40

Santa Rosa

54

Vaughn

60

Fort Sumner SM

285

E X I C O

70

L L A N O

LUBBOCK

Lincoln NF
Fort Stanton
Lincoln SM

Roswell

380

E S T A C A D O

Rio Hondo

Mescalero IR.

82

Artesia

Lincoln NF   Rio Peñasco

Hobbs

285

180

T E X A S

GUADALUPE MTS.

Carlsbad

Carlsbad Caverns NP

Guadelupe Mountains NP

180

0   60 Mi.

Pecos R.

N
W   E
S

The Mission of La Purísima Concepción de Cuarac, constructed before 1633 and

The twelve pueblos of Tiguex along the Rio Grande date from the early fourteenth century. One of the Tiguex pueblos that has survived is fourteen miles from present-day Albuquerque. It was visited by Coronado's lieutenant Hernando de Alvarado in 1540, who mistook the squash he saw growing there for watermelon and named the pueblo Sandía (Spanish for watermelon). Coronado spent the winter of 1540 in the Tiguex pueblos, possibly in the one just north of Albuquerque now preserved in ruins as the Coronado State Monument. His mistreatment of the people of the pueblos planted the seeds of ill will that drove the Spanish out of New Mexico during the Pueblo Revolt of 1680. It is often said that the first European to enter New Mexico, in 1536, was Alvar Núñez Cabeza de Vaca, who had been shipwrecked and spent years wandering through the Southwest. Historians doubt that he entered New Mexico, but his inflated tales of rich cities inspired Spanish expedi-

abandoned in 1674, a casualty of intense drought in the region and Apache raids.

tions into the territory. Missionaries and would-be colonizers helped blaze El Camino Real (the Royal Road) up the Rio Grande valley. In 1598 Juan de Oñate, the first successful colonizer, extended the trail to the northern pueblos of the Rio Grande.

After he probed into New Mexico and was arrested in 1807, Lieutenant Zebulon Pike was escorted out of the territory down the Rio Grande to El Paso. His published observations increased American interest in the territory. General Stephen Watts Kearny followed roughly the same route down the Rio Grande after he took Santa Fe in 1846. Before heading west, he detached Philip Saint George Cooke and his Mormon Battalion to blaze a trail to California. Cooke crossed into present-day Arizona through the Guadalupe Pass in the extreme southwestern corner of New Mexico. The Royal Road was also the Civil War invasion route of the army of Confederate general Henry Hopkins Sibley. Sibley needed to pass

This photograph, taken in 1909, shows "an 85,000 wool-clip, Roswell, N.M;" a frontier center for sheep as well as cattle.

heavily defended Fort Craig, one of the posts built to protect traffic in the Rio Grande valley. Sibley won a narrow victory at the Battle of Valverde after luring Fort Craig's commander, Edward R. S. Canby, and his forces into the open. He then continued north to Albuquerque and Santa Fe. A dawn battle and the loss of his supply train at Glorieta Pass forced him to withdraw.

After the Civil War, the U.S. Army had its hands full protecting travelers, settlers, miners, stagecoaches, cattle ranchers, and railroaders from the Indians. The Apache and their cousins, the Navajo, were among the most fierce, clever, and stubborn Indians the army ever faced. The famed Apache leaders—Geronimo, Mangas Coloradas, Nana, and Victorio—raided and plundered, then eluded pursuers by fading away into the mountains of southwestern New Mexico, Arizona, and Mexico. In 1863 Kit Carson launched a campaign against the Navajo from New Mexico. After his victory, the Indians were forced to make "the Long March" from Fort Defiance in Arizona to the Bosque Redondo reservation near Fort Sumner, New Mexico, where, it was hoped, they would become farmers. The experiment was singularly unsuccessful; five years later the Indians who survived were repatriated to Arizona.

Fort Sumner and the reservation were a lucrative market for Texas beef, and in 1866 cattlemen Charles Goodnight and Oliver Loving blazed the Goodnight-Loving Trail from Fort Belknap, Texas, along the Pecos River to Fort Sumner and from there north to Colorado. To supply Indian agencies in Arizona, the "Cow King of New Mexico," John Chisum, ran his cattle from Roswell to Las Cruces along the Chisum Trail, and then into Arizona. In a struggle for commercial supremacy known as the Lincoln County War of 1878–1881, Chisum was first the ally and then the enemy of William Bonney (better known as Billy the Kid), who made his reputation as an outlaw rustling Chisum's cattle.

The arrival of the railroad was preceded by the Butterfield Overland Mail Company stage line, which crossed almost the entire southern portion of the state in its run from Missouri to San Francisco. In addition to being the exact halfway point on this stage line, Mesilla was the principal town in the territory the United States acquired in the Gadsden Purchase from Mexico in 1853; as a result, it was declared the capital of the Confederate Territory of Arizona when Major John Baylor marched into southern New Mexico late in the spring of 1861. Within thirty years railroads changed the character of New Mexico. In the southeastern portion of the state, Charles B. Eddy's Pecos Valley Railroad brought farmers to settlements on the Great Plains: Carlsbad (then named Eddy), which it reached in 1891; Roswell, in 1894; and Portales, in 1898. A new city center sprang up in Albuquerque when the Atchison, Topeka & Santa Fe Railroad, New Mexico's foremost line, bypassed Old Town in 1880. From there, it traveled the Rio Grande valley south to Rincon, where it cut southwest to Deming about the same time the Southern Pacific reached El Paso in 1881. For a time it looked as if there would be two parallel lines through the southwestern part of the state, but an agreement was reached to use one set of tracks. In 1908 the Santa Fe Railroad opened the Belen Cutoff from Clovis to Belen to Gallup, which eliminated the difficult climb through the Raton Pass. Route 60, the Ocean-to-Ocean Highway, opened in 1917, the first numbered highway to cross the country. In New Mexico it parallels the Belen Cutoff almost to the Rio Grande; from Magdalena it follows an old cattle trail west through the mountains.

Southern New Mexico's clear air, sunny skies, and wide open spaces have attracted a number of scientific endeavors. In 1930 Robert Goddard arrived in southeastern New Mexico to pursue his experiments in rocketry after being banned from Massachusetts for firing his frightening missiles. That same year the astronomer Clyde Tombaugh discovered the planet Pluto by examining telescopic photographs of the heavens from New Mexico. In 1942 the White Sands Proving Ground for testing rockets opened, and in 1945 the world's first atomic explosion took place at Trinity Site, located far into the desert. In Albuquerque the Sandia National Laboratory provides casings for atomic weapons and also pursues research into peaceful uses of nuclear energy and alternate forms of energy such as solar power. On the San Agustin Plains west of Magdalena, the world's largest radio telescope—twenty-seven two-and-a-half-ton antennas known as the Very Large Array—has extended the known limits of the universe. Such activity has changed both the character and the image of New Mexico.

Mesquite trees in front of the Church of San Felipe de Neri, constructed in 1793 on Albuquerque's Old Town plaza.

The tour of southwestern New Mexico begins in Albuquerque, heads west to Zuni Pueblo, then makes a long run south, passing through the Gila National Forest to Silver City. From there it crosses the southern part of the state to Las Cruces on the Rio Grande and then follows the old Camino Real, or Royal Road, north back to Albuquerque. The loop through southeastern New Mexico goes from Albuquerque to the Salinas National Monument with head-quarters at Mountainair, then south to Alamogordo. From there it follows a circuitous route eastward through Lincoln, Roswell, and Carlsbad to Hobbs. The final major stop on the way back to Albuquerque is Fort Sumner.

ALBUQUERQUE

The center of historic Albuquerque is a quiet oasis known as Old Town. Tiwa-speaking Indians had occupied a pueblo on this site as early as 1350, and in 1632 a Spanish settler is believed to have built a house here, but neither it nor the pueblo escaped destruction in the Pueblo Revolt of 1680. Old Town's plaza, located in the center of the town founded by Governor Francisco Cuervo y Valdés early in the eighteenth century, was dedicated when the governor and others flung stones and grass to the four points of the compass and shouted "Long live the king!" It was not until 1779, however, when Spanish authorities ordered the colonists to group together for protection from Indians, that the plaza actually began to take shape. At first, livestock was corralled into it at night; later it became an open-air market. The plaza remained the center of town until a new city center sprang up around the railroad when it arrived in 1880, about one-and-a-half miles east of Old Town.

In 1706, the year Albuquerque was officially founded, a church was built on the west side of the present plaza. It apparently fell into disrepair in 1790 and was replaced by the **Church of San Felipe de Neri** on North Plaza in 1793. The church's high windows and thick walls were built to protect against Indian attacks. The towers on the church, added between 1855 and 1865 to make it look more European, are often described as "folk Gothic," while the church itself is an amalgam of Gothic, Spanish Colonial, and Pueblo Revival styles. The church's **Rectory** on its east side was also built in 1793, but the second story, the brick fronting, and portico were added in the latter half of the nineteenth century. The **Sister Blandina Convent** (North Plaza and Romero) was erected in 1881 to house the Sisters of Charity. It was the first two-story adobe building in Old Town. In 1906 the merchant Charles Mann built the **Charles Mann Barn** (200 Block north of Romero, private), a simple adobe structure, and purchased the **Florencio Zamora Store** (301 Romero, private), which was built between 1893 and 1898 from soft pugmill brick. The store is built on the foundation of the first San Felipe de Neri Church.

A number of historic buildings in Old Town now house shops on the ground floor. The brick **Jesús Romero House** (204 Romero) was built in both Prairie and Mediterranean styles in 1915 by its prominent namesake. It was the last home constructed on the plaza. In 1893 Romero also built the **Jesús Romero Store** (121 Romero), which has elements of the Queen Anne style. Dating from the same era, the **Manuel Springer House** (2036 South Plaza) was built in the Queen Anne style with projecting bay windows; its original lines have since been covered up by additions and adaptations. Springer, like Romero, was a merchant who kept his business in Old Town after the center of the city shifted east. The 1898 **Herman Blueher House** (302 San Felipe) was once a large, Italianate-style residence whose original lines have been obscured by pueblolike adaptations. Blueher, who came to Albuquerque in 1882 as a hired hand, was its first dealer in farm equipment. Another prominent Old Town residence is the large **Cristóbal Armijo House** (2004 South Plaza, private), constructed between 1880 and 1886 in the Italianate and Queen Anne styles. The wealthy Armijo was one of the founders of the First National Bank in New Town. In the 1930s and 1940s, Old Town was discovered by artists, who were followed there by tourists. Many of the section's old buildings were redone in the Pueblo Revival style in the 1950s.

Albuquerque Museum

Located since 1979 in a new solar-heated building just north of Old Town, the Albuquerque Museum features an extensive permanent exhibit on local history entitled "Four Centuries: A History of Albuquerque." The objects on display—squash blossom necklaces, branding irons, carved Spanish Colonial furniture—represent the many cultures that have shaped the city. The exhibit features a *repostero,* or armorial wall hanging, that was made in approximately 1665

OPPOSITE: *Stylized tile and terra-cotta Indian war shields with iconic birds, whirling logs of the four winds, and clouds—the Navajo symbols for freedom, happiness, and life—decorate Albuquerque's "Pueblo Deco" style KiMo Theater.*

for the eighth duke of Alburquerque. The hanging, embroidered with the Alburquerque coat of arms, was presented to the city in 1956 on its 250th anniversary by the eighteenth duke of Alburquerque.

> LOCATION: 2000 Mountain Road NW. HOURS: 9–5 Tuesday–Sunday. FEE: None. TELEPHONE: 505–243–7255.

The nearby **New Mexico Museum of Natural History** (1801 Mountain Road NW, 505–841–8837) has among its exhibits on natural history full-size models of dinosaurs and a simulated volcano.

The **KiMo Theater** (421 Central Avenue NW, 505–848–1370), built in 1927, is a regional variation on the moving picture palaces that sprang up across the country in the 1920s. The KiMo's style has been dubbed Pueblo Deco, a fanciful mix of the Pueblo Revival and Art Deco styles. On the exterior, its deep-set doors, stucco-imitating adobe walls, and false *vigas* (protruding log cross beams) are in the Pueblo Revival tradition. Inside, the decor gives way to fantasy: murals depicting the Seven Cities of Cibola, air vents that look like Navajo rugs, war drum chandeliers, and lamps of longhorn steer skulls with glowing amber eyes. The KiMo was restored in the late 1970s and is now a performing arts center.

The museum at the **Indian Pueblo Cultural Center** (2401 12th Street NW, 505–843–7270) is divided into two sections, Pueblo history from prehistoric times to the present, and contemporary arts and crafts from the Pueblo. Throughout the museum, step-by-step techniques of various crafts are displayed. Traditional Indian dances are performed on selected weekends. The center, owned and operated jointly by New Mexico's nineteen Indian pueblos, works to promote understanding of the traditional culture and heritage of the Pueblo Indians. When the **University of New Mexico** (Central Avenue and Las Lomas, University, and Girard boulevards, 505–277–0111) opened in the summer of 1892, it rented rooms in a preparatory school until its first building, **Hodgin Hall,** was completed later that year. Originally a square, red-brick, Richardsonian Romanesque building, Hodgin Hall was remodeled in 1908 when President William Tight decreed the entire campus be in the Spanish-Pueblo style. In 1938 the immense **Zimmerman Library,** with a reading

OPPOSITE: *The Pueblo motif of the KiMo Theater is carried through to the smallest detail, even the lobby doorhandles.*

room shaped like the interior of a pueblo church, was completed; it was designed by the Santa Fe architect John Gaw Meem, who built many other pueblo-style structures on campus and in the state over the next thirty years. The library includes special rooms on Southwestern material and a room containing Meem's archives. The **Maxwell Museum of Anthropology** (Rodondo Drive at Ash Street, 505–227–4404) has distinguished collections on the native and prehistoric cultures of the Southwest.

Off Central Avenue (Route 66) at Wyoming Boulevard, the **National Atomic Museum** (505–844–8443) is located on the Kirtland Air Force Base. The exhibits here emphasize the World War II Manhattan Project that developed the atomic bomb at Los Alamos and the first atomic explosion at the Trinity Site near White Sands, New Mexico. Models of the first two atomic bombs, Little Boy and Fat Man, are part of what is touted as the "world's most complete collection of atomic weapons."

PETROGLYPH STATE PARK

Known as the West Mesa, this seventeen-mile serpentine stretch of volcanic rock west of Albuquerque contains some 15,000 petroglyphs, or prehistoric pictures: white or gray lines chipped into the dark rock. Anasazi petroglyphs date from A.D. 700 to 1200. Between the fourteenth and seventeenth centuries, the Tiwa carved animals, birds, people, flute players, and kachina figures. The state park protects only seventy-two acres of this important repository of prehistoric art, and some of the best petroglyphs are on private land beyond the park's boundaries. In June 1988 the New Mexican congressional delegation introduced a bill proposing that most of this area be brought under federal protection as the Petroglyph National Monument. It would be the first national monument devoted to prehistoric art.

LOCATION: 6900 Unser Boulevard NW. HOURS: 9–5 Daily; extended hours in summer, call for exact times. FEE: Yes. TELEPHONE: 505–823–4016.

CORONADO STATE MONUMENT

Twelve hundred rooms of this fortresslike, multistoried Rio Grande pueblo called Kuaua were excavated by the University of New Mexico in the 1930s. Since then, the square kiva has been reconstructed with reproductions of the many-colored ceremonial frescoes that were discovered inside. Kuaua was one of twelve pueblos—a grouping called Tiguex—along the west bank of the Rio Grande. Historians believe that Coronado stopped at Kuaua or at a pueblo nearby during the winter of 1540–1541. The Indians rebelled against Spanish mistreatment when, according to chronicler Pedro de Casteñada, a soldier ordered an Indian to hold his horse and then "ravished or had attempted to ravish his wife." The pueblo was still hostile when Coronado visited it again in April 1542 to winter over before returning to New Spain. Kuaua, built about 1325, was populated until the end of the sixteenth century, when the Spanish consolidated many pueblos by force. There is a self-guiding trail through the monument. A small museum at the visitor center displays many of the original frescoes, examples of some of the finest murals in North American prehistoric art.

LOCATION: Route 44, 1 mile northwest of Bernalillo. HOURS: 9–5 Daily. FEE: Yes. TELEPHONE: 505–867–5351.

PUEBLO OF ISLETA

The Tiwa-speaking Indians living here were originally called Tauweaga, or Kick-Flaking Stone Place People. The pueblo was established in the first half of the thirteenth century. When the first Franciscan priest arrived in 1581, it had a population of 1,500 living in two- and three-story buildings. A mission church was built in 1613. The pueblo was unusual in that it did not participate in the Pueblo Revolt of 1680, probably because a large Spanish garrison was stationed here. Governor Antonio de Otermín and other Spanish refugees fled to Mexico after escaping from Santa Fe. When the Spanish returned to this pueblo, they found the church partially destroyed. The present **Mission of Saint Augustine,** a handsome adobe structure with two bell towers and two bell niches above the main entrance, was completed in 1720. Father Juan de Padilla, one of the two priests of Coronado's expedition who stayed behind to Christianize the Indians, is buried under the altar. According to legend, his coffin pops out of the ground from time to time with the body perfectly preserved. Today Isleta has the largest population of any pueblo, with 3,000 residents.

LOCATION: Route I-25, 14 miles south of Albuquerque. HOURS: *Visitor Center:* 8–5 Daily. FEE: None. TELEPHONE: 505–869–3111.

San Esteban del Rey, a seventeenth-century mission church with massive walls nine feet thick, overlooks the pueblo of Acoma, one of the oldest continuously occupied settlements in the New World. OPPOSITE: *The San José Mission at Laguna Pueblo.*

ACOMA PUEBLO

Located dramatically atop a steep 365-foot-high mesa, Acoma, also called Sky City, is one of the oldest continuously inhabited villages in the United States. Dates of its original settlement vary from A.D. 600 to 1150. The pueblo already had been established for many centuries when Hernando de Alvarado of the Coronado expedition stopped there in 1540 and reported that the pueblo was "one of the strongest ever seen, because the city is built upon a very high rock. The ascent was so difficult that we repented climbing to the top." In 1598 Juan de Zaldívar, the nephew of Juan de Oñate, New Mexico's first Spanish colonizer, was killed when he went to Acoma to demand tribute. On January 12, 1599, his brother Vicente and seventy Spanish soldiers attacked the pueblo, killing 800 Indians and inflicting harsh punishment on the survivors.

Between 1629 and 1640, the **San Esteban del Rey Mission** was built under the direction of Friar Juan Ramírez. Virtually all the con-

struction materials, including the earth for the 2,000-square-foot cemetery, had to be carried up to the mesa. According to legend, Ramírez was allowed into the pueblo after he miraculously saved an Indian infant who had fallen off a cliff. San Esteban, 150 feet long with walls 60 feet high, is one of the most beautifully constructed and situated mission churches in New Mexico. Enchanted Mesa, the legendary home of the Acoma people, rises 400 feet from the plains a few miles east of Acoma. Fewer than twenty families live in the old village today. At the foot of the mesa, there is a large, well-organized visitor center with a permanent exhibit entitled "One Thousand Years of Clay: Pottery, Environment, and History." Shuttle buses to the mesa depart regularly. Events and celebrations take place throughout the year.

> LOCATION: 12.5 miles southwest of the junction of Routes I-40 and 23. HOURS: June through August: 8–7 Daily; September through May: 8–4:30 Daily. FEE: Yes. TELEPHONE: 505–552–6604.

About five miles toward Albuquerque, exit 114 off Route I-40 leads to **Laguna Pueblo** (505–552–6654). Founded in 1699 by refugees from other pueblos fleeing the Spanish reconquest of New Mexico, Laguna is actually six villages spread out around the original settlement, Old Laguna. The **San José Mission,** a stone church covered with adobe, has an interior that has been elaborately decorated by Indian artisans and includes a carved and painted altar and a large hide painting of Saint Joseph and the Christ Child. In 1800, in the midst of a severe drought, Laguna Pueblo borrowed and then refused to return a painting of Saint Joseph from nearby Acoma Pueblo that was said to have miraculous powers. After fifty years Acoma took Laguna all the way to the U.S. Supreme Court and won the painting back. When the Acoma pueblo Indians went to retrieve the painting, they found it propped against a tree about midway between the two pueblos. Legend has it that Saint Joseph, having heard about the decision, had started home on his own.

EL MORRO NATIONAL MONUMENT

It is thought that the people of the northern plateau country deserted that region to build the well-fortified pueblo called Atsinna on top of

OPPOSITE: *El Morro, a massive sandstone mesa within the Navajo Indian Reservation in northwestern New Mexico, is the site of the ruins of the Atsinna pueblo.*

the mesa known as El Morro about A.D. 1275. They left their ancestral home because the area was becoming increasingly arid, culminating in a major drought from 1276 to 1299. The threat of hostile invasion from the Athabascan to the north or from other neighboring pueblos also may have precipitated the move. Early in the fourteenth century, when the drought had abated, they returned down the Zuni River. The excavated remains of Atsinna can be seen atop the mesa today, but the main attraction is the 200-foot-high **Inscription Rock,** where from prehistoric times passers-by have left drawings, comments, and signatures, creating a unique register of historical time. The petroglyphs on the base of the rock probably date from the time of the Atsinna. The earliest recorded European inscription was left by Juan de Oñate, *adelantado* of the new Spanish colony, who wrote "Paso por acquí el adelantado Don Juan de Oñate del descubrimiento de la mar del sur a 16 de Abril de 1605." (The Adelantado Don Juan de Oñate passed by here coming from the discovery of the Sea of the South, the 16th of April of 1605). The over 500 legible names include Diego de Vargas (1692), reconqueror of New Mexico; Lieutenant James Simpson (1849), the military observer who made one of the first scientific reports on prehistoric sites; and Edward F. Beale (1857), commander of the famed camel corps. El Morro, which means "the bluff" in Spanish, was made a national monument in 1906.

LOCATION: Route 53, east of Ramah. HOURS: 8–5 Daily. FEE: Yes. TELEPHONE: 505–783–4226.

Zuni Pueblo, the largest Indian pueblo, is located ten miles west of the junction of Routes 602 and 53 (505–782–5581). It was one of the Seven Cities of Cibola that Coronado was seeking on his 1540 expedition. Instead of cities of gold, however, Coronado found poor settlements. At the time the Zuni people inhabited at least six pueblos, including one located fifteen miles southwest at Hawikuh. In 1670 this settlement was abandoned; the ruins can be visited with a Zuni guide. The Zuni of all six pueblos over time consolidated at what is today Zuni Pueblo. The modern village of Zuni, sprawled along the highway, surrounds the old pueblo called Halona. The Zuni are renowned for their silversmithing and the fetishes that they carve. Their black-and-red-on-white pottery decorated with animal designs has also experienced a resurgence in the last few decades.

OPPOSITE: *Red rock sandstone formations within the Zuni Reservation.* OVERLEAF: *A Zuni tribal dance.*

Hornos, communal bee-hive ovens brought to New Mexico by the Spanish, line the wall of the church at Zuni Pueblo.

Socorro was one of the largest towns in New Mexico during the silver boom in the 1880s. Although it lost much of its population and most of its forty-four saloons after silver prices plummeted in 1893, the town survived as a farming and ranching center. A local hero of the boom days was Sheriff Elfrego Baca, who allegedly held off eighty armed Texas cowboys after he had arrested one of their drunken companions. The town has many interesting buildings dating from the nineteenth century. After an earlier mission church was destroyed in the Pueblo Revolt of 1680, the **Mission of San Miguel** (403 El Camino Real) was built between 1819 and 1821. The interior of the handsome twin-towered adobe church has carved beams and corbels.

SAN ANTONIO

After the Civil War, a merchant named Augustus Hilton built a store here and established a local stage line to mining towns. Before long, he was known as the "Merchant King of San Antonio." In 1907 Hilton converted part of his store into a rooming house, perhaps inspiring his son, Conrad Hilton, born in San Antonio in 1887, to go into the hotel business.

A marker south of San Antonio on Route I-25 marks the approximate location of the **Valverde Battlefield,** the first major engagement of the Civil War on New Mexican soil. The Confederate army of General Henry Hopkins Sibley clashed here with the Union forces occupying Fort Craig under General Edward R. S. Canby. Finding Fort Craig heavily defended, the Confederates crossed to the east side of the Rio Grande on February 19, 1862, to lure the Union army into the open. The two sides met at Valverde on February 21 in a close contest, until some poorly trained Union militia refused to cross the river, and the Union army was forced to withdraw to Fort Craig. Sibley's army, running low on rations, continued north to Albuquerque, Santa Fe, and eventual defeat on March 28 at Glorieta Pass.

TRUTH OR CONSEQUENCES

Until 1950 this town was named Hot Springs for the thermal springs that were the main attraction of this local resort. That year it accepted an offer to name itself Truth or Consequences on the tenth anniversary of the popular radio show of the same name, receiving much publicity and an annual fiesta with Hollywood stars. Opponents challenged the name change in several elections but lost. The town's **Ralph Edwards Park** honors the program host who came up with the scheme. The **Geronimo Springs Museum** (325 Main Street, 505–894–6600) has examples of Mimbres pottery, exhibits on local history, and mementoes of the radio program.

SILVER CITY

After Captain John Bullard opened the first silver mine—Legal Tender—here in 1870, the settlement's name was changed from La Ciénaga de San Vicente (Saint Vincent's Marsh) to Silver City. Bullard was later killed fighting the Apache, and the townspeople named a mountain and a main street after him. Silver City was also the boyhood home of Billy the Kid. Early photographs of the town as well as Indian artifacts and antiques are on display at the **Silver City**

Museum (312 West Broadway, 505–538–5921). The museum is housed in the mansard-style mansion built in 1880–1881 by the local businessman Henry B. Ailman. **Western New Mexico University** (1000 West College, 505–538–6336) was established in Silver City in 1893, the year that the silver boom ended. The **Fleming Hall Museum** (505–538–6386) on its main campus has a collection of rare Mimbres and Casa Grande Indian pottery, as well as historical photographs and military artifacts.

Twelve miles south of Silver City on Route 90, a viewpoint overlooks the open-pit mine of the Phelps-Dodge Corporation. This was once the site of the model mining town of **Tyrone,** designed in 1916–1917 in the Spanish Colonial style by the New York architect Bertram Grosvenor Goodhue. Known as the "million-dollar mining camp" (and later, after the mine closed in 1921, as the "million-dollar ghost town"), Tyrone had a modern hospital, a library, substantial homes with indoor plumbing, and a railroad station with chandeliers in the waiting room. The town was destroyed in the 1960s in order to open up a new pit. Present-day Tyrone is located north of the pit.

The ghost town of **Pinos Altos** (seven miles north of Silver City on Route 15), on the road leading to Gila National Monument, sits practically atop the Continental Divide. Gold was discovered in 1860 in nearby Bear Creek, but Indian raids discouraged development at first. In one raid the Apache leader Mangas Coloradas lured the miners out of camp by placing young Indian women on a hill in full view of the camp. When the miners climbed up to investigate, the Indians ambushed them from both sides. Indian attacks decreased after the Civil War, and mining continued in Pinos Altos until the 1920s. Today the opera house, a saloon, and a mill have been restored.

GILA CLIFF
DWELLINGS NATIONAL MONUMENT

In 1884 Adolph Bandelier visited the cliff dwellings at the headwaters of the Gila River and became the first scientist to report on the ruins. Bandelier concluded that the Mogollon who lived there were "in no manner different from the Pueblo Indians in general culture," and that they had learned how to build on the cliffs from Anasazi, who had drifted into the region from the north. The Mogollon, like the Anasazi, were farmers, hunters, and gatherers. (These conclusions are not universally accepted today.)

Most of the forty-two rooms in five caves about 175 feet above the canyon floor originally had roofs in addition to the protection afforded by the overhanging cliffs. About a dozen families lived here from about 1280, when dendrochronology, or tree-ring dating, of the roof timbers reveals they were built, to 1300, when the cliff dwellings were abandoned. The Mogollon had lived in pithouses elsewhere in the area from about A.D. 500. In approximately 1000 they began building surface homes. The cliff dwellings are located within the **Gila National Forest,** a 3.3-million-acre preserve. Gila (pronounced HEE-la) may be a corruption of an Apache word meaning mountain. After their raids the Apache would take to these mountains for refuge. One of their most famous leaders, Geronimo, lived on the upper Gila River as a boy. There is a self-guiding trail through the monument and information is available at the visitor center.

LOCATION: Route 15, 42 miles north of Silver City. HOURS: *Visitor Center:* Memorial Day through Labor Day: 8–5 Daily; Labor Day through Memorial Day: 8–4:30 Daily. *Cliff Dwellings:* Memorial Day through Labor Day: 8–6 Daily; Labor Day through Memorial Day: 9–4 Daily. FEE: None. TELEPHONE: 505–536–9461.

SHAKESPEARE

The town of Shakespeare was called Ralston during its first silver boom in the early 1870s after William Ralston, president of the Bank of California, who laid out the town in lots and blocks, staked all claims, and hired men to keep out independent miners. The silver proved to be in small pockets, however, and mined out quickly. Some men associated with Ralston attempted the great diamond hoax, scattering diamonds about to create another boom to revive their fortunes. Depression and depopulation occurred in the mid-1870s until William George Boyle in 1879 renamed the town Shakespeare and started a mining company and the second silver boom, which lasted until 1893 when depression struck again with falling silver prices. Today Shakespeare is an unusually well-preserved ghost town that includes an old store, a saloon, and the Stratford Hotel, where Billy the Kid supposedly once worked as a dishwasher. The town is privately owned and offers tours (505–542–9034).

DEMING

Deming, founded in 1881 at the junction of the Santa Fe and Southern Pacific railroads, was named for Mary Deming, the wife of a Southern Pacific investor. Water for the flourishing fields comes from the Mimbres River, which goes underground twenty miles north of town and flows into Mexico. The **Deming Luna Mimbres Museum** (301 South Silver Street, 505–546–2382) has a varied collection, including pottery and baskets of the Mimbres Indians, early railroad artifacts, an antique doll collection, and period rooms. It is housed in a former National Guard armory, built in 1916.

COLUMBUS

On March 9, 1916, eighteen Americans were killed when the Mexican revolutionary Pancho Villa and 500 followers attacked the military outpost at Deming. In retaliation General John "Black Jack" Pershing and 6,000 men marched from Fort Furlong in Columbus into Mexico on March 15. They were supported by trucks and airplanes in the first mechanized action in U.S. military history. After a clash with the Mexican Army, the U.S. called off the chase, but the National Guard remained on alert along the Mexican border until Villa stopped his raids in 1917. Some of Camp Furlong's original adobe buildings remain at **Pancho Villa State Park** (Route 11, three miles south of town, 505–531–2663), although the park is best known for more than 5,000 varieties of desert flowers and cacti. The **Columbus Historical Museum** (Route 11, 505–531–2620) is housed in the restored 1902 Southern Pacific depot and has exhibits on Villa's raid and the Punitive Expedition, as Pershing's move into Mexico was called.

MESILLA

Although now part of Las Cruces, Mesilla once was the more important community of the two before the railroad passed it by. It was founded in 1850 by New Mexicans who preferred to remain under Mexican rule after the Mexican War. In 1853, however, the Gadsden Purchase made the entire Mesilla Valley part of the United States. New Mexican territorial governor David Meriwether attended a flag-raising ceremony in the town plaza on July 4, 1854, that made American sovereignty official. In 1858 Mesilla became the halfway point on the Butterfield Overland Mail Company's Missouri-to-California route. On the inaugural trip, there was heavy betting on which stage would reach Mesilla first, since both runs—one from Tipton, Missouri, the other from San Francisco—began at precisely the same time. (The stage from the west won.) What is now the restaurant **La Posta** (off Route 28), an adobe building constructed in 1807, was a way station on the Butterfield route. Mesilla became the Confederate capital of the Territory of Arizona, which extended from Texas to California, in 1861 when Captain John Robert Baylor captured nearby Fort Fillmore for the South. Major General James H. Carleton retook Mesilla for the Union in 1862. Many of the buildings on Mesilla's old plaza have been restored. The brick **San Albino Church,** with two massive towers, was built in 1906 over the foundations of an adobe church that dates to 1856. The 1905 **Fountain Theater** was named for Colonel Albert Jennings Fountain, an important Republican who mysteriously disappeared in 1896 during a cattle-rustling dispute. Pat Garrett, the sheriff who tracked and killed Billy the Kid, came out of retirement to hunt Fountain's killers. Billy the Kid also was tried and convicted in Mesilla.

LAS CRUCES

A cluster of crosses marking the graves of travelers killed by Apache raiders in 1787 gave this settlement on the Camino Real its name. After the Treaty of Guadalupe Hidalgo ended the Mexican War in 1848, there was some doubt as to whether Las Cruces was in the United States or Mexico (Texas also had claims on the area), but the town became indisputably part of the United States with the Gadsden Purchase of 1853. The College of Las Cruces, which opened in 1888, eventually became New Mexico State University.

Although Las Cruces today is a modern city, there are several noteworthy historic buildings, including the 1850s **Amador Hotel,** now a bank, at Water and Amador streets. It was built in 1853 by Don Martin Amador, a stage driver on the Santa Fe Trail. In its heyday the hotel, patronized by men from Forts Selden and Fillmore, served many functions, with a dance hall, a casino, and a variety theater. When needed, the dining room was converted into a courtroom. The Victorian **Armijo House** on the north side of the Loretto Mall was built in 1877.

Fifteen miles north of Las Cruces, **Fort Selden State Monument** (exit 18 off Route I-25, 505–526–8911), now in ruins, was the site of a fort built in 1865 to protect wagon trains and later the railroad. Some black troops (known as Buffalo Soldiers) were stationed here in a campaign against the Indians. One of the most famous U.S. soldiers, General Douglas MacArthur, lived here as a boy from 1884 to 1886 while his father was fort commander. The fort was closed in 1891. There are old photographs displayed along a trail through the ruins, and period military equipment is exhibited in a small museum.

The undulating dunes of the **White Sands National Monument** (Route 70/82, 505–479–6124) contain one of the few deposits of pure gypsum in the world. There is a sixteen-mile round-trip drive through the monument, and rangers lead walking tours of Lake Lucero: Dry winds carry the grains of gypsum from the lake to the dunes. A visitor center offers exhibits on the monument.

ALAMOGORDO

Alamogordo was founded in 1898 as a railroad town; its phenomenal growth since 1950 is due to space-age research at the nearby White Sands Proving Grounds and the Air Force Missile Development Center at Holloman Air Force Base. The first atomic bomb, developed under great secrecy at Los Alamos in northwestern New Mexico, was exploded on July 16, 1945, at the **Trinity Site** on the White Sands Missile Range about 150 miles from Alamogordo. The test gave the world its first look at the dreaded mushroom cloud that has since become the symbol of nuclear destruction. Tours from Alamogordo to the site are made biannually (505–437–6120). The **International Space Hall of Fame** (two miles east via Route 54, 505–437–2840) honors nearly 100 space pioneers from fourteen countries. There are interactive exhibits and displays of space equipment, space suits, and launch vehicles and other spacecraft.

The resort community of **Cloudcroft** high in the Sacramento Mountains dates to the turn of the century when the Alamogordo & Sacramento Mountain Railway was completed in order to haul timber from the mountains to El Paso. In 1901 the railroad-owned **Lodge** (off Route 82, 505–682–2566) at Cloudcroft was opened as a summer resort for wealthy El Pasoans. This rustic two-story building burned down in 1909, and a new lodge was completed at an even higher elevation in 1911. The lodge is one of the leading historic hotels in the Southwest.

THREE RIVERS

Three Rivers was once part of the ranch belonging to Mrs. Susan Barber, the widow of Alexander McSween, a casualty of the Lincoln County War. Known as the "Cattle Queen of New Mexico," Mrs.

Barber, according to the *WPA Guide to New Mexico,* "rode as hard and shot as straight as any man, and never asked for quarter." Her ranch later became part of the Tres Ríos Ranch belonging to the prominent New Mexican politico Albert B. Fall, who was once described as an "astute, cool, suave defender of the special privileged interests." Fall became embroiled in the Teapot Dome Scandal when he was secretary of the interior under President Warren Harding.

Three Rivers Petroglyph Site

There are more than 500 petroglyphs—images that have been pecked, chiseled, or carved into the volcanic rock surface—along this ridge near the base of the Sacramento Mountains about twenty-eight miles south of Carrizozo off Route 54. The abstract designs, as well as the representations of people, animals, fish, and reptiles, were made between 900 and 1400 by the Jornada branch of the Mogollon people. Many of the pictures—gray-white lines that stand out against the black rock—are visible from a path that runs for

Mogollon petroglyphs at Three Rivers, with the Sacramento Mountains in the background. OVERLEAF: *White Sands National Monument, a vast sea of brilliant gypsum.*

about a mile along the top of the ridge; others can be seen by climbing over the rocks. Neither the meaning of the art nor why the
Mogollon chose this particular spot is clear. Perhaps sentries at posts
looking out over the plains passed the time by sketching on the
rocks; perhaps the place and the pictures had spiritual meaning for
the Mogollon; or perhaps the artists were inspired by the tranquility
and beauty of the place. A trail leads through the sites of a prehistoric village. There is also a replica of an early Mogollon pithouse
and two partially reconstructed pueblo dwellings.

West of Lincoln and two-and-a-half miles south of Route 380 on the
banks of the Rio Bonito, **Fort Stanton** (private) was established in
1855 to protect settlers in the area. It was abandoned early during
the Civil War, occupied by Kit Carson in 1863, and rebuilt in 1868.
Troops were sent from there to quell the fighting in the Lincoln
County War but, uncertain which side to take, mostly stood by and
watched. Since the turn of the century, the post has been used as a
government medical facility.

LINCOLN STATE MONUMENT

The Lincoln County War of 1878 put the town of Lincoln on the
map and gave birth to the curious story of Billy the Kid, a local gunslinger and cattle thief transformed by legend into a Robin Hood of
the Wild West. The town, originally a small Spanish farming community called Las Placitas del Río Bonito, was settled in the 1850s, and
the round stone *torreón*, or defensive tower, that still stands dates
from this early period. In 1869 the town became Lincoln and the
seat of Lincoln County; by that time, it had changed because of the
influx of Anglo farmers and ranchers—among them John Chisum,
who ran 80,000 head of cattle—and the establishment of Fort
Stanton ten miles away. Although Chisum did accuse the merchant
L. G. Murphy of rustling his cattle, the "war" had its origins in a dispute between rival merchants: Murphy and his partner, James J.
Dolan, on the one hand and John Tunstall, an English rancher, and
Alexander McSween, his lawyer, on the other. McSween and Tunstall
had opened a rival store that threatened Murphy-Dolan economic
control of the area. With huge government contracts at stake,
Murphy's close connections with the powerful Santa Fe Ring in the
territorial capital added a political dimension to the affair that put
local law enforcement on his side.

The "war" began on February 18, 1878, when Tunstall was killed by a posse of Dolan's men. Instead of arresting the murderers, Sheriff William Brady jailed William H. Bonney, alias Billy the Kid, who had been working for Tunstall. Once released, Billy returned to Lincoln with five henchmen, captured and killed two of Tunstall's murderers, and later killed Brady in an ambush in the middle of town. More killings followed. Finally, a five-day battle in the middle of town ended when Billy and others made a daring escape after being besieged in McSween's burning house. With both McSween and Tunstall dead and the Dolan-Murphy faction the clear winners, Billy the Kid was arrested for killing Sheriff Brady. The new territorial governor, Lew Wallace, promised Billy amnesty in return for his testimony against the Murphy group in another murder. Billy, however, grew tired of waiting and simply walked out of jail. He then tried to collect the $500 he claimed Chisum owed him for his support. When no money was forthcoming, Billy turned to stealing cattle belonging to Chisum and other ranchers and to killing more people in the process. The new sheriff of Lincoln County, Pat Garrett, captured Billy after a gunfight, but the outlaw escaped from jail before he could be hanged for murdering Brady. On July 14, 1881, Garrett surprised Billy at the Maxwell Ranch at Fort Sumner and shot him dead.

Much of the town lining Route 380 has been preserved as Lincoln State Monument. The **Lincoln County Courthouse,** from which Billy the Kid made a daring escape, also served as the Murphy-Dolan store. The courthouse is now a museum of local history, displaying such relics as the wooden marker from the grave of the Kid's mother, Katherine Antrim; Sheriff Garrett's boot last, and a bugle belonging to a "Buffalo Soldier"—one of the black Indian fighters stationed at Fort Stanton. The **Wortley Hotel** is a reconstruction of the original hostelry owned by Sheriff Pat Garrett and others. The **Tunstall Store** has a display of merchandise and an exhibit of early documents relating to the Lincoln County War. **Dr. Wood's House,** a frontier doctor's home and surgery, is the property of the Lincoln County Heritage Trust (505–653–4025) started in 1976 by the petroleum magnate Robert O. Anderson and the western painter Peter Hurd. The trust also owns the **Montaño Store** and the **Luna House.** Replicas of the town's earliest form of architecture, jacal adobe, can be seen outside: posts driven into the ground and then covered and chinked with adobe. Across from the courthouse, the privately owned **La Paloma Museum** (505–653–4828) contains the private collection of Western artifacts that proprietor Roman Maes has compiled over the past fifty years. It is an extensive accumulation of both the predictable (barbed wire) and the surprising (a full-size scaffold); many items fall somewhere between the two: a Colt Lightning .38, flatirons, ox shoes, bullet molds, hoops for hoop skirts, and most of a blacksmith shop.

LOCATION: Route 380. HOURS: Summer: 9–6 Daily; travelers should check in advance to see if open in winter. FEE: Yes. TELEPHONE: 505–653–4372.

SALINAS PUEBLO MISSIONS NATIONAL MONUMENT

In 1980 Gran Quivira National Monument and two state monuments—Abó and Quarai—were combined as Salinas Pueblo Missions National Monument. Salinas ("salt mines" in Spanish) is a reference to the salt deposits found in the region. This part of the Spanish empire was known as the Salinas Jurisdiction. The three ruins are closely related. All were large Indian pueblos before the arrival of the Spanish and it is speculated that all three became major settlements when the Spanish tried to consolidate the Indians to make it easier to rule and convert them. Each settlement was abandoned before the Pueblo Revolt of 1680; exploitation by the Spanish, drought, disease, and attacks by the Apache and Comanche scattered the residents to other Rio Grande pueblos.

Today the center of each site is the ruin of an immense mission church, making for incongruous landmarks on the desert floor. The voluminous spaces of the church interiors must have made an overwhelming impression on Indians accustomed to the tiny, cramped rooms of the pueblos. The writer Charles F. Lummis's description of Quarai, written in the late 1800s, could apply to all three ruins today: "An edifice in ruins, it is true, but so tall, so solemn, so dominant in that strange, lonely landscape, so out of place in that land of adobe box huts, as to be simply overpowering. On the Rhine it would be a superlative, in the wilderness of the Manzano it is a miracle." The park headquarters and orientation center are in the old **Shaffer Hotel** in the town of Mountainair, once known as the "Pinto Bean Capital of the World." This unusual structure was the work of folk

artist Pop Shaffer, who decorated it with animal and Indian designs. A restaurant, also colorfully decorated by Shaffer, is open.

LOCATION: *Park Headquarters and Orientation Center:* One block south of the junction of Routes 60 and 55, Mountainair. HOURS: 8–5 Daily. FEE: None. TELEPHONE: 505–847–2585.

Quarai

Work on the **Misión de la Purísima Concepción Cuarac** (Church of the Immaculate Conception) began about 1628. Foundations 7 feet deep and 6 feet wide support the walls. The interior of the church is 100 feet long, and the transept 50 feet wide. The interior walls were originally plastered white. The sacristry was still roofed when Major James Carleton visited in 1853; he described corbels "carved into regularly curved lines and scrolls." The self-guiding trail also leads past the ruins of the chapel and the unexcavated sites of the Indian pueblo. Quarai is located off Route 55 eight miles north of Mountainair.

Abó

When Major James Carleton saw the ruins of Abó in 1853, he wrote: "Abó belongs to the region of romance and fancy; and it will be for the poet and the painter to restore to its original beauty this venerable temple." Today the original beauty can only be imagined but the massive ruins of the **Mission of San Gregorio de Abó** help the viewer envision how impressive this structure must have once been. The sandstone rock walls were supported on the west by two exterior buttresses and a bell tower that rose fifty feet, and the rectangular sockets high in the wall that supported the massive roof beams can be seen. There were three stone altars spanning the width of the sanctuary. When the mission was excavated, an Indian kiva, or sunken ceremonial chamber, was found in the midst of the mission complex. There is a theory that the Indians built this kiva when the priest was away and that he ordered it destroyed on his return. Abó is located off Route 60, nine miles west of Mountainair.

OVERLEAF: *The ruins of the Mission of San Gregorio de Abó, built in the 1620s near a pueblo located on a pass opening onto the Rio Grande valley, are now part of the Salinas Pueblo Missions National Monument.*

Gran Quivira

Why this pueblo was named Gran Quivira is uncertain. When Juan de Oñate visited in 1598, he named it Pueblo de las Humanas, or the Pueblo of the Striped Ones, because the Indians painted stripes across their noses. Somehow, after the pueblo was abandoned in the 1670s, the place became confused with Quivira, the fabled city that lured Coronado to the Great Plains in 1541 in yet another disappointing quest for riches. Although in ruins, Gran Quivira has the stately presence of an architectural monument. The first church, known as the **Chapel of San Isidro** (though probably called San Buenaventura), was built between 1630 and 1636. It was destroyed by Apache raiders in September 1670. Father Diego de Santander arrived in 1659 to build the massive church known as **Mission of San Buenaventura,** a cruciform building 138 feet long with walls about 5 feet thick. The church still had not been completed or used in 1672 when the pueblo was completely abandoned. Recent research into the probable construction sequence now suggests that it is at best tenuous whether a mission dedicated to San Isidro ever existed. There are also seventeen multiroom house mounds at the site in addition to a large kiva and a number of smaller ones. The roof of the large kiva probably extended two feet above the level of the plaza. There is also archaeological evidence that the kivas had been burned, probably on order of the priests. Gran Quivira is located on Route 55, twenty-six miles south of Mountainair.

FORT SUMNER STATE MONUMENT

Only a visitor center exists here to tell the story of this historic fort built in 1862 by General James Carleton as a resettlement center for Navajo and Apache. Colonel Kit Carson, charged with the roundup, pursued the Navajo relentlessly, even though he once called them "the most noble and virtuous tribe within our Territory." After dislodging them from Canyon de Chelly and forcing their surrender at Fort Defiance, Carson led more than 7,000 Navajo on the 400-mile "Long March" to a twenty-one-acre reservation at Bosque Redondo (Round Grove of Cottonwood Trees) near Fort Sumner. The experiment in resettlement was a failure. There were raids by the

OPPOSITE: *Grey limestone ruins at Gran Quivera, a once-extensive pueblo, within Salinas National Monument.*

Comanche, crop failures, and food shortages, and thousands of
Navajo became ill and died. The survivors were returned to their
tribal lands in Arizona in 1868.

The fort was sold to Lucien Maxwell, the extravagant, high-living
former owner of the Maxwell Land Grant near Cimarron. He converted the officers' quarters into a twenty-room mansion. After his
death in 1875, his son Peter inherited the property. Billy the Kid was
shot and killed by Sheriff Pat Garrett in this house in 1881. **Billy the
Kid's Grave** is located in the graveyard of this state monument. The
bosque redondo has survived and is a haven for migratory birds.
There are floor plans of the original fort displayed at the visitor center. A private museum off the grounds exhibits old photographs.

LOCATION: 4 miles south of Route 60, southwest of Fort Sumter.
HOURS: Variable, check in advance. FEE: Yes. TELEPHONE:
505–355–2573.

ROSWELL

Settled by a professional gambler, Roswell became an important cattle center after the Civil War. The Chisum Trail—not to be confused
with the Chisholm Trail—over which John Chisum moved his cattle
west started here. The Goodnight-Loving Trail of Texas cattlemen
Charles Goodnight and Oliver Loving, which took cattle north to
military posts and mining camps, also passed through Roswell. The
entire town eventually came under the ownership of another cattle-
man, Captain Joseph Lea, who helped found the **New Mexico
Military Institute** (North Main and College Boulevard,
505–622–6250) in 1891. The institute's **General Douglas L. McBride
Military Museum** has displays on twentieth-century American military history. A stately Roswell landmark since its construction in
1910, the **Chaves County Historical Museum** (200 North Lea
Avenue, 505–622–8333), formerly the home of James Phelps White,
now stands amidst towering elms as a reminder of turn-of-the-century life in southeastern New Mexico. The museum is maintained by
the Chaves County Historical Society to promote the discovery, collection, exhibition, and preservation of archaeological, historical,
and cultural materials relating to southeastern New Mexico and particularly Roswell and Chaves County. The museum's first floor contains period furnishings, and the second floor features exhibits of
clothing, toys, and crafts from the late nineteenth and early twentieth centuries.

Marsden Hartley's Landscape: New Mexico, *painted in 1920, is part of the collection of the Roswell Museum and Art Center (detail).*

From 1930 until 1941, Robert Goddard conducted his important rocket experiments in the desert near Roswell. There is an exact replica of Goddard's liquid fuel rocket laboratory as it existed in 1931 in the Goddard wing of the **Roswell Museum and Art Center** (11th and Main streets, 505–624–6744). The museum contains an unusual combination of space-age artifacts and Southwestern art. The space suit of the moon-walking astronaut and former senator Harrison Schmitt is also exhibited. In addition to exhibits on rocketry and space sciences, there is also a planetarium. The permanent art collection includes works by Georgia O'Keeffe, Marsden Hartley, Stuart Davis, John Marin, and the two important leaders of the art colony at Taos, Ernest Blumenschein and Andrew Dasburg. There are also works by contemporary artists.

CARLSBAD CAVERNS NATIONAL PARK

In the foothills of the Guadalupe Mountains, the seventy-three-square-mile national park protects a series of spectacular underground rooms created by groundwater eating through a limestone reef formed some 250 million years ago when this part of New Mexico was submerged under the sea. Within the huge rooms (fourteen football fields could fit within the Big Room alone) are a fascinating repository of stalactites and stalagmites that frequently merge into weird and beautiful formations. The caves are also home to countless bats that emerge each evening (when they are not migrating) in great spiraling clouds. There is some evidence that prehistoric man lived in and around these caves. The credit for rediscovering them generally goes to a cowboy named Jim White, who began exploring this area in 1901. White's enthusiastic reports about the caves finally reached government officials; their investigations led to the creation of the national park in 1930. In 1933 the Carlsbad Bat Guano Company began making fertilizer from the guano mined from the cave, an industry that lasted for twenty years. Early tourists to the cave were lowered in guano buckets.

LOCATION: Routes 62/180 and 7, 27 miles south of Carlsbad. HOURS: June through August: 8:30–5 Daily; September through May: 8:30–3:30 Daily. FEE: Yes. TELEPHONE: 505–785–2232.

HOBBS

Named for a Texan who built a dugout here in 1907, Hobbs sprang up overnight in the "Black Gold Rush" that followed the discovery of oil in 1930. (Before the streets were paved, oil was used to keep the dust down.) Although oil prices plummeted shortly thereafter in the Great Depression, the town recovered rapidly: The first oil well drilled in the mid-1930s, **Midwest Number 1,** is still pumping oil. The Lee County Airport is also home to the **Confederate Air Force Museum** (Route 62/180, three miles west of town, 505–393–9915), which houses a collection of World War II aircraft in flying condition. The organization's unusual name comes from the fact that its members "rebelled" against the government's policy of scrapping World War II fighter planes.

OPPOSITE: *Stalactites and stalagmites at the Kings Palace entrance to Carlsbad Caverns, which was once known as the Bat Cave because of its most visible inhabitants. The Caverns extend at least twenty-one miles and as deep as 1,037 feet below the surface, and its temperature remains a steady 56 degrees throughout the year.*

SOUTHERN ARIZONA

OPPOSITE: *Saguaro cactus, preserved in the Saguaro National Monument near Tucson. This Sonoran desert plant can grow up to fifty feet high and can live for 200 years.*

F rancisco Vásquez de Coronado was the first European to lead a major exploration of the American Southwest; in 1540 he passed from Mexico into what is now southern Arizona in search of the fabled Seven Cities of Cibola. His expedition trekked to the headwaters of the Little Colorado River, the Grand Canyon, and eventually Kansas before he concluded the golden cities did not exist. Although he was disgraced by his failure to return with riches, he contributed immensely to knowledge about the region. Coronado found southern Arizona to be dry and mountainous and inhabited by the Apache, Papago, and Pima Indians. The Pima are possibly descendants of the Hohokam, a comparatively advanced prehistoric people who had been cultivating the land by irrigating as early as the year A.D. 1. The western Apache, mounted on horses introduced to the Plains by the Spanish, proved to be the most intractable and resistant to white ways. Led by such warriors as the great Cochise, they kept the southern Arizona frontier in turmoil until another leader, Geronimo, surrendered in 1886.

Of the Jesuit missionaries who began spreading the faith among the Indians in southern Arizona in the late 1600s, Father Eusebio Francisco Kino left the most enduring legacy: a string of missions, including Guevavi, the first mission on Arizona soil (now gone), and the surviving San Xavier del Bac and San José de Tumacacori, plus a number of settlements. As he made his way west along the Gila River, Father Kino made a lasting contribution to southern Arizona's economy by introducing his parishioners to cattle ranching. After Father Kino died in 1711, discontent spread among the Indians of the northern frontier, and in 1751 the Pima rose up, killing many settlers and missionaries. Spanish troops were sent in to subdue them, and the next year a presidio, or garrison, was established at Tubac. In 1767 the Jesuits, who had fallen into disfavor at the Spanish court, were banished from the territory and replaced with Franciscans. The presidio was moved to Tucson in 1775.

In 1846 Colonel Philip St. George Cooke raised the first American flag over Tucson. Cooke was commander of the Mormon Battalion, which was made up of Latter-day Saints volunteered by Brigham Young to fight in the Mexican War. The battalion's mission, admirably accomplished, was to build a road from Santa Fe to California. Tucson and southern Arizona did not become indisputably American, however, until the Gadsden Purchase of 1853, when the United States acquired from Mexico almost 30 million

At an 1886 meeting between Geronimo, facing camera at left, and General George Crook, wearing a pith helmet at right, the Apache agreed to end their raids and to live on a reservation. PAGES 150-151: *After the Spanish introduced sheep to the Southwest, the Navajo became known for their fine woolen weaving, a craft they had learned from the Pueblo Indians. This blanket was inspired by Hopi designs.*

acres of land along the Arizona and New Mexico borders. Soon afterward residents in Tucson complained to Congress that Arizona was "cut off among savage tribes," with "no law, no courts, no vote, no representation in any legislative body."

In early 1862 Tucson was occupied briefly by a small force of Confederate cavalry under Captain Sherod Hunter. In April, a handful of Rebel sentries clashed with the advance guard of a 2,000-man Union column from California led by Colonel James Carleton at Picacho Pass, forty-two miles northwest of Tucson. This engagement, described as the westernmost battle of the Civil War, was really a skirmish from which the badly outnumbered Confederates quickly withdrew. On May 20, 1862, Union forces charged into Tucson only to learn that the Rebels had withdrawn a week earlier. Although Tucson remained in Union hands for the rest of the war, its citizens were suspected of secessionist sympathies. Thus Prescott, not Tucson, was made the capital when President Lincoln signed the bill on February 24, 1863, making Arizona a territory separate from New Mexico.

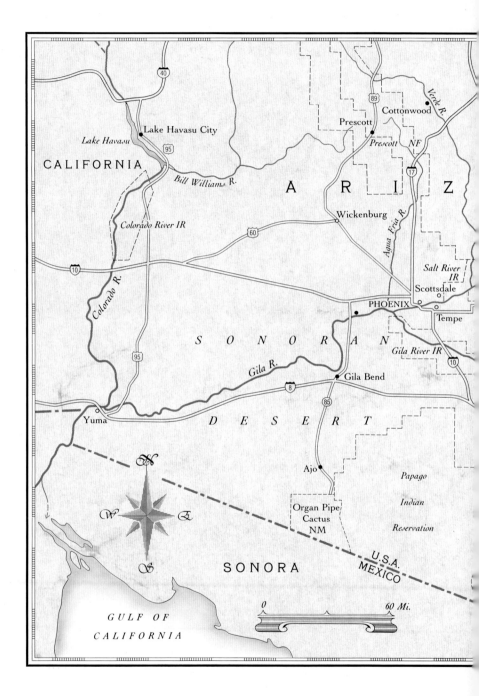

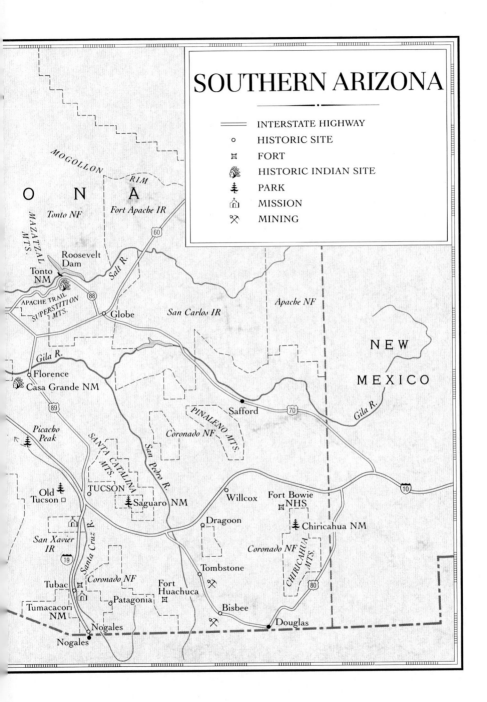

SOUTHERN ARIZONA

—— INTERSTATE HIGHWAY
○ HISTORIC SITE
⊞ FORT
🏵 HISTORIC INDIAN SITE
🌲 PARK
🏛 MISSION
⚒ MINING

MOGOLLON RIM

O N A

MAZATZAL MTS.

Tonto NF

Fort Apache IR

Roosevelt Dam

Salt R.

60

Tonto NM

APACHE TRAIL

SUPERSTITION MTS.

88

Globe

San Carlos IR

Apache NF

NEW

MEXICO

Gila R.

Florence
Casa Grande NM

89

Safford

70

Gila R.

Picacho Peak

SANTA CATALINA MTS.

Coronado NF

PINALENO MTS.

San Pedro R.

Old Tucson

TUCSON

Saguaro NM

Willcox

Fort Bowie NHS

10

Dragoon

Chiricahua NM

San Xavier IR

Santa Cruz R.

19

Coronado NF

CHIRICAHUA MTS.

Tombstone

Tubac

Coronado NF

Fort Huachuca

80

Tumacacori NM

Patagonia

Bisbee

Douglas

Nogales

Nogales

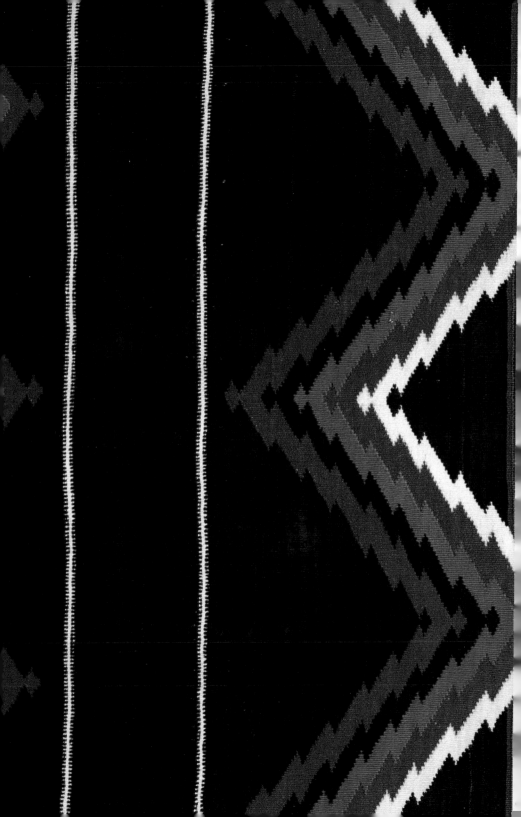

Central Arizona abounds in evidence of the prehistoric people given by modern Native Americans the name Hohokam ("people who have gone") because they disappeared. That departure occurred about A.D.1400. In the Salt Valley—where Phoenix is today—the Hohokam had built canals for irrigation, and in 1867 Jack Swilling got the idea to put the remnant of this intricate network back to work. He founded the Swilling Irrigating Canal Company and within six months had opened enough of the canals to begin farming on a substantial scale. The hard-drinking Swilling was an interesting character—Confederate deserter, miner, rancher, and Indian fighter—who died in the Yuma prison, accused of robbing a stagecoach. His use of the Hohokam canals turned Phoenix into the breadbasket for the entire territory and influenced the development of the territory after the Civil War.

In 1867 the territorial capital was moved to Tucson, where it remained for ten years before returning to Prescott. The discovery of precious metals at Tombstone, Bisbee, and elsewhere in southern Arizona brought prosperity and growth to Tucson, which by 1880 numbered 7,000 people. On March 20 of that year, the Southern Pacific Railroad reached Tucson, setting off a public celebration; Charles Crocker, who with Collis P. Huntington, Leland Stanford, and Mark Hopkins formed the Big Four who financed the line, drove in a silver spike. In 1888, for the first time, the value of copper exceeded that of all other precious metals mined in the state. Almost all the copper mines were located in southern Arizona. By 1889 Phoenix had developed enough political clout to wrest the state government away from Prescott; from that point on Arizona's capital stayed put.

Arizona petitioned for statehood as early as 1902. After the Senate passed a bill in 1910 permitting the writing of a constitution in preparation for statehood, a constitutional convention was held in Phoenix. On August 22, 1911, President Taft vetoed the constitution on the grounds that it allowed voters to recall judges, which he felt would threaten the independence of the judiciary. Arizona duly amended the constitution and, on February 14, 1912, was admitted to the Union as the forty-eighth state. It then reinstated the recall provision. Although Tucson, one of the state's oldest cities, was never

OPPOSITE: *A desert garden of balloon flowers and jumping cholla, photographed near Tucson by Eliot Porter.*

to match upstart Phoenix's extraordinary growth, both cities prospered and grew in the twentieth century. Agriculture, irrigation, manufacturing, tourism, and in recent years, retirees all contributed to the prosperity of southern Arizona. In World War II the deserts of the region attracted military airfields and prisoner-of-war camps. (In December 1944 nineteen German submariners tunneled out of an internment camp outside Phoenix, the largest POW escape on American soil.) But nothing has contributed as much to the postwar growth of these two metropolitan centers as the development of the now-essential ingredient of desert living: modern air conditioning.

This tour starts in Tucson and its environs, then heads east to the Chiricahua National Monument. The route then turns south, through Bisbee, Tombstone, Coronado National Memorial, Fort Huachuca, Patagonia, Nogales, and north, to Tubac. The tour next travels north toward Phoenix and its satellite cities of Tempe and Scottsdale before covering the more distant sites.

TUCSON

Four mountain ranges—the Santa Catalina, Rincon, Santa Rita, and Tucson—form a protected valley around Tucson. Jesuit missionaries had visited the Papago village of Chuck Son ("at the foot of dark mountain") in the 1690s; that dark mountain is today called Sentinel Peak. Since 1915 it has borne a huge whitewashed *A* placed there by University of Arizona students. The Spanish changed the town's name to Tucson when they built a garrison, Presidio San Augustín del Tucson, on the west bank of the Santa Cruz River in 1776. In 1864 Tucson was officially incorporated, and one of its most popular citizens, Virginia-born William Oury, a former Texas Ranger and survivor of the Battle of the Alamo, was appointed mayor. In 1871 Oury was indicted for leading a band of vigilantes to raid a group of sleeping Apache at Camp Grant on the San Pedro River, northeast of Tucson. The toll: seventy-seven women and eight old men killed. (The young Apache men were not in the camp.) The Camp Grant Massacre caused headlines and outrage across the country, but Oury was easily acquitted. In 1881 Tucson received its first telephone exchange, and in 1885 two professional gamblers

OPPOSITE: *Tucson's Spanish Colonial Revival Pima County Courthouse, completed in 1928, is constructed over a portion of the wall of the town's Spanish presidio.*

and a saloon keeper donated forty acres of land for a university, now
the University of Arizona. In 1920 Phoenix surpassed Tucson as
Arizona's largest city, but the Old Pueblo, as Tucson is called, has
hardly stood still. Since World War II, it has experienced astounding
growth, but a number of its historic buildings still stand.

Tucson's official birthdate, August 20, 1775, is commemorated
by the **Parque Veinte de Agosto** (the "Twentieth of August Park"), at
Church Street between Congress and Broadway in the **El Presidio
Historic District** in downtown Tucson. Here fly the five flags that
have been raised over the city: the royal crest of Spain, the Mexican
flag, the Stars and Stripes, the Stars and Bars of the Confederacy,
and the flag of the state of Arizona. The **Presidio San Augustín del
Tucson,** established in 1776, covered ten acres surrounded by adobe
walls three feet wide at the base and about twelve feet high. One
entrance is where Almeda and Main avenues cross today. The south
half of the garrison was a large public plaza and drill ground, Plaza
de las Armas, which is now **El Presidio Park** (between Almeda and
Pennington). The **Levi Manning House** (450 West Paseo Redondo,
private), located just west of El Presidio Historic District, was built in
1907 for Manning, a mayor of Tucson remembered for his efforts to
curb gambling in the wide-open city.

The modern **Tucson Museum of Art** (140 North Main Avenue,
602–624–2333) and five of Tucson's oldest houses are located on
the Plaza of the Pioneers. The museum's main gallery, which is
below the street level, is used for changing exhibits, but there also is
a permanent display of pre-Columbian and Western art. The museum also maintains historic houses for the public. The **Edward Nye
Fish House** (120 North Main Avenue) was built in 1868 with adobe
walls two-and-a-half feet thick and ceilings fifteen feet high. Fish was
a leading merchant; his wife, Maria Wakefield, who became a prominent educator, was the first Anglo woman married in Tucson. The
house is now an art gallery. The **Stevens House** (150 North Main
Avenue) was built in 1856 by another leading merchant, Hiram
Stanford Stevens, who married the daughter of his Mexican washer-
woman. When Stevens was ruined by a drought that wiped out his
ranch in 1893 he tried to shoot his wife, but the bullet was deflected
by the Spanish comb in her hair. He then shot and killed himself.
The house is now a restaurant. The western section of **La Casa
Cordova** (140 North Main Avenue, behind the Tucson Museum),
on the east side of the plaza, was built about 1848, with two other

sections added later. The adobe building, with a foot-thick dirt roof supported by *vigas* (pine beams) and saguaro (cactus) ribs, has been restored as a museum of Mexican heritage. Off the courtyard where the cooking was done are an 1850s family room furnished with Hispanic items and a typical 1880s bedroom with such Anglo influences as plastered walls and paneled doors. The **Leonardo Romero House** (101 West Washington) was built in the 1860s and now houses the museum school. The fifth house in the complex, the **Sam Hughes House** (233 North Main, private), was built by the sixth Anglo to have lived in Tucson. Hughes arrived in 1858 and in 1862, when he was 32, he married a 12-year-old girl. They enlarged the house gradually to accommodate their fifteen children.

John C. Frémont House Museum

Frémont, who came to Arizona in 1878 as the fifth territorial governor to restore his fortunes, may not have lived here. The adobe house, built about 1860 by the Sosa family, has been carefully restored and is an excellent example of the Sonoran style: a single-story house with thick adobe walls and a patio in the rear where the cooking was done. The house is built around a central entryway, or *zaguán*, which originally connected the roadway with the corral in the rear. The parlor, study, music room, dining room, and bedroom are furnished with antiques, many from the Victorian era, including a Mathusek square grand piano dating from about 1860. The exposed saguaro and ocotillo ribs in the ceiling would have been covered with mud when the house was occupied. One bedroom has a cotton manta spread across the ceiling, a common way of preventing dirt and bugs from falling on the people below.

LOCATION: 151 South Granada Avenue, in the Tucson Convention Center Complex. HOURS: 10–4 Wednesday–Saturday. FEE: None. TELEPHONE: 602–622–0956.

The **Saint Augustine Cathedral** (192 South Stone Avenue), with its sandstone facade, was built in 1896 and modeled after the Cathedral of Querétaro in Mexico. There is a bronze statue of Saint Augustine above the entry along with renderings of the saguaro, nopal, yucca, and horned toad found in the Arizona desert. South and west of the cathedral is the **Barrio Histórico,** a remarkable concentration of more than 150 adobe buildings of the 1880s, many of which have been or are being restored. The area is bounded by Stone Avenue, the railroad west of Main Avenue, Cushing (14th Street), and 18th Street. Because the district was not controlled by the city in its early days, it was known as the Barrio Libre ("free neighborhood"). The **Montijo House** (116 Cushing Street, private) was built during the Civil War and remodeled for a prominent Mexican ranching family in the 1890s. On Main Avenue between Simpson and Cushing is **El Tiradito** ("the castaway"), also known as the Wishing Shrine; it is dedicated to the memory of a young shepherd who fell in love with his mother-in-law and was killed on this spot by her husband when he discovered the two together. The young man was buried here in unconsecrated ground. Residents of the barrio began to light candles for his soul and for answers to their own prayers—often help for wayward children—in the belief that their prayers would come true if the candle stayed lighted through the night.

University of Arizona

Established in 1885, before the territory even had a high school, the university did not graduate more than ten students a year for its first two decades; today it has over 36,000 students. The oldest building on campus, **Old Main,** a two-story brick building with a long gallery porch, was completed in 1891. The **University Museum of Art** (Olive Road, north of 2d Street, 602–621–7567) has one of the best collections of sculpture in the Southwest, including sixty-one bronze and plaster models by Jacques Lipchitz. The Samuel H. Kress Collection consists of Renaissance and seventeenth-century European masterpieces. A collection of American art includes works by Edward Hopper, Stuart Davis, and Reginald Marsh. The **Arizona State Museum** (Park Avenue and University Boulevard, 602–621–6302) was founded in 1893 by the territorial legislature as a division of the territorial university. Its collections include artifacts from early Indian cultures: Anasazi textiles, Hohokam pottery, and Navajo blankets. In 1974 the photographer Ansel Adams agreed to give his archives to the university if they would be made available to the public for study. Today the collection at the **Center for Creative Photography** (Olive Road, north of 2d Street, 602–621–7968) com-

OPPOSITE: *A Mojave doll, probably made near Yuma in the first decade of the twentieth century for sale to tourists, now in the collection of the Arizona State Museum.*

prises the complete archives, including correspondence and other memorabilia, of such other twentieth-century masters as Louise Dahl-Wolfe, Andreas Feininger, Harry Callahan, W. Eugene Smith, and Edward Weston. In addition, more than 1,000 nineteenth- and twentieth-century photographers are represented.

LOCATION: University Boulevard and Park Avenue. TELEPHONE: 602–621–5130.

Arizona Historical Society Museum

The state's oldest cultural institution, the Arizona Historical Society, Tucson, has built up a collection of over 3,000 artifacts and half a million photographs. The early 1900s copper-mining exhibit includes a re-created tunnel with sound effects, a walk-in miner's cabin, an assay office, an ore-dumping car, and a 10,000-pound stamp mill. Other exhibits trace the history of Arizona from the Hohokam people to the present. Period rooms concentrate on the furnishings and decorative arts of the Victorian era. The arched portal and rose-window frame in front of the building are from the original Saint Augustine Cathedral in downtown Tucson.

LOCATION: 929 East 2d Street. HOURS: 10–4 Monday–Saturday, 12–4 Sunday. FEE: None. TELEPHONE: 602–628–5774.

The **Saguaro National Monument** protects the magnificent saguaro cactus, found only in the Sonoran Desert, which can grow to fifty feet and live nearly 200 years. The monument is divided into two parts on either side of Tucson. **Saguaro National Monument East** (3693 South Old Spanish Trail, 602–296–8576), the older and larger of the two parks, has mostly very young and very old plants; **Saguaro National Monument West** (2700 North Kinney Road, 602–883–6366) has a denser population of large tracts of plants that resemble people standing quietly on a desert mountainside.

East of Tucson, the **Pima Air Museum** (6000 East Valencia Road, 602–574–9658) is the third-largest collection of historic aircraft in the world and the largest privately funded air museum. On display

OPPOSITE: *Hohokam petroglyphs, dating from* A.D. *900-1400, atop Signal Hill in the Tucson Mountain District of Saguaro National Monument. The site preserves large stands of the distinctive saguaro cactus, the state flower of Arizona.*

are a full-scale model of the 1903 Wright Flyer and a mockup of the X-15, the world's fastest aircraft. The more than 150 planes on exhibit include models by the country's leading manufacturers—Boeing, McDonnell Douglas, Fairchild, Grumman, Lockheed, Sikorsky, and others. About twenty miles south of Tucson, in Green Valley, is the **Titan Missile Museum** (1580 West Duval Mine Road, off Route 19, 602–791–2929), a preserved Titan II missile site complex that was active from 1963 to 1982. The museum includes a missile complex complete with silo and control center.

FORT LOWELL MUSEUM

Established in 1866 in downtown Tucson, Fort Lowell was moved in 1873 to this spot on Rillito Creek seven miles northeast of town. The purpose of the move was to set the troops at a distance from the temptations of town and to spare the citizenry "the outrages of a depraved and drunken soldiery," in the words of one newspaper editor. Fort Lowell was an important army post in the effort to control the Apache and was also a supply point for other posts in southern Arizona. By the time Geronimo surrendered in September 1886, one-fourth of the U.S. Army was stationed in Arizona. After the troops departed in 1891, the fort was abandoned and allowed to deteriorate; only the adobe ruins are visible today. The museum building is an accurate reconstruction of the commanding officer's quarters with a parlor, dining room, and office with displays of photographs, maps, uniforms, and equipment.

> LOCATION: Fort Lowell Park, Craycroft Road and Fort Lowell Road. HOURS: 10–4 Wednesday–Saturday. FEE: None. TELEPHONE: 602–885–3832.

MISSION SAN XAVIER DEL BAC

The architect of this splendid Spanish Baroque monument is unknown. Nor is anyone certain why the right tower is unfinished (to symbolize that the preaching of the gospel is never ending, one theory goes). The mission was founded by the indefatigable Jesuit missionary Eusebio Francisco Kino in 1700. "Anybody might have [founded] it," he said, "but His whisper came to Me." Father Kino died in 1711, and the church he built was destroyed in the Pima Revolt of 1751. The present church, begun in 1783, was not completed until 1797—thirty years after the Jesuits had been expelled

· from the area by the Spanish crown. The white stucco covering the fired adobe bricks makes the whole church shimmer in the intense desert light. The twin towers frame both the elaborately carved stone portal and the circular dome over the crossing. The interior is much more elaborate than most Spanish mission churches: There are frescoes inside the dome, and the altar is backed by an intricately carved brick and polychromed stucco retablo. The church, which was restored between 1906 and 1909 and again between 1949 and 1958, is located on the San Xavier Indian Reservation and is actively used by the Papago community.

LOCATION: Off Route I-19 and Mission Road, 9 miles southwest of Tucson. HOURS: 9–5 Daily. FEE: None. TELEPHONE: 602–294–2624.

Old Tucson (201 South Kinney Road, twelve miles west of Tucson in Tucson Mountain Park, 602–883–6457) makes no claim to historical

Mission San Xavier del Bac is the most sophisticated example of Spanish Colonial architecture in the southwest. It was constructed between 1783 and 1797 by Franciscan missionaries on the site of an earlier mission established by the Jesuit Father Kino in 1700.

authenticity, but as the self-styled "Hollywood in the desert," it is of considerable importance to the history of film. It was created at a cost of $250,000 in 1939 for the filming of the epic western *Arizona,* starring Jean Arthur and William Holden, and today includes saloons, a frontier mission, a Mexican plaza area and numerous other reconstructed historic sites and movie fronts, as well as the Simmons Gun Museum with more than 1,000 historic weapons, a kachina exhibit, and the Reno, an 1872 steam engine built for Nevada's famed Virginia & Truckee Railroad. Such well-remembered films as *Winchester 73* (1950), *Gunfight at the OK Corral* (1957), and *Rio Bravo* (1958) were made on its sets. In 1958 Old Tucson opened to the public, and the setting continues to be used for films, documentaries, television, and commercials.

The **Arizona-Sonora Desert Museum** (2021 North Kinney Road, 602–883–1380), fourteen miles west of Tucson, is part zoo, with over 200 species of animals on view, part historical museum, and part arboretum. The museum also has an earth sciences center with an artificial limestone cave.

AMERIND FOUNDATION

Located about midway off Route I-10 between Benson and Willcox, the Amerind Foundation is an archaeological research facility and museum chartered in 1937. In 1905 its founder, William Shirley Fulton, an amateur archaeologist from Connecticut, began making regular trips to excavations in Arizona before purchasing the property (the FF Ranch) on which the Amerind Foundation is situated. (The name is a contraction of American and Indian.) Although many of the artifacts on view were gathered during foundation-sponsored excavations in the Southwest and Mexico, a variety of cultures are represented; the museum's holdings include notable collections of White Mountain Apache baskets, *bultos* (religious figures hand-carved by the Indian parishioners of the early Spanish missions), nineteenth-century Navajo weavings, and Plains Indian beadwork and costumes. The art gallery, located in a separate building, has paintings by William Leigh and a sculpture by Frederic Remington.

LOCATION: Off Route I-10 (exit 318), in Dragoon. HOURS: June through August: 10–4 Wednesday–Sunday; September through May: 10–4 Daily. FEE: Yes. TELEPHONE: 602–586–3666.

Named for Civil War general Orlando B. Willcox, who was later commander of the Department of Arizona, **Willcox** is a cattle-ranching center whose surrounding hills once harbored a wide variety of outlaws. While he was unarmed and probably inebriated, Warren Earp, an Earp brother not present at the O. K. Corral, died in 1900 in Willcox after challenging an enemy to a gunfight. His killer was acquitted after arguing that it was inconceivable that an Earp would not be carrying a weapon. One mile north of town, the **Cochise Information Center and Museum of the Southwest** (1500 North Circle I Road, 602–384–2272) has exhibits on local history, including Apache displays, a cowboy hall of fame, and memorabilia donated by Rex Allen, a western movie star of the 1950s.

About thirty miles south of Willcox, Route 666 leads to the **Cochise Stronghold,** a canyon where the Apache chief and his warriors hid out. In the nearby town of **Cochise,** six miles south on

The ruins of Fort Bowie, established in 1862 to guard the eastern entrance to Apache Pass, which because of Apache raids was one of the most dangerous points on the immigrant trail to California. The fort was abandoned in 1896.

Route 666, the adobe **Cochise Hotel** (602–384–3156), built in 1882 to accommodate passengers on the Southern Pacific, still operates. In 1899 more than $10,000 was stolen from a Southern Pacific train passing through Cochise; the law enforcement officer from Willcox in charge of investigating the crime was the culprit.

FORT BOWIE NATIONAL HISTORIC SITE

A mile-and-a-half-long footpath leads to the stabilized ruins of this former army stronghold guarding Apache Pass. The fort was built after Brigadier General James Carleton and his California volunteers were attacked by Apache on July 15, 1862, not long after they had taken Tucson for the Union. A year earlier the pass had been the scene of the Bascom affair, in which an inexperienced second lieutenant, George N. Bascom, attempted to arrest the friendly Apache chief Cochise and several others for crimes against a rancher. Cochise escaped, but the incident, which was followed by the killing of captives on both sides, set off more than ten years of Apache warfare, as Cochise undertook to drive settlers from the region. Undefeated in battle, he made peace in 1872. Fort Bowie was later used in the army's campaign to capture Geronimo. The ranger station has exhibits of old photographs, and signs identify the location of the buildings, stage station, and battles.

> LOCATION: Apache Pass Road, off Route 186. HOURS: 8–4:30 Daily. FEE: None. TELEPHONE: 602–847–2500.

CHIRICAHUA NATIONAL MONUMENT

These extraordinary rock formations—towering spires, huge rocks balanced one on the other, and tall, narrow columns—were probably caused by a combination of volcanic eruptions and erosion some 25 million years ago. The Indians called the Chiricahua (chee-ree-KAH-wa) Mountains the "land of the standing-up rocks," and the Chiricahua Apache took refuge here during hostilities with whites. After Geronimo surrendered in 1886, Bonita Canyon was settled by Swedish immigrants Neil and Emma Erickson. Their daughter Lillian and her husband turned the homestead into a guest ranch and worked to have the area made a national park. The eighteen-

OPPOSITE: *Chiricahua National Monument preserves a landscape resulting from millions of years of erosion, volcanic activity, and other geologic changes.*

The Faraway Ranch house, occupied by members of the pioneering Erickson family from 1888 until the late 1970s.

square-mile Chiricahua National Monument was created in 1924, and the Riggs's homestead, named **Faraway Ranch** because, according to Lillian, its was so "god-awful far away from everything," has been restored. The visitor center offers exhibits on the geology and history of the area.

LOCATION: Off Route 186, 37 miles southeast of Willcox. HOURS: *Visitor Center:* 8–5 Daily. FEE: Yes. TELEPHONE: 602–824–3560.

BISBEE

Copper was discovered at Bisbee in 1875 by a prospector, who went away disappointed because he was hoping for silver and gold. Two years later George Warren established the first claim but later lost it in a fit of drunken self-confidence after betting that he, on foot, could outrace another man on horseback. The town was named for Judge DeWitt Bisbee, who financed the Copper Queen Mine in

1880 with a group of San Francisco businessmen. In 1880 a minister and physician, Dr. James Douglas, an agent of Phelps-Dodge and Company, purchased property bordering the Copper Queen Mine for his firm, and when rich ore was found on the boundary, the two companies merged to avoid legal battles. In 1898 Captain Jim Hoatson, a mining foreman from Michigan, established the Calumet and Arizona Company, an important rival of Phelps-Dodge.

In the meantime, the town of Bisbee was growing up the slopes of Mule Pass Gulch. The settlement was still subject to Indian attacks when the first school was established in a miner's shack above the landmark Castle Rock; four blasts from a whistle warned that potentially hostile Indians had been spotted in the vicinity, and the children would be rushed to a mining tunnel for safety. Nearly fifty saloons, gambling dens, and brothels were located in a side canyon known as Brewery Gulch, a contrast to the more staid community that was developing nearby. Brewery Gulch declined as families replaced the single miners and as mining became more mechanized, requiring fewer workers.

By the turn of the century Bisbee had a population of 20,000 and was Arizona's largest and wealthiest city. Miners' wages—and the prosperity of the town—were tied to the price of copper, and in the early twentieth century there were frequent labor disputes. In 1917 armed sheriff's deputies rounded up 1,286 striking miners, loaded them into boxcars, and after a three-day train trip, abandoned them in the desert near Columbus, New Mexico. The incident, which has gone down in history as the "Bisbee deportation," caused outrage nationwide, and Felix Frankfurter (later a U.S. Supreme Court justice) was sent to Bisbee as a federal investigator. Still, the deportation broke the back of the union movement for decades.

Tours of the town, the **Queen Mine,** and the **Lavender Pit,** the open-pit copper mine (950 feet deep and over a mile long), leave regularly from the Queen Mine tour office (602–432–2071) off Route 80. The Lavender Pit, named for Harrison Lavender, a Phelps-Dodge executive, is so large that a whole section of homes and businesses had to be removed to make way for it. The **Bisbee Mining and Historical Museum** (5 Copper Queen Plaza, 602–432–7071) is located in the two-story headquarters building of the Copper Queen Consolidated Mining Company, built in 1897; the oak-paneled office of the general manager is preserved, and there is an exhibit of historic photos. Pieces of mining equipment are displayed outside, including an elevator cage used to lift small ore cars and miners from the mine. A permanent exhibit interpreting Bisbee's transformation from mining camp to urban center will open in early 1991.

The **Bisbee Restoration and Historical Society Museum** (37 Main Street), located in the 1915 Fair Store Building, has memorabilia related to Bisbee's past. Among the antique furniture, clothing, mining equipment, and household items are a blackjack table and dealer's chair from a gambling house in Brewery Gulch. The ten-room **Muheim Heritage House** (207 Youngblood Hill, 602–432–4461) was built in stages between 1898 and 1915 by the enterprising Swiss immigrant Joseph M. Muheim, a saloon keeper, entrepreneur, and cofounder of the Miners and Merchants Bank. Muheim, his wife, and their four children lived in the house; it was occupied by the youngest son, Henry, until 1976. The house is restored with the origi-

An 1883 photograph of the Bisbee copper smelter, now in the collection of the Bisbee Mining and Historical Museum.

nal furnishings and is open to the public. In 1905 Muheim built the downtown **Muheim Block** (13–17 Brewery Avenue), which once housed the Bisbee Stock Exchange and, in the basement, one of the finest restaurants in the West, the Edelweiss Cafe.

The **Copper Queen Hotel** (11 Howell Avenue), now restored and still operating as a hotel, was built by the Copper Queen Mining Company in 1902. The building, with its stucco exterior, windows trimmed with brick, and tile roof, is a splendid relic of the time when Bisbee was the destination of mining executives, politicians, and other celebrities and dignitaries. John Wayne once stayed in Room 10. The four-story Art Deco **Cochise County Courthouse** (Quality Hill at Tombstone Canyon) was built in 1931 with a concrete frieze over the entryway depicting two miners. The **Miners' Monument** at the foot of Quality Hill, a statue of a miner holding a hammer and chisel, is made of cast concrete sprayed with copper. It is mounted on a block of granite that was used for drilling contests in the 1890s.

TOMBSTONE

For all the impact it has had on the national imagination, Tombstone, the wide-open mining town of fact and folklore, had a remarkably short heyday—a mere five or six years in the early 1880s. The San Pedro Valley was still controlled by hostile Apache when Edward L. Schieffelin set off from Fort Huachuca to prospect for gold and silver in 1877. Scornfully forewarned that he would find "nothing else but his tombstone," he discovered silver ore soon afterward and christened the spot Tombstone. Schieffelin was soon joined by his brother Al and an experienced miner named Richard Gird. When Edward struck silver again, Al reportedly told him, "You're a lucky cuss," and so Schieffelin named the claim, one of the richest in the state, the Lucky Cuss Mine. Schieffelin's knack for composing colorful names also accounts for the Toughnut and Good Enough Mines in the district he founded.

The Schieffelins soon sold out, and the mines were developed with Eastern money. By 1881 the town was a thriving community of 5,000 people, renowned for its gambling dens, dance halls, brothels, and saloons. As the 110 liquor licenses issued in 1882 attest, the town had no shortage of watering places; the classiest one was the gray frame **Crystal Palace Saloon** on Allen Street, Tombstone's main thoroughfare. The building, which dates from 1879, has been

restored to reflect its original appearance with furnishings that include the original tin ceiling and a reproduction of the mahogany bar removed when the saloon closed during Prohibition.

The **Bird Cage Theater,** built in 1881, contained a theater, saloon, gambling house, and brothel all under one roof; the *New York Times* once described it as the "wildest, wickedest night spot between Basin Street and the Barbary Coast." The one-story adobe building retains all of its original fixtures and furnishings, including the hand-painted stage and wallpaper. Still intact are the fourteen birdcage compartments suspended from the ceiling in which the ladies of the establishment plied their trade, as well as the furniture in the room in which the longest poker game in history—eight years, five months, and three days in duration—was played. One hundred forty bullet holes riddle the walls and ceilings of this notorious emporium.

Despite the bawdy nightlife and the lawlessness, most of the residents in Tombstone were "perfectly good citizens; lawyers, doctors, mine workers—butchers, bakers and candlestick makers . . . and a couple of editors," according to John Clum, founder, editor, and publisher of the Tombstone *Epitaph.* An ardent advocate of law and order, Clum started the newspaper in 1880; his belief that "no tombstone is complete without its epitaph" provided its unusual name. The *Epitaph* survived early competition from the Tombstone *Nugget* and is now a monthly journal of Western history. The **Tombstone Epitaph Office** (5th Street between Fremont and Allen streets, 602–457–2211) displays old issues of the newspaper and early printing equipment. **Saint Paul's Episcopal Church** (3d and Safford streets) serves as a symbol of Tombstone's moral facet. The church, with a frontier-style steeply pitched roof, was built in 1882 by the Reverend Endicott Peabody, the esteemed founder of the Groton School in Massachusetts, during his tenure as pastor here.

Tombstone Courthouse State Historic Park

Tombstone's original courthouse, a two-story red-brick building with prominent stone quoins built in 1882, was the scene of trials and hangings that have become part of the town's considerable store of legends. In 1884, for example, a mob lynched John Heath, an

OPPOSITE: *The Tombstone Courthouse, which between 1882 and 1929 was the scene of the many trials and hangings associated with the notorious town of Tombstone and Cochise County.*

accused murderer. The coroner later ruled that he died of "strangulation, self-inflicted or otherwise." The building, which closed in 1929 when the county seat was moved to Bisbee, opened as a museum in the 1950s. Today the courtroom looks much as it did when the courthouse was built; both the judge's bench and the prisoner's dock are original. Some of the courthouse papers used as props in films have been retrieved from Hollywood. Only a conjectural reconstruction of the gallows stands in the courtyard because the original was burned for kindling in 1909.

> LOCATION: 219 East Toughnut Street. HOURS: 8–5 Daily. FEE: Yes. TELEPHONE: 602-457-3311.

On the corner of Fremont and Allen streets stands the **O. K. Corral,** site of the 1881 gunfight that assured Tombstone a permanent place in the annals of the Wild West. Because of the tangled events leading up to the shootout—secret alliances, greed, and corrupt politics—as well as Hollywood embellishments of it, the true story of the gunfight may never be known. Most sources agree that the shootout culminated a feud between the Earp brothers and Ike Clanton's gang. Virgil Earp, the U.S. deputy marshal of Tombstone, his brother Wyatt, a deputy marshal and quarter-owner of the Oriental Saloon, and their brother Morgan, also a deputy, rode with John "Doc" Holliday, a dentist who had come West to cure his tuberculosis. The Clanton "ranchers" (Ike Clanton, his brother Billy, and Frank and Tom McLaury) repeatedly defied the Earps' authority by smuggling cattle across the nearby Mexican border. Antagonism between the two factions intensified in the spring of 1881 when bandits killed two men while attempting to rob the Wells Fargo stagecoach. A witness identified three of the four gunmen as friends of Ike Clanton. According to one theory, Wyatt Earp, eager for the publicity the capture would bring, promised Clanton the reward money if he would reveal the robbers' whereabouts. Before Earp could arrest the criminals, they were killed during other exploits. Soon afterward, Earp and Clanton both suspected that the other had broken the secrecy surrounding the deal.

When rumors began to spread, the situation grew even more complicated. Witnesses claimed that the unidentified gunman had coughed while galloping away from the scene, thus suggesting the consumptive Holliday as the prime suspect. Holliday's possible role

has led some to theorize that Wyatt Earp, in cahoots with Holliday
and Ike Clanton, had planned the stagecoach robbery. In exchange
for a share of the future reward money, Clanton provided three gunmen who did not know they were being set up; Earp would make
the arrest and reap the local glory. In any case, by October the Earps
and Clantons had publicly vowed to shoot each other on sight. At
2:30 P.M. on October 26, the Clanton gang arrived at the Fremont
Street entrance to the O. K. Corral. Marshal Virgil Earp made his
way to disarm them, as an ordinance forbade citizens from wearing
arms in town. Sheriff John Behan beat him to the corral, ordered
the rustlers to drop their guns (to no avail), and declared that he
had "disarmed the cowboys" when he met the black-clad Earps on
Fremont Street. As he approached the Clanton gang, Wyatt said,
"You sons-of-bitches, you have been looking for a fight and now you
can have it." Virgil's command to "give up your arms or throw them
up" was immediately followed by a thirty-second barrage of bullets,
and when the gunfire ended, Tom and Frank McLaury and Billy
Clanton lay dying in Fremont Street. Morgan and Virgil Earp had
been wounded while Ike Clanton had ducked into C. S. Fly's photo
studio and escaped unhurt, as had Wyatt Earp. Clanton charged the
Earps with murder, but Judge Wells Spicer exonerated them, stating
that the homicides were "fully justified" as "necessary acts done in
the discharge of an official duty." Life-size mannequins now mark
the location of the gunfighters at the O. K. Corral.

The three men "hurled into eternity," as the *Epitaph* described
the casualties, are buried in **Boothill Cemetery,** located just outside
Tombstone overlooking the town and the surrounding desert.
Violence in Tombstone escalated after reprisals and more shootings
followed the gunfight. More than 250 people are interred in the
graveyard; most died prematurely by murder, hanging, mishaps,
encounters with Indians, or suicide. The town lapsed into relative
peacefulness after President Chester A. Arthur threatened to impose
martial law and John Slaughter, a man with a reputation for not taking prisoners alive, became sheriff.

One-third of the business district burned in 1881 after a barrel
of bad whiskey was ignited by a bartender's cigar, but the town was
soon rebuilt. The same year, miners began to encounter a serious
flooding problem at the 500-foot level; the flooding worsened
despite costly attempts to drain the tunnels with huge Cornish
pumps imported from England. Then came labor troubles and

falling silver prices. In 1886 another fire destroyed the pumps in the Grand Central mine, a blow from which Tombstone never recovered. Mining finally ended in the early 1900s; one estimate puts the total earnings of Tombstone's silver veins at some $40 million. Yet "The Town Too Tough to Die" never became a ghost town. Today it is a thriving commercial center with many authentic vestiges of its wild and woolly past.

CORONADO NATIONAL MEMORIAL

This 5,000-acre national memorial in the Huachuca Mountains, next to the Coronado National Forest, commemorates the journey of Francisco Vásquez de Coronado north from Mexico along the San Pedro River in 1540. The view of the river valley from 6,800-foot Coronado Peak is nearly as unspoiled today as it was then. Coronado was searching for the fabled Seven Cities of Cibola, but after two-and-a-half years he returned to Mexico and reported that the golden cities were actually seven small towns. An Indian guide who had urged the expedition ever onward with promises of gold just over the horizon was strangled to death on Coronado's orders. There is a small museum at the visitor center with exhibits relating to Coronado's trek.

LOCATION: Montezuma Canyon Road, off Route 92. HOURS: 8–5 Daily. FEE: None. TELEPHONE: 602–366–5515.

FORT HUACHUCA

Set up as a temporary camp in 1877 to protect travelers and settlers from Apache raids, Fort Huachuca became a permanent installation in 1886 during the campaign against Geronimo, who surrendered in August of that year. Today the post is still active; the **Fort Huachuca Museum** (Boyd and Grierson Streets, 602–533–5736) is located in the Old Post, a group of frame-and-adobe military buildings dating back to 1880 that line the parade ground. The museum contains old photographs of the fort, Indian artifacts, dioramas, and military artifacts. One room is devoted to the Buffalo Soldiers, as the Indians called the black U.S. Army troops stationed on the frontier. Black regiments were frequently used for Indian fighting, and between 1870 and 1890 fourteen of their soldiers were awarded Congressional Medals of Honor.

PATAGONIA

The name of this ranching and one-time mining center comes from the Spanish *patagón* ("big foot"), which is what the Spaniards called the local Indians. Set among some of the most spectacular rolling ranchland in the state, Patagonia is home of the **Stradling Museum of the Horse** (350 McKeown Avenue, 602–394–2264), a collection of carriages that also includes a 400-year-old Mexican ox cart, saddles, harnesses, books, paintings, and other artifacts and paraphernalia relating to the horse through history.

Several ghost towns in the vicinity of Patagonia are remnants of mining activity in the area. **Mowry,** once the site of a productive silver and lead mine, was purchased by Lieutenant Sylvester Mowry in 1859. During the Civil War, he was imprisoned at Fort Yuma, accused of using lead from the mine to make bullets for the Confederates.

NOGALES

Although Nogales Pass has been used for more than 2,000 years, the two towns of that name—one in Mexico, the other in the United States—were not founded until 1880, when a Mexican set up a roadhouse on the Mexican side and an American established a trading post north of the border. The first railroad to cross the Mexican border came through here in 1882. Thousands of U.S. soldiers were stationed in Nogales during the decade of the Mexican Revolution, from 1910 to 1920. Exhibits relating to the history of southern Arizona and northern Sonora in Mexico are displayed in the **Pimería Alta Historical Society** (223 Grand Avenue, 602–287–5402), which is housed in the picturesque former city hall. "Pimería Alta," meaning the upper country of the Pima, is the name by which the area was called in the days of Spanish colonization.

TUMACACORI NATIONAL MONUMENT

In 1691 the Pima invited the Jesuit missionary and explorer Father Eusebio Francisco Kino to visit the village of Tumacacori, where he established a mission outpost, or *visita,* of a larger mission at

OVERLEAF: *Cholla and pricklypear cacti growing in Montezuma Pass in the Huachuca Mountains, part of the Coronado National Memorial.*

Guevavi. He wrote that "very good beginnings were made in spiritual and temporal matters." In 1753 the Pima moved the village to its
present site and built a small church, **San José de Tumacacori.**
When Father Nacisco Gutiérrez, a Spanish Franciscan, arrived in
1794, he vowed to build a church the equal of San Xavier del Bac to
the north. Although the church was never finished, it was in use by
1822. Apache raids forced the Pima parishioners to leave
Tumacacori in 1848.

Although not as elegant as San Xavier del Bac, San José de
Tumacacori is a fine example of Spanish Colonial Baroque architecture. On the right of the entrance is the baptistry, its nine-foot-thick
adobe walls supporting a three-story bell tower. The church
entrance has an arched doorway framed by pilasters and a semicircular gable end. Tumacacori was made a national monument in
1908 to protect the church, which was then in ruins. The monument's patio garden, containing herbs, flowers, desert plants, and
fruit trees, was planted in 1939; it is similar to the gardens found in
the eighteenth-century missions of northern Sonora, Mexico. As
models in the visitor center show, there once was a closed courtyard
on the east side of the church, which was surrounded by priests'
quarters, storerooms, and classrooms.

LOCATION: Exit 29 off Route 19, 3 miles south of Tubac. HOURS: 8–5
Daily. FEE: Yes. TELEPHONE: 602–398–2341.

TUBAC

After the Pima Revolt of 1751, the Spanish established a presidio, or
garrison, on the Santa Cruz River at Tubac, the first permanent
Euro-American settlement in Arizona, to protect missionaries and
settlers. The second commander of the presidio, Juan Bautista de
Anza, set off from here to open the route to San Francisco, a settlement he founded in 1776. That same year the garrison at Tubac was
moved to Tucson, leaving the settlement, which was abandoned in
1783, helpless before Apache attacks. After soldiers—actually Pima
Indians commanded by Spanish officers—returned in 1787, settlers
returned, and Tubac prospered until 1830, when Apache attacks
again caused its decline.

OPPOSITE: *The ruins of San José de Tumacacori, dedicated by its Franciscan builders*
in 1822, only a few years before the order was expelled from its churches by the
Mexican government after achieving independence from Spain. Local parishioners
continued services there until the 1840s.

Tubac has been a mining town since its beginning, but it boomed after the Gadsden Purchase of 1853 when the colorful Charles D. Poston developed the Heintzelman mine in the vicinity. Of the community, which was mostly Mexican, Poston wrote: "We had no law but love, and no occupation but labor; no government, no taxes, no public debt, no politics. It was a community in a perfect state of nature." The Civil War caused the mine to close, and Tubac became a quiet farming community despite Apache raids that lasted until about 1890. In 1948 an art school opened, and the town became an artists' colony. In 1973 in **Tubac State Historic Park** (River Avenue, 602–398–2252), archaeologists excavated about half of the house of Tubac's first commandant, which was built in the early 1750s. Today a section of the foundations and lower walls of the commandant's house can be seen from an underground viewing area. The visitor center displays models of the presidio; other exhibits include the press on which Arizona's first newspaper, *The Weekly Arizonian,* was printed in 1859. The **Old Tubac School,** built in 1885, is also open to the public as part of the park.

In 1989 the Center for Spanish Colonial Archaeology in Tubac created **El Presidio de Tubac Archaeological Park** (602–398–9622) on seventeen acres south of the state park. The new park contains the ruins of more than fifty buildings from the time when the town was under Spanish colonial and Mexican rule.

S O U T H-C E N T R A L   A R I Z O N A

From about 200 B.C. until their unexplained disappearance in A.D. 1450, the agricultural Hohokam Indians farmed the Gila and Salt River valleys in south-central Arizona, frequently using canals for irrigation. Today the same sources of water have made this region the population center of the state, with over half the people in Arizona living in the region surrounding Phoenix. The Pima and the Maricopa followed the Hohokam and lived in relative harmony with white settlers, but the fierce Apache raiders slowed settlement—and mining—in the region. Beautiful cacti, such as the giant saguaro, grow in the deserts of the region. Its mountain ranges, by no means the highest in the state, are extremely rugged and provide spectacular backdrops for the desert scenery.

OPPOSITE: *Casa Grande was built by the Hohokam in the early fourteenth century using unreinforced caliche formed by hand into courses two feet high. Its ruins are protected by a steel canopy.*

CASA GRANDE RUINS NATIONAL MONUMENT

In his diary of 1694, Father Eusebio Francisco Kino, the Jesuit missionary, wrote of his first visit to "the Casa Grande—a four-story building as large as a castle and equal to the finest church in the lands of Sonora." The **Casa Grande,** or "big house," is the largest building constructed by Hohokam Indians. The walls of the tower are four-and-a-half-feet thick at the base and taper to one-and-three-quarters feet at the top. Scholars are uncertain about the purpose of the Casa Grande, but holes in three walls apparently were for astronomical observation. The Hohokam built the Casa Grande in about 1320 from caliche, a hard subsoil containing some calcium carbonate, using more than 600 floor and roof beams made from imported trees. Exhibits at the monument's visitor center include a map of the extensive system of irrigation canals built by the Hohokam.

LOCATION: Route 87, 1 mile north of Coolidge. HOURS: 7–6 Daily. FEE: Yes. TELEPHONE: 602–723–3172.

FLORENCE

Settled in 1866 by Levi Ruggles, Florence grew so fast as a trading center that it came close to being selected as the territorial capital. Once the railroad passed it by, however, growth stopped, although in 1909 convicts completed the new state prison there to replace the dungeons previously in use in Yuma. Exhibits relating to the prison, such as hangmen's nooses and a gas chamber chair, are among the more conventional items, including barbed wire and Indian pottery, displayed at the **Pinal County Historical Museum** (715 South Main Street). Today Florence retains many of its original adobe buildings, including its first courthouse, built by Ruggles in 1878. The building is operated as a museum called the **McFarland Historical State Park** (Main and Ruggles streets, 602–868–5216). Charles D. Poston, a pioneer, explorer, miner, and politician who helped Arizona attain territorial status, is buried on **Poston's Butte,** northwest of town.

PICACHO PEAK STATE PARK

The 3,374-foot Picacho Peak was a prominent landmark for westward-bound travelers, including the Mormon Battalion that built the first road across the territory in 1848. On April 15, 1862, Union and Confederate forces skirmished here in what some historians say is the westernmost conflict of the Civil War. On the Union side, a detachment commander and two soldiers were killed. The Confederates retreated. The landmark's name is redundant, since *picacho* is a Spanish word meaning "peak."

LOCATION: Picacho Peak Road, off Route I-10 at milepost 219. HOURS: 8–5 Daily. FEE: Yes. TELEPHONE: 602–466–3183.

GLOBE

Globe came into existence after silver was discovered on the San Carlos Indian Reservation, home of the Apache; the initial strike included a sizable boulder of almost pure silver that was said to have the outlines of the earth's continents on it. When the twelve-mile strip containing the claims was taken from the reservation, the Apache declared war, and their raids on the settlement continued until Geronimo signed a peace treaty in 1886. Although the silver was soon exhausted, copper was abundant, and the local Old Dominion mine became one of the most important in the world after the Lewisohn Brothers of New York purchased the company in 1895. A section of an early underground mine is reproduced in the **Gila County Historical Museum** (1330 North Broad Street, 602–425–7385), along with period rooms and artifacts from the **Besh-Ba-Gowah Ruins** (Jesse Hayes Road, 602–425–0320), which were the home of the prehistoric Salado Indians from 1225 to 1400. The foundations and remaining walls at the site give some idea of the settlement, which consisted of over 200 rooms and seven plazas.

TONTO NATIONAL MONUMENT

The Salado (Spanish for salted) Indians migrated from northeastern Arizona to this place near the Salt River. The culture is noted for its black-and-white pottery, known as Gila polychrome, and its cotton weaving. The Salado began building these cliff dwellings above slopes covered with saguaro cacti in the early 1300s. The monument and the Tonto Basin in which it is located are named for a band of nineteenth-century Apache. The three major sites—Upper Ruin, Lower Ruin, and Lower Ruin Annex—were declared a national monument in 1907 to protect them from pot hunters and population pressures resulting from the construction of Roosevelt Dam. A self-guided half-mile trail leads from the visitor center to the nine-

teen-room Lower Ruin. The larger, forty-room Upper Ruin can be visited only with a monument ranger.

LOCATION: Route 88, 5 miles east of Roosevelt. HOURS: 8–5 Daily. FEE: Yes. TELEPHONE: 602–467–2241.

The forty-four-mile **Apache Trail** (Route 88) was once an Apache warpath; today it is a scenic, twisting road that winds around the Superstition Wilderness. Soon after it leaves Apache Junction, the road passes **Lost Dutchman State Park** (Route 88, four miles north of Apache Junction, 602–982–4485), named for a supposedly valuable gold deposit worked by a German immigrant, Jacob Waltz, who reputedly killed several men to keep its location secret. Waltz revealed the location on his deathbed, but the mine was never found, despite the efforts of legions of gold seekers. Of all the stories of lost mines in Arizona, this one is the most enduring, despite geologists' reports that gold is unlikely to be found in that region. One theory holds that Waltz invented the story to cover the fact that he was selling gold stolen by miners from the Vulture Mine near Wickenburg. Two miles farther north, the trail passes **Weaver's Needle.** The 4,553-foot craggy pinnacle, a landmark for prospectors, is named for the famous frontier scout Pauline Weaver. The road passes **Roosevelt Dam,** completed in 1911 and, at 280 feet, still the highest masonry dam in the world.

PHOENIX

The flags of Spain, Mexico, and the United States, as well as the Confederate flag, had flown over Tucson by the time Phoenix was established in 1870. The name, chosen by the English adventurer and scholar Darrel Duppa, was meant to be prophetic: Duppa saw the city growing up from the ruins of the prehistoric Hohokam civilization just as the mythical bird had risen from its own ashes. Phoenix more than lived up to its name. In a mere nineteen years, it grew powerful enough to wrest the territorial capital away from Prescott; today it is both the largest city in Arizona and the ninth-largest in the country. Phoenix's potential for growth was evident almost from the beginning. In 1872 the Phoenix correspondent of a California paper wrote: "When it has become the capital city of the

OPPOSITE: *Ruins of the lower house, a large pueblo constructed in an easily defended cliff location by the Salado Indians, in the Tonto National Monument.*

*A doorway and window in the ruins of the upper house at Tonto National Monument,
built by the Salado Indians in the cliffs a thousand feet above the Salt River.*

Territory, which it will, undoubtedly, at no very distant day, and
when the 'iron horse' steams through our country on the Texas
Pacific road, Salt River Valley will be the garden of the Pacific, and
Phoenix the most important inland town." In 1881 Phoenix, with a
population of almost 2,000, was incorporated; in 1887 the railroad
(a branch of the Southern Pacific from Maricopa) arrived, and in
1889 the territorial capital moved here from Prescott.

The desperate quest for water—the key to the growth of any
desert city—was alleviated in 1911 when the Roosevelt Dam was
completed. The competition for the waters of the Colorado River,
which enters the state about midway along the northern border, cuts
through the Grand Canyon, and forms the western boundary with
California, became so intense as to almost cause warfare. In 1922
the Arizona National Guard was sent to prevent construction of a
dam at Park, California, but the troops were called off when the U.S.
Supreme Court ruled the state powerless to stop the construction.

So much of Phoenix's heritage was lost in the city's phenomenal
growth after World War II that today it gives the impression of being

a completely modern city, but vestiges of the past remain in a few historic houses, museums, and other sites. The granite, tuff, and malapay building that today houses the **Arizona State Capitol Museum** (Adams Street and Seventeenth Avenue, 602–542–4675) opened in 1900 as the territorial capitol. It is now restored to its appearance in 1912, the year Arizona achieved statehood, and houses a collection of artifacts and documents relating to state history and a wax figure of Governor George Hunt in his office. The Winged Victory weathervane atop the copper dome was once a favorite target for pistol-packing cowboys. The state government left the building in 1974 for offices in a new building. The **Arizona History Room** in the downstairs office of the First Interstate Bank of Arizona (100 West Washington Street, 602–271–6879) is a reconstruction of the first chartered bank in the Arizona Territory and includes original fixtures, furniture, tellers' cages, and spittoons; bank records are also displayed.

The Roosevelt Dam, completed in 1911 just below the confluence of Tonto Creek and Salt River.

An 1887 photograph of an Arizona stage being loaded in front of the Commercial Hotel in Phoenix.

Heritage Square (6th and Monroe streets), a block of eight restored houses from the late nineteenth century, includes the elegant **Rosson House** (139 North 6th Street, 602–262–5071), built in 1895 with a wraparound verandah and hexagonal turret. It was the home of Dr. Ronald Rosson, an army doctor. The other houses contain shops, offices, and restaurants, except for the **Stevens House** (602 East Adams Street, 602–253–9337), currently the Arizona Doll and Toy Museum, and the **Silva House** (628 East Adams Street, 602–236–5451), built in 1900, half of which is maintained in turn-of-the-century period and which contains a series of exhibits by Salt River Project on such subjects as Arizona history, communications, power development, and water supply.

Heard Museum

More than 75,000 objects representing southwestern culture from prehistoric times to the present are displayed at this museum. The museum's featured exhibit is titled "Native Peoples of the Southwest: The Permanent Collection of the Heard Museum." Divided into three geographic sections—the Desert, the Uplands, and the Colorado Plateau—the exhibit includes a reconstruction of a Hohokam pithouse, a display of Pima basketry pottery from the Mogollon, Salado, and Sinagua peoples, a reconstruction of an Apache wickiup, and a Navajo hogan. The exhibit's fourth section, the Kachina Gallery, contains over 400 dolls, one of the largest collections in the world. Sculpture, including the work of the contemporary Apache artist Allan Houser, is displayed in the sculpture court and in the museum patios. The museum also displays and actively promotes the work of other contemporary Indian artists both in its exhibit galleries and at its only sale show, the Biennial Native American Fine Arts Invitational. Indian dancers and musicians frequently perform in the museum amphitheater.

The museum was founded by Dwight and Maie Heard, who moved to Phoenix in 1895 to seek relief for Dwight's lung congestion. He became a real estate developer, the publisher of *The Arizona Republican,* and an early promoter of irrigation in the Salt River Valley. He also planted palm trees imported from Egypt along Phoenix's streets. The Heards built an adobe, hacienda-style museum to display their collection to the public; it opened three months after Dwight Heard's death in 1929.

LOCATION: 22 East Monte Vista Road. HOURS: 10–5 Monday–Saturday, 1–5 Sunday. FEE: Yes. TELEPHONE: 602–252–8840.

The **Arizona Historical Society–Central Arizona Division** (1242 North Central Avenue, 602–255–4470) occupies the 1917 Ellis-Shackleford House, which was built from "tapestry," or wire-cut, bricks and had such innovative touches for the day as solar hot-water heat, automatic flush toilets, a central vacuum system, and electric outlets. The society operates the **Museum on Wheels** (302 Latham Avenue, 602–255–3047), which displays photographs and artifacts concerning Arizona history. A new, larger museum is scheduled to open in 1991.

In north Phoenix, on the Arizona State Fairgrounds, the **Arizona Mineral Museum** (Seventeenth Avenue and McDowell Road, 602–255–3791) has examples of all the ores found in Arizona, old mining tools and assay kits, and lapidary displays. In east Phoenix the **Arizona Military Museum** (5636 East McDowell

From the extensive collection of the Heard Museum: A Hopi tableta, or ceremonial headgear, made from wood in the early 1900s (above); a Navajo silver bow guard, also crafted in the early 1900s (opposite top); and a selection of intricate basketry from various tribes (opposite bottom).

Road, 602–267–2676) has a collection of military artifacts from
Spanish colonial times to the present. The museum is housed in a
building in the National Guard complex, about seven miles from
downtown, that was used to confine captured German submariners
during World War II. In December 1944 twenty-five officers and
enlisted men escaped, triggering the largest manhunt in Arizona
history. All were recaptured. The **Hall of Flame Museum** (6101 East
Van Buren Street, 602–275–3473) has a collection of firefighting
equipment from around the world dating to 1725.

Pueblo Grande Museum

The centerpiece of this unusual museum and park is the remains of
the Hohokam civilization of desert farmers that flourished between
the eighth and the fourteenth century. The ruins, one of the few
Hohokam archaeological sites open to the public, were discovered
by the anthropologist Frank Hamilton Cushing in 1887. From the
excavations visitors can see remains of the Hohokam canals and an
oval depression, probably a ball court similar to those found in
Mexico. The museum displays Hohokam artifacts and cooking utensils in a reconstructed pueblo room.

LOCATION: 4619 East Washington Street. HOURS: 9–5
Monday–Saturday, 1–5 Sunday. FEE: Yes. TELEPHONE: 602–275–1897.

TEMPE

In 1870 Charles Trumbull Hayden began operating a ferry land-
ing, flour mill, and store on the Salt River, the nucleus of a com-
munity that was first called Hayden's Ferry and later renamed
Tempe supposedly because a visitor said it reminded him of the
Vale of Tempe in Greece. Hayden's son was the longtime Arizona
congressman Senator Carl Hayden. Exhibits on the history of
Tempe are displayed at the **Tempe Historical Museum** (3500 South
Rural Road, 602–731–8377) and include an old post office, old
farm tools and vehicles, toys, clothing, and furniture. In 1886 the
Arizona Normal School, now **Arizona State University** (Rural Road
and Apache Boulevard, 602–965–5728), opened in Tempe with
thirty-three students. Growth was slow until after World War II;
now it is one of the largest universities in the country. The circular
Gammage Center for the Performing Arts (Mill Avenue and

Apache Boulevard, 602–965–3434), completed in 1964, was one of Frank Lloyd Wright's last commissions; Wright died in 1959.

SCOTTSDALE

Named for its developer, an army chaplain named Winfield Scott, Scottsdale began in 1888 after the Arizona Canal had opened sections of the Salt River valley for irrigation. A two-room schoolhouse, built in 1909 near the center of the original settlement, is occupied by the chamber of commerce (Brown Avenue and Main Street, 602–945–8481). Scottsdale, which calls itself the "West's Most Western Town," began as a sedate community whose citizens strove to keep out saloons and gambling dens. Scottsdale's reputation as a center for creative people was enhanced in 1938 when the architect Frank Lloyd Wright established a winter headquarters for his Wisconsin school and studio, Taliesin (a Welsh word meaning "shining brow"). In 1947 Paolo Soleri came to Taliesin West, as the Scottsdale branch was called, as a student; in 1956 he started his own **Cosanti Foundation** (6433 Doubletree Road, 602–948–6145), where he researches the design of energy- and space-efficient cities, a science he calls "arcology" (a word derived from architecture and ecology). Here in a complex of earth-formed concrete structures are drafting studios, crafts workshops, and display areas with original Soleri sculptures, graphics, sketches, and windbells. The foundation is building **Arcosanti** (602–632–7135), an energy-efficient city, near Cordes Junction, sixty-five miles north of Phoenix.

Taliesin West

Soon after he began to purchase the 600 acres of desert at the foot of the McDowell Mountains, Frank Lloyd Wright wrote that it was "a grand garden the like of which in sheer beauty of space and pattern does not exist, I think, in the world." Here Wright built a winter camp in 1937–1938. The camp buildings consisted of stone walls, redwood beams, and canvas roofs. Much of the canvas has been replaced with a more permanent plastic. The associates and students at Taliesin West carry on Wright's work as an architectural firm, Taliesin Associated Architects, and as the Frank Lloyd Wright School of Architecture. As in Wright's day, the students live communally and work on the grounds and in the kitchen, as well as

in the drafting room. As Taliesin West is a winter camp, students sleep in tents in the desert.

LOCATION: 13201 North 108th Street at Cactus Road. HOURS: October through May: 10–4 Daily; June through September: 9–11 A.M. Daily. FEE: Yes. TELEPHONE: 602–860–8810.

In north Scottsdale is a re-creation of a western town called **Rawhide** (23023 Scottsdale Road, 602–563–5111), with about twenty-five replicas of western buildings from the 1880s. The complex also has a museum with such relics as Geronimo's moccasins and one of Wyatt Earp's guns.

WICKENBURG

Wickenburg, on the Hassayampa River, came into existence to process gold from the Vulture Mine fourteen miles away. Henry Wickenburg discovered gold here in 1863 when, according to one story, he bent down to pick up a vulture he had just shot and noticed gold in the rocks. Soon there were eighty mines operating in the area, and Wickenburg had become Arizona's third-largest city. Today many buildings from the early 1900s are still standing along **Frontier Street,** including the railroad depot and the brick Hassayampa Building. In the Apache language, Hassayampa means "river that runs upside down," a reference to the fact that the river flows beneath the ground. There is a legend that anyone who drinks from the river will never tell the truth again. The **Desert Caballeros Western Museum** (20 North Frontier Street, 602–684–2272) has period rooms, an early street scene, Indian exhibits, dioramas explaining the Vulture Mine, and a gallery of Western art. Before Wickenburg had a jail, prisoners were chained to the **Jail Tree,** a mesquite that still stands at Tegner and Center streets.

YUMA

In 1540 Hernando de Alarcón, the Spanish navigator, proceeded up the Colorado River past the site of present-day Yuma in hopes of resupplying Coronado, who had in the meantime struck off in a

OPPOSITE *and* OVERLEAF: *Taliesin West, designed by Frank Lloyd Wright, who sought to create a building as "nobly simple in outline as the region itself is sculptured . . . the man-made building heightening the beauty of the desert."*

different direction. Father Eusebio Kino, the beneficent pioneer and missionary, made the first of several trips into the region in 1683. He and other Spanish explorers discovered that the best crossing of the Colorado River lay just below the confluence with the Gila River. In around 1779 Father Francisco Garcés established two missions on the California side of the river. He was part of a Spanish colonizing experiment that included a military detachment and a group of civilian settlers, the idea being that a combination of the three elements—military, ecclesiastical, and civilian—would result in a successful and stable settlement. Instead, the combination produced discord and angered the local Quechan Indians, who slaughtered most of the colony, including Father Garcés, in an uprising on July 18, 1781. The revolt ended Spanish colonizing in the area.

American mountainmen operated in the area in the early 1800s, but Colonel Stephen Kearny, guided by Kit Carson, was the first to claim the land for the United States; he passed through in 1846 with a force of 100 men on his way to California during the war with Mexico. Kearny was followed by Colonel Philip Cooke and his Mormon Battalion, which built the important road between Santa Fe and California. "Cooke's Road" was used by forty-niners on their way to the California gold fields, and in 1851 Fort Yuma was built on the California side of the river to protect the Yuma Crossing from Indian attacks. The next year the first river steamer arrived at the fort. In 1854 Colonel Charles D. Poston laid out a town, which he called Colorado City, on the site of present-day Yuma. After being flooded out eight years later, the settlement was rebuilt on higher ground and seemed to join another settlement, called Arizona City; later both sites were united as Yuma. The discovery of gold in 1858 along the Colorado and Gila rivers swelled Yuma's population, and by 1880 it was, after Tucson, the territory's second-largest city. In the 1860s the journalist J. Ross Browne reported on Yuma's torrid summer weather: "I have even heard the complaint made that the thermometer failed to show the true heat because the mercury dried up. Everything dries; wagons dry; men dry; chickens dry; there is no juice left in any thing, living or dead, by the end of summer."

OPPOSITE: *The Yuma Territorial Prison, now a State Historical Park, where some 3,000 prisoners whose crimes ranged from poligamy to murder were incarcerated between 1876 and 1909.*

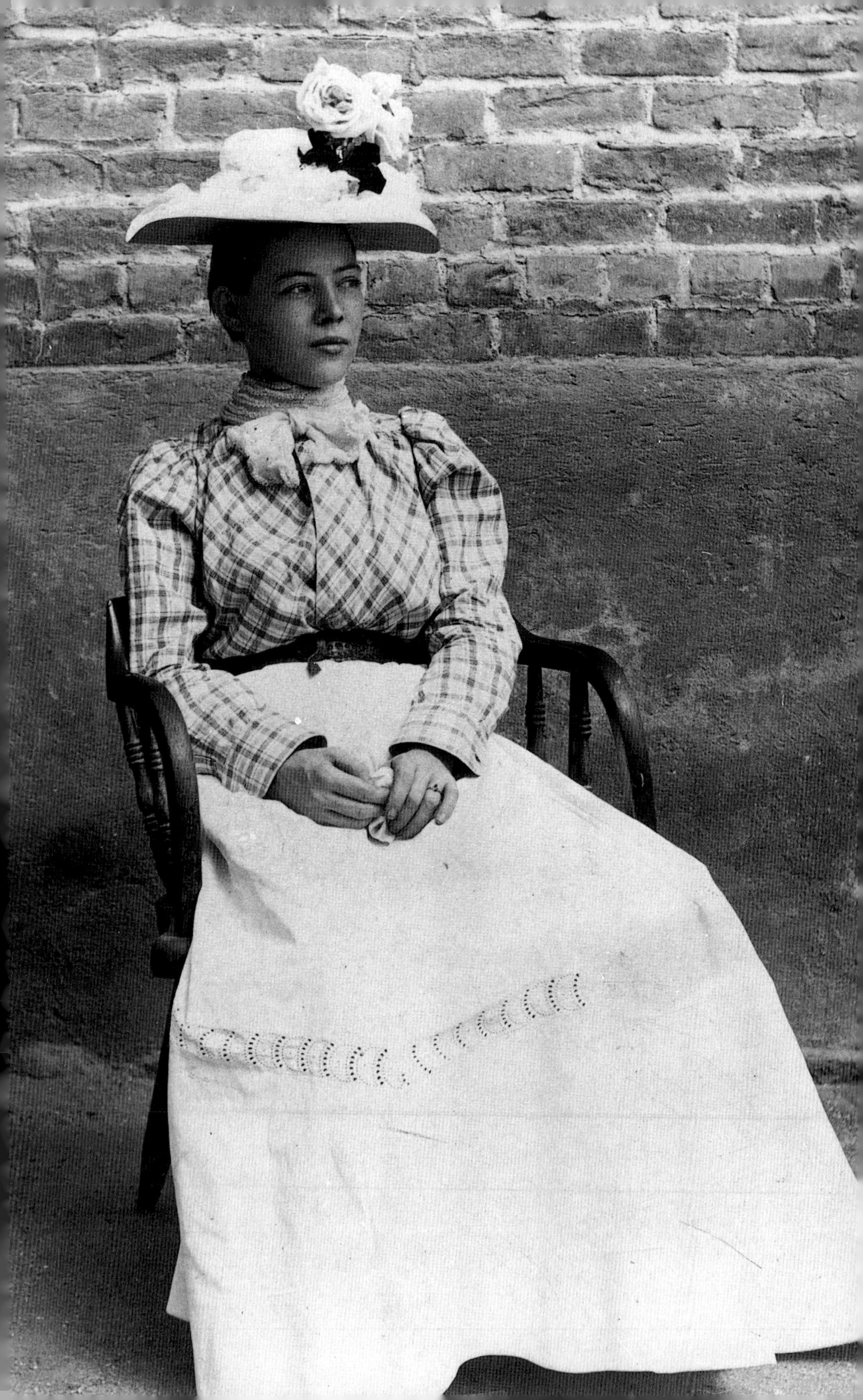

The **Arizona Historical Society/Century House Museum and Gardens** (240 Madison Avenue, 602–782–1841), built of adobe in 1871, displays photographs and artifacts relating to the history of the lower Colorado River region. It also has an aviary and extensive gardens of exotic and desert plants. The **Adobe Annex,** or Mellon House (248 Madison Avenue, 602–782–1841), was built in 1890 for a Colorado River steamboat captain, Jack Mellon. Both houses are owned and operated by the Arizona Historical Society. In 1876 the Yuma Territorial Prison was built; it became one of the town's main economic assets. In cementing California and Arizona in 1877, the Southern Pacific Railroad built a bridge across the Colorado. Irrigation, which was first attempted about the turn of the century, became widespread after the Laguna Dam was built in 1909, and Yuma became an agricultural center.

Yuma Territorial Prison State Historic Park

This formidable place of incarceration, built in 1876 on the banks of the treacherous Colorado River in the midst of the desert, was Arizona's response to the lawlessness that pervaded the territory. The early prisoners constructed the stone-and-adobe walls themselves and carved dungeons out of solid rock for difficult prisoners. A guard tower overlooking the walls held a Lowell battery gun capable of firing 600 rounds a minute. Local Indians were paid fifty dollars a head for capturing escaped prisoners. During one attempted breakout in 1887, a prisoner who was about to murder the warden was shot dead by another convict, Barney Riggs. Riggs was later pardoned and became a noted Texas gunslinger. The prison closed in 1909. The cell blocks, guard tower, and prison graveyard are open to visitors, and a museum displays photographs and tells the story of some of the 3,040 men and 29 women who were incarcerated here. Artifacts made and used by the prisoners are also on exhibit.

LOCATION: Prison Hill Road. HOURS: 8–5 Daily. FEE: Yes. TELEPHONE: 602–783–4771.

OPPOSITE: *Pearl Hart, one of the most popular prisoners in the Arizona Territorial Prison in Yuma, was convicted of robbing several stagecoaches in 1899.*

NORTHERN ARIZONA

OPPOSITE: *A solitary rider in the sand dunes near Second Mesa, site of several pueblos within Arizona's Hopi Indian Reservation.*

Although Arizona came to statehood late (the forty-eighth state, it was admitted in 1912), it was widely inhabited by ancient peoples. Nowhere is this more evident than in northern Arizona, where a wealth of prehistoric ruins have somehow survived the erosion of time and destruction by vandals, looters, and pot hunters. Particularly outstanding are the cliff dwellings now known as the Navajo National Monument, intricately built pueblos that were one of three centers of the Anasazi, who lived here for fifty years in the latter half of the thirteenth century. The Sinagua, probably a related but distinct people, were displaced from their homeland in 1064 by a volcanic eruption that occurred close to present-day Flagstaff; they returned several decades later to find the soil enriched by the volcanic fallout. The remains of the settlements where they lived for the next century and a half are now Wupatki National Monument.

The Hopi of today consider many of the Anasazi and Sinagua ruins to be their sacred ancestral homes, and it seems likely that the Hopi absorbed some of those prehistoric people who had abandoned their pueblos and disappeared. The Hopi too are an ancient people, and their village of Old Oraibi, founded about 1150, may be the oldest continuously populated settlement in the country. Although they participated in the Pueblo Revolt of 1680 against their Spanish occupiers, the Hopi were a predominantly peaceful people who lived, then as now, in relative isolation amid the mesas of northeastern Arizona. Their main enemies have been the more aggressive Navajo, with whom they still have territorial disputes.

To quell the Navajo, whose raids were making life miserable for their neighbors, especially the Hopi and Zuni, the U.S. government built Fort Defiance in 1851 near the present Arizona–New Mexico border, but the tribe continued to defy white authority. On April 30, 1860, nearly 1,000 Navajo warriors attacked the fort but were beaten back. In 1863 almost 8,000 Navajo surrendered after Colonel Kit Carson's foray into Arizona, which succeeded in penetrating Navajo defenses in the narrow canyons of Canyon de Chelly. The Navajo were marched off on the punishing "Long Walk" 300 miles to Fort Sumner in New Mexico, where they were incarcerated for four years. The Navajo are closely related to the Apache, who terrorized the Arizona frontier and territory. General George Crook's winter campaign of 1872–1873 against the Apache resulted in the surrender of most of the tribe, but others continued to resist for another decade.

A Dash for the Timber, *an 1889 painting by Frederic Remington.* PAGES 210–211:
*Wuptuki National Monument preserves the ruins of Hopi buildings constructed of the
red sandstone that occurs naturally throughout the region.*

As soon as President Abraham Lincoln signed the bill creating
the Arizona Territory in 1863, the appointed governor, John N.
Goodwin of Maine, and other officials left on a three-month tour of
the settled areas of Arizona. They established a temporary capital
near Fort Whipple but soon moved both the fort and the government south to the site of present-day Prescott, on Granite Creek, to
be closer to the mining activities there. Prescott was named the capital because many of the citizens of the more likely candidates,
Tucson and Tubac, supported the Confederacy in the Civil War. The
territorial government took a census (which established that there
were 4,187 whites in the territory), appointed a legislature, and
named Charles Poston congressional delegate. The capital, which
came to be known as the "capital on wheels," moved to Tucson in
1867, back to Prescott ten years later, and finally to Phoenix in 1889.

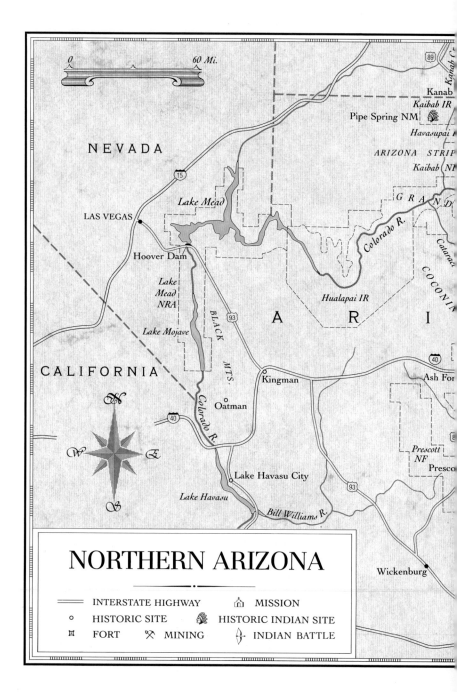

0   60 Mi.

NEVADA

Kanab
Kaibab IR
Pipe Spring NM
Havasupai
ARIZONA STRIP
Kaibab NF

15

Lake Mead

LAS VEGAS

Hoover Dam

Lake
Mead
NRA

Lake Mojave

BLACK

93

MTS.

CALIFORNIA

Colorado R.

40

Oatman

Kingman

GRAND

Colorado R.

Cataract

COCONIN

Hualapai IR

A   R   I

40

Ash For

Prescott
NF

Presco

Lake Havasu City

93

Lake Havasu

Bill Williams R.

Wickenburg

NORTHERN ARIZONA

——— INTERSTATE HIGHWAY   🏠 MISSION

○ HISTORIC SITE   HISTORIC INDIAN SITE

⊟ FORT   ✗ MINING   INDIAN BATTLE

89

Kanah Cr.

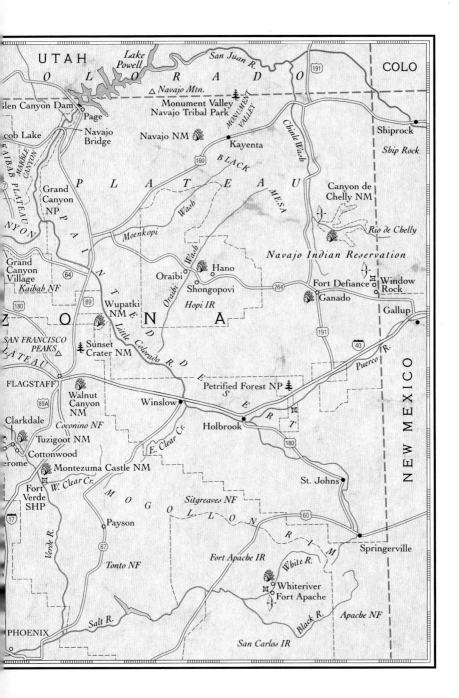

A mule team hauling a wagon across the Little Colorado River in 1885.

The Arizona Strip—the narrow, northernmost section of the state between the Grand Canyon and the Utah border—and the shores of the Little Colorado River attracted many Mormons from Utah. In the early 1880s, the mines of Jerome in central Arizona began producing silver, the start of an economic bonanza that lasted through World War I. Development accelerated in 1883 when the Atlantic & Pacific Railroad completed a line across northern Arizona to the Colorado River. A spur to the Grand Canyon in 1901 opened up that scenic wonder to tourism.

This chapter begins near the Colorado border in Page and proceeds southward through Lee's Ferry to the Grand Canyon. It continues eastward to the Navajo and Hopi reservations before moving west along Route 40 through Flagstaff and Kingman. After a detour to Lake Havasu City, the tour resumes in Prescott, proceeds to Jerome and moves in a southeasterly direction to Payson and Whiteriver.

A R I Z O N A   S T R I P

The Colorado River and the Grand Canyon almost completely iso-
late this barren, mountainous, hauntingly beautiful section from the
rest of the state. In heritage, history, and temperament more a part
of Utah, the Arizona Strip was settled by Mormon farmers and
ranchers seeking to enlarge the Mormon sphere of influence and to
practice polygamy free of persecution. Today Paiute live on the
Kaibab Reservation; they came to the strip some time after the prehistoric pueblo people about 1,000 years ago. The strip also contains
nine separate wilderness areas as well as the northern rim of the
Grand Canyon National Park. This part of the Grand Canyon, reach-
able by road only by taking a long detour through northern
Arizona, is about 1,000 feet higher than the opposite rim and offers
an entirely different perspective on the chasm.

PAGE

This planned community was developed in the 1960s to house the
workers on the Glen Canyon Dam. Since it is on the east side of the
river, it is not technically part of the Arizona Strip, but neither does
it belong to the Navajo Reservation that begins just east of it. The
John Wesley Powell Memorial Museum (6 North Lake Powell
Boulevard, 602–645–9496) is devoted to the intrepid Civil War
major who led the first expedition down the Colorado River and
through the Grand Canyon in 1869 and repeated the feat in 1871.
Displayed in front of the museum is a slightly-larger-than-life-size
replica of the pine rowboat that Powell used on his first expedition.
The replica was constructed for the film about the expedition, *Ten
Who Dared.* Inside the museum are portraits of Powell, many photographs of his expeditions, pioneer artifacts, Indian arts and crafts,
and Powell's letter to the president, dated May 8, 1894, resigning as
director of the U.S. Geological Survey "by reason of wounds that
require surgical operation." Powell had lost an arm at the Battle of
Shiloh in the Civil War, and the amputation had been done so badly
that he still felt pain over thirty years later.

LEES FERRY

This town was settled by Mormons in 1869; a break in the canyon
wall made it the only feasible crossing of the Colorado River in this

section of Arizona. The town is named for John D. Lee, who began operating a ferry here in 1872. In 1877 Lee was executed by a firing squad for his part in the Mountain Meadows Massacre of 1857, in which a force of Mormons and Indians slaughtered the non-Mormon members of a wagon train in southern Utah. The ferry continued to operate until the **Navajo Bridge,** a graceful span that crosses the Colorado River 467 feet above the water, was completed five miles downstream in 1929.

PIPE SPRING NATIONAL MONUMENT

Pipe Spring got its name when William Hamblin shot out the bottom of a companion's pipe in an extraordinary feat of marksmanship. The Mormons tried to settle Pipe Spring as early as 1863 but were driven off by the Navajo. After peace was established in 1870, the Mormons built a fortified ranch house over the springs, possibly to prevent Indians from using the water. Called Winsor Castle, after the ranch superintendent Anson P. Winsor, the structure—two stone houses connected by high stone walls—forms a fortified courtyard. Arizona's first telegraph office opened in Winsor Castle in 1871. The first operator later married David King Udall; their grandsons are the Arizona politicians Stewart and Morris "Mo" Udall. Today the ranch house has been restored, and pioneer crafts are demonstrated on the grounds and in the outbuildings. There is also a visitor center with exhibits on the history of the ranch.

> LOCATION: Off Route 389, 14 miles west of Fredonia. HOURS: 8–4:30 Daily. FEE: Yes. TELEPHONE: 602–643–7105.

GRAND CANYON NATIONAL PARK

With its ever-shifting hues and its layers of cliffs, valleys, and pinnacles laid bare to the eye, the Grand Canyon is a geological spectacle caused by the mighty Colorado River cutting through the rising Colorado Plateau. Its size alone is awe-inspiring: over 200 miles long and, on the average, 10 miles wide and a mile deep. Although the Anasazi lived in and around the Grand Canyon as early as the twelfth century, it was unknown to European-Americans until

OPPOSITE: *Winsor Castle, a fort built by the Mormons to protect the water supply at Pipe Spring.*

Indians led a party from Coronado's expedition there in 1540. In 1776 the explorer and priest Francisco Garcés spent several days in a Havasupai village in the canyon. He wrote: "I am astonished at the roughness of this country, and at the barrier which nature has fixed therein." A few trappers hunting beaver traversed the canyon's rim in the 1820s, and in 1857 Lieutenant Joseph C. Ives traveled up the Colorado River from the Gulf of California in a small steamer. He was shipwrecked at Black Canyon, near the present site of the Hoover Dam, and proceeded with his party overland to the western part of the canyon. Ives was unimpressed by what he saw: "Ours has been the first and will doubtless be the last party of whites to visit this profitless locality."

Ives's prediction held for about twelve years, until the one-armed Civil War hero John Wesley Powell led a party of nine down the Green and Colorado rivers in 1869. The men spent most of the month of August navigating the uncharted rapids of the Grand Canyon. Before they began their descent, Powell wrote, "We are now ready to start on our way down the Great Unknown. . . . We have an unknown distance yet to run; an unknown river to explore. What falls there are, we know not; what rocks beset the channel, we know not; what walls rise over the river, we know not." He led a second expedition down the Colorado in 1871 with the mission of mapping the Colorado Plateau for the federal government.

Prospectors attracted by the mineral potential of the canyon in the 1880s soon found tourists more profitable than mining. A few primitive hotels were built, and a trail down into the canyon opened. Tourism increased markedly in 1901 when the Santa Fe Railroad built a spur line from Williams, Arizona, to Grand Canyon Village, and in 1905 the Fred Harvey Company opened the rustic but elegant El Tovar Hotel. When President Theodore Roosevelt visited the Grand Canyon in 1903, he said: "You can not improve on it. The ages have been at work on it, and man can only mar it." Roosevelt created the Grand Canyon National Monument in 1908; it became a national park in 1919. Since then the park has been enlarged and adjacent areas protected, but maintaining the Grand Canyon from man's incursions is a task requiring constant vigilance. Over 3 million tourists a year visit the park, creating traffic jams,

OPPOSITE: *Desert View is the highest point on the southern rim of the Grand Canyon.*

wear and tear on the facilities, and ecological damage. As late as 1963, conservationists had to fight a government plan to build two dams across the Colorado and flood over 150 miles of the canyon.

Although few visitors to the canyon pay much attention to **Grand Canyon Village,** it is an official historic district, and many of its buildings tell the story of the area's development. In particular the **El Tovar Hotel,** named for an officer in Coronado's expedition, is by itself a worthy destination; the naturalist John Burroughs wrote of meeting a woman there who "thought that they had built the canyon too near the hotel." Built by Hopi workers with local limestone blocks and logs from Oregon, the hotel was designed as a combination "Swiss chalet and Norway villa," and the amenities included meticulous service, Craftsman furniture in every room, and fresh flowers—grown in the hotel's own greenhouse—on every table. Nearby is the **Hopi House,** designed by the Fred Harvey Company architect, Mary Jane Colter, as a place for Hopi artisans to produce and sell their work. The pueblo-style building is based on the Hopi village of Old Oraibi.

Among the earliest entrepreneurs to settle on the rim of the canyon were the photographers Ellsworth and Emery Kolb, who began building the **Kolb Studio,** a log-and-shingle building that hangs over the edge of the canyon rim, in 1904. Here the enterprising brothers sold scenic views, showed a film of their 1911 trip down the Colorado River, operated a soda fountain, held Wednesday night dances, and resisted all attempts to remove them. Emery Kolb continued to operate the studio, which is closed, until he died in 1976. The studio is located at the head of **Bright Angel Trail,** once a toll path into the canyon controlled by another early promoter, Ralph Cameron. Cameron and his brother staked mining claims along the rim and the trail, thereby controlling some of the canyon's most desirable building sites.

In 1914 the Fred Harvey Company built the **Lookout Studio** on the rim to compete with the Kolbs. This unobtrusive, aesthetically pleasing building of rough-cut limestone still operates as a tourist shop. Other historic structures include the **Buckey O'Neill Cabin,** now part of Bright Angel Lodge. This simple log cabin, the oldest surviving structure on the rim, was built in the 1890s by O'Neill, the

OPPOSITE: *Male kachina doll, circa 1880, carved from the root of a cottonwood tree and sewn with sinew.*

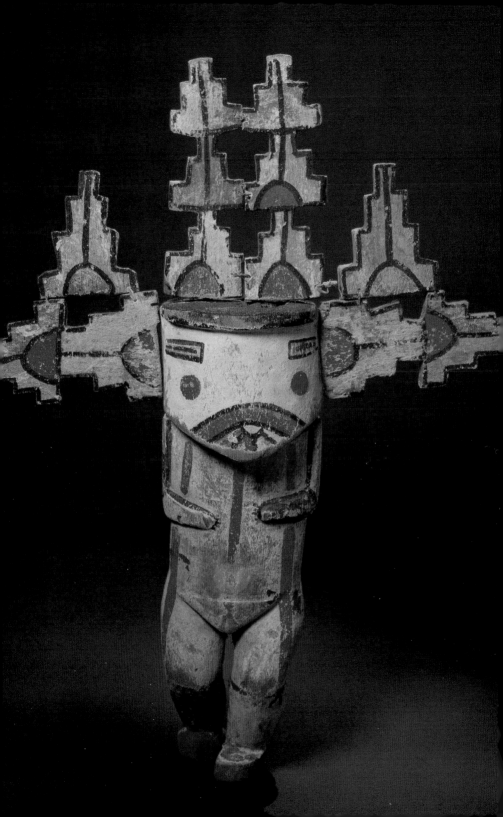

Prescott mayor and Roughrider who was killed by a sniper in Cuba.
O'Neill was part owner of a copper mine near the canyon. The log-
and-shingle **Santa Fe Railroad Station** was built by the railroad in
1909 and closed when service ended in 1968. Nearby, the **First
National Park Service Administration Building,** built of stone and
rough-cut pine in 1921, is a fine example of the style that came to be
known as "rustic." Near the east entrance of the park, the unusual
seventy-foot **Desert View Watchtower** was built by the Fred Harvey
Company in 1932. At 7,500 feet, Desert View is the highest point on
the South Rim and offers spectacular views of the canyon and the
Painted Desert to the east. Farther west on East Rim Drive is the prehistoric **Tusayan Ruin,** an Anasazi site that was occupied by some
twenty inhabitants for about twenty-five years starting in 1185. The
remains of some of its fifteen rooms can be seen from a self-guided
trail. The ruins are not as spectacular as other prehistoric sites in
the region, but they are an important reminder that the canyon had
been home to native peoples for centuries before European-
Americans discovered it.

> LOCATION: *North Rim entrance:* Route 67; *South Rim entrances:* Route
> 180/64 and Route 64. HOURS: 24 hours Daily; North Rim closed
> mid-October through mid-May. FEE: Yes. TELEPHONE:
> 602–638–7888.

THE   NAVAJO   RESERVATION

The Navajo, who speak a language closely related to that of the
Apache, migrated from the Great Plains to the Southwest in the sixteenth century. After they acquired horses in the early seventeenth
century, they expanded their territory, often at the expense of their
neighbors, particularly the Hopi and Zuni. (In 1837 they raided the
Hopi village of Oraibi and killed many inhabitants.) The Navajo were
a loosely knit people; even after some tribes made peace with the
United States, others continued raiding white settlements. In 1863
Colonel Kit Carson led an expedition that penetrated the Navajo
stronghold at Canyon de Chelly and persuaded many Navajo to surrender. Early the next year more than 8,000 of them were forced on

OPPOSITE: *Keet Seel was once the largest Anasazi village in Tsegi Canyon.*

the punishing, 300-mile "Long Walk" from Fort Defiance to Fort Sumner in New Mexico. They were repatriated by the Navajo Treaty of 1868, which also gave them a reservation of 3.5 million acres. Today more than 100,000 Navajo live on the reservation, which has been increased over the years to more than 15 million acres. The tribal headquarters is located at Window Rock, Arizona. The tribe operates its own utilities, public works, police force, newspapers, and other services. In 1973 it built two campuses—at Shiprock, New Mexico, and Tsaile, Arizona—for the Navajo Community College.

The Navajo remain superb craftspeople. Navajo rugs, particularly, woven on handmade looms that have changed little over the centuries, are the ultimate expression of traditional Indian crafts. The patterns often bear the names of the places where they originated; Two Grey Hills (in New Mexico), for example, is particularly prized. The Teec Nos Pos pattern developed in the northeast corner of Arizona.

A traveler coming from the Grand Canyon or Flagstaff can loop through the Navajo and Hopi reservations by first visiting Navajo National Monument near the Utah border, then proceeding to Canyon de Chelly National Monument via Routes 59 and 191. From there the tour goes south on Route 191 to the junction with Route 264 and east to Ganado and Window Rock, then backtracks west along Route 264 through the Hopi mesas.

NAVAJO NATIONAL MONUMENT

Navajo National Monument preserves a principal home of the Kayenta Anasazi, the prehistoric people who lived here for half a century, until 1300. About 1250, the Anasazi moved from villages in the open to the cliff dwelling of the canyon. Heavy summer thunderstorms caused erosion, created arroyos, and lowered the water table, making farming impossible. The same kind of change in climate probably drove this group out of their cliff dwellings some fifty years later. The Kayenta were the premier potters of the Anasazi, making the most advanced, multicolored pottery of the culture. It is speculated that pottery was their principal trading product. In 1909 John Wetherill, guide, interpreter, and Indian trader, was named the first custodian of the monument. Two years earlier Wetherill had guided the archaeologist Byron Cummings on an expedition that discovered Betatakin and Inscription House. Wetherill's appoint-

From 1250 to 1300, the Anasazi lived in the cliffs at Keet Seel and farmed the valley below. OVERLEAF: *Navaho crossing the bottomland of Canyon de Chelly; photographed by Edward Curtis, circa 1920.*

ment continued his family's long connection with the monument; in 1895 his brothers, Al and Richard, discovered Keet Seel, the largest cliff dwelling in Arizona. The 135 connected rooms of **Betatakin,** which means "ledge house" in Navajo, are tucked into the cliffside, protected by a south-facing alcove that measures 452 feet high, 370 feet wide, and 135 feet deep. Tree-ring dating shows that the first families moved in about 1250. By 1269 they were cutting timbers to expand the village, probably in preparation for a large group that joined them in 1275. Twenty-five years later the dwelling was abandoned. Betatakin can be viewed at a distance from an overlook at the end of the half-mile-long Sandal Trail. To visit the ruin, visitors must take a guided tour with a park ranger on a two-and-a-half-mile trail that drops 700 feet. Also situated in a cliff alcove, **Keet Seel,** one of the best-preserved cliff dwellings in Arizona, has 155 rooms and 6 kivas. Unlike Betatakin, which was built in discernible stages, Keet Seel was constructed at random as its inhabitants came and went. The site was occupied as early as A.D. 950 by small groups, and materials from their houses were used in the construction of the later

cliff dwelling. The name is Navajo for "broken pottery," given to the site no doubt for the abundance of pottery shards found there. Not more than twenty people per day are allowed to visit the site, which is reached by a primitive eight-mile trail. A permit is required and must be applied for in advance.

The seventy-four-room **Inscription House** ruin is built partially of adobe. Its doorways are primarily T-shaped, a style found in pre-historic ruins elsewhere but only marginally at Betatakin and Keet Seel. It derives its name from a faint inscription scratched into the plaster bearing the date 1861, which was probably left by a Mormon party passing through. This ruin is closed to the public.

LOCATION: Route 564, 9 miles off Route 160. HOURS: 8–5 Daily. FEE: None. TELEPHONE: 602–672–2366.

CANYON DE CHELLY NATIONAL MONUMENT

The riverbeds and sheer sandstone cliffs of Canyon de Chelly have protected and sheltered Indians since the Anasazi came here about 2,000 years ago. The canyon was formed by the Rio de Chelly, which rises near the Arizona–New Mexico border and empties into the Chinle Wash just west of the monument. During the Pueblo period, from A.D. 700 to 1300, the Anasazi built cliff dwellings here. After the Anasazi disappeared, the canyon was occupied—at least in the summer—first by the Hopi and then, after 1700, by the Navajo. (The name Canyon de Chelly, pronounced d'SHAY, is probably a corruption of the Navajo *tsegi*, meaning "rocky canyon.") The 131-square-mile national monument also includes the adjoining **Canyon del Muerto,** "canyon of the dead," so named after U.S. cavalry soldiers found mummified bodies in one of its caves.

The Navajo's defiant independence and predations against their neighbors caused the Spanish and later the United States to mount military expeditions against them. In 1805 a column commanded by Antonio Narbona, who later became governor of the province of New Mexico, fought a day-long battle with the Navajo in Canyon del Muerto in which more than 100 Navajo women and children were killed after they took refuge in a shelter, now called **Massacre Cave,** near the top of the canyon. The place from which the Spanish fired into the cave is now a viewpoint on the canyon rim.

OPPOSITE: *View from Sliding Rock overlook in Canyon de Chelly with traditional Navaho home, or hogan, in foreground.*

During the American Civil War Brigadier General James H. Carleton, military governor of New Mexico, dispatched Colonel Christopher "Kit" Carson and a force of 1,000 men against the Navajo. The expedition was a success: Some 8,000 Navajo surrendered and were marched, on the so-called Long Walk, to Fort Sumner in New Mexico, where they stayed under guard for four years before being returned to their homelands. Today Canyon de Chelly belongs to the Navajo nation, which administers it with the National Park Service. In summer Navajo families, whose homes are scattered along the valley, farm and graze sheep on the bottomland.

There are over 700 prehistoric sites in the monument. These were first recorded when Lieutenant James H. Simpson of the Corps of Topological Engineers accompanied a military expedition against the Navajo in 1849. Simpson named the canyon's best-known site Casa Blanca, or **White House Ruins,** for the wall of white

Navajo petroglyphs at Canyon de Chelly depict a party of Spanish soldiers on horseback led by Lieutenant Antonio Narbona. In the winter of 1804–1805, Narbona's

plaster across its upper portion. With sixty rooms, it is one of the largest ruins in the monument—and the most accessible, via a trail that descends 500 feet down the canyon wall. This is the only trail visitors can take unaccompanied by a guide. Located twenty-one miles northeast of the visitor center, **Mummy Cave**—actually two adjacent caves in Canyon del Muerto—is the largest ruin in the monument. The eastern cave contains fifty-five rooms and four kivas, the western cave contains twenty rooms, and a ledge connecting the two has fifteen rooms and a tower house. Mummy Cave is located about 300 feet up a talus slope. The traces of a hand-and-toe trail cut into the rock from the top of the slope to the ruin are still visible. Other principal ruins include Canyon del Muerto's **Antelope House,** a forty- to fifty-room village that is known for the tan-and-white half-scale antelopes painted high on a nearby cliff. The antelopes are possibly the work of a Navajo artist who lived in

party massacred more than one hundred Navajo men, women, and children, whom they trapped in Massacre Cave .

the canyon in the 1830s. Excavations at **Big Cave,** also in Canyon del Muerto, have produced remains of the Basket Maker–period Anasazi who lived here from A.D. 331 to 835. Among the relics uncovered was a buried pair of arms and hands with three abalone shell necklaces wrapped around the wrists; their significance remains a mystery. Paved drives provide viewing points for major ruins along both canyons. Information on scheduled hikes and other programs is available at the visitor center at the entrance to the monument.

> LOCATION: Route 7, 3 miles east of the junction of Routes 7 and 191. HOURS: *Visitor Center:* May through September: 8–6 Daily; October through April: 8–5 Daily. FEE: For authorized guides. TELE-PHONE: 602–674–5436.

The **Hatathali Museum** (602–724–6156) at the Tsaile campus of Navajo Community College, east of the Canyon de Chelly, claims to be the only Indian museum run by Indians. It is located on two floors of the Hatathali Center, an unusual, six-sided, hogan-shaped building at the east entrance of the campus.

GANADO

The Spanish called this town Pueblo Colorado after prehistoric ruins nearby, that were inhabited by the Anasazi from A.D. 800 to 1300. The name of the town was changed to Ganado by the Indian trader John Lorenzo Hubbell in honor of his friend the tribal chieftain Ganado Mucho ("many cattle").

Hubbell Trading Post National Historic Site

Hubbell settled here in 1876, when he was 23 years old, and built the present trading post in 1883. He was an honest trader and an enthusiastic promoter of Navajo crafts, and when Ganado became part of the Navajo Reservation he was allowed to keep the trading post and the 160 acres he homesteaded. Hubbell died in 1930; his son and daughter-in-law ran the store until 1967, when the National Park Service purchased it.

OPPOSITE: *The rug room at the Hubbell Trading Post; Navaho weavers still study the designs in these 100-year-old rugs.*

The Hubbell Trading Post, in operation for more than a century.

The trading post's long stone main building is little changed from the days when Hubbell operated it. Inside, the shelves are still lined with canned goods, flour, sugar, candy, Pendleton blankets, and tobacco. Saddles, harnesses, and hardware hang from the ceiling. Navajo rugs and blankets are piled high in the rug room, and some of the designs for the rugs hang from the walls. Behind the trading post, the Hubbell house—its floors covered wall to wall with Navajo rugs, baskets hanging from the ceiling—evokes the era of the Indian trader, who acted as a go-between for the Indians and the outside world. The paintings of the artist E. A. Burbank, who spent several months as a guest of the Hubbells, hang on the walls. Hubbell and his family are buried on the hill behind a stone hogan.

LOCATION: Route 264, 1 mile west of Ganado. HOURS: May through September: 7:45–6 Daily; October through April: 8–5 Daily. FEE: None. TELEPHONE: 602–755–3475.

WINDOW ROCK

Named for a natural arch almost fifty feet wide in a sandstone ridge nearby, Window Rock became the Navajo tribal administration center in the early 1930s. Navajo arts and crafts and exhibits relating to the tribe's history are displayed at the **Navajo Tribal Museum** (Route 264, 602–871–6673) in the Navajo Arts and Crafts Enterprise Building. There is also a reconstructed trading post. A few miles north is the town of **Fort Defiance,** named for a fort established in 1851 in an attempt to subdue the Navajo. After Kit Carson's foray into Navajo country in 1863, nearly 8,000 Navajo surrendered here the following year and were then marched over 300 miles to Fort Sumner in New Mexico. Nothing remains of the fort today.

THE   HOPI   RESERVATION

In Hopi legend, their people entered into a world of darkness when they left the realm of caves beneath the Grand Canyon. They created the sun from a shield of bleached deerskin and the moon from a ball of white silk spun by a spider. The name *Hopi* is a form of their word *hopituh*, which means "peaceful people." In 1540 Pedro de Tovar, one of Coronado's captains, became the first European to visit the Hopi pueblos. Later that year the Hopi guided Captain García López de Cárdenas to the Grand Canyon.

The Hopi, who are still located on three fingerlike mesas—First, Second, and Third mesas—that are extensions of the larger Black Mesa to the north, were relatively undisturbed by the westward expansion of white settlers. Franciscan missionaries built the first church at the village of Awatovi in 1629; it and several other churches and *visitas* (mission outposts) were destroyed in the Pueblo Revolt of 1680. Tewa Indians fleeing the avenging Spanish were permitted to establish a village, Hano, on the condition that it guard the approach to First Mesa. When the village of Awatovi allowed the Franciscans to build another church after the Spanish reconquest of New Mexico in 1692, other Hopi attacked and destroyed the village, killing some 700 residents. Awatovi has never been rebuilt. It can be visited today only with a Hopi guide and permission from the **Cultural Preservation Office** (602–734–2441) in

the village of Kykotsmovi. The Awatovi massacre ended the influence of the Christian church among the Hopi and left them free to
follow their traditional beliefs. Many Hopi are farmers and practice
a kind of "dry farming" in which fields are not usually plowed, but
rather windbreaks are placed at intervals to retain soil and mois-
ture. The Hopi raise corn, beans, squash, melons, and other crops.
They also produce a sturdy brown-and-red pottery, exquisite silver
work, weavings, and baskets.

The Hopi Reservation was created in 1882; since then it has
been completely surrounded by additions to the Navajo
Reservation. In 1975 Congress partitioned nearly 2 million acres
that had been designated a joint-use area. The partition was a Hopi
victory; putting it into effect by the year 1995 will mean removing
some 8,000 Navajo. Today nearly 6,000 Hopi live in the nine main
villages atop the three mesas and in other modern towns. Along the
First Mesa, the village of **Hano** is indistinguishable from the adjoining **Sichomovi,** but it is really a Tewa village. At the end of the mesa
is **Walpi,** a small, ancient pueblo of about thirty families that is constructed of sandstone blocks. On the approach to Walpi, the mesa
narrows to fifteen feet.

Along the **Second Mesa** is **Shongopavi.** According to tradition,
it was the first village on all the mesas, although it existed in a location lower than the present pueblo. Its close neighbor, **Shipaulovi,**
is on the eastern end of the mesa. **Shongopavi,** the largest on the
Second Mesa—over 700 residents—was founded after the Pueblo
Revolt of 1680 to protect the inhabitants of the mesa from Spanish
reprisals. The **Hopi Cultural Center** (Route 264, 602–734–6650) is
a pueblo-style complex completed in 1971 to provide facilities,
information, and lodging for visitors. The museum includes permanent exhibits of silver, basketry, weaving, and kachina dolls.
Among the pottery is the much-imitated work of Poligaysi
Qoyawayma (Elizabeth White), who designed and executed ollas,
bean pots, windbells, and other pieces with signature ears of corn
superimposed on the side. The photographic archive includes
photographs of pueblo life taken by Dr. Frederick Momsen in
1901.

OPPOSITE: *Edward Curtis photographed this man from Walpi, an ancient Hopi town
located on First Mesa that has changed little since the time of the Spanish. From
1896 to 1930, Curtis took some 40,000 photographs of American Indians and their
settlements, collected in his massive work,* The North American Indian, *comprising
twenty volumes of text, each with an accompanying portfolio of plates.*

Atop the **Third Mesa** is **Old Oraibi,** one of the oldest continuously inhabited towns in the United States, which dates back to 1150. At the turn of the century, it was one of the largest villages on the reservation, but dissension caused a split in the community. At issue was accommodation with the U.S. government, particularly regarding education of Hopi children. Those who wanted to remain isolated and retain old customs were finally evicted in 1906; they founded the towns of **Hotevilla** and **Bacabi.** When the federal government insisted that they return to Oraibi so their children could attend school, twenty-five families complied. The others—over fifty families—refused to move, so the government jailed the men and forcibly took the children to boarding school.

C E N T R A L   A R I Z O N A

The pine forests of the central part of Arizona contrast with the deserts and arid mountain ranges found elsewhere in the state. Besides timber, the area is rich in minerals. When Arizona was separated from New Mexico in 1863, Governor John Goodwin set up a temporary capital at Fort Whipple before moving it seventeen miles south to present-day Prescott. Fort Whipple later was used in campaigns against the Apache, whose raids were interfering with mining and settlement in the region.

PETRIFIED FOREST NATIONAL PARK

The well-traveled Lieutenant A. W. Whipple, passing through in 1853, described the area as a place "where trees have been converted into jasper," and the forest of petrified wood—some 225 million years old—and the ever-shifting hues of the Painted Desert are still the main attractions here. But the park, which became a national monument in 1906, also contains prehistoric ruins and many fine petroglyphs. Near the main entrance, the seventy-five-room **Puerco Ruin** was occupied intermittently from 1100 to 1400. A petroglyph at the ruin clearly depicts a heron swallowing a frog. On the southern end of the park, **Agate House** is a small seven-room pueblo constructed of blocks of petrified wood. Two rooms have been recon-

OPPOSITE: *Arizona's Petrified Forest National Park encompasses five regions containing the world's largest preserve of petrified wood.* OVERLEAF: *Blue Mesa at Petrified Forest.*

structed. **Newspaper Rock,** an overlook located about midway along the park drive, is a fine collection of petroglyphs.

LOCATION: East of Holbrook between Routes I-40 and 180. HOURS: June through August: 6 AM–7 PM Daily; September through May: 8–5 Daily. FEE: Yes. TELEPHONE: 602-524-6228.

FLAGSTAFF

Thomas Forsyth McMillan, who arrived with a flock of sheep in the spring of 1876, was Flagstaff's first permanent settler. A band of colonists from Boston, inspired to make the trip by exaggerations contained in Samuel Cozzens's book *Marvellous Country,* were the next to arrive. On July 4, 1876, the nation's centennial, the colonizers stripped a tall pine tree of its branches and flew a flag from it. The flagstaff became a familiar landmark and the source of the city's name. According to the census of 1880, Flagstaff had a population of sixty-seven. During the construction of the Atlantic & Pacific Railroad, which reached Flagstaff in 1882, John Young (son of the Mormon leader Brigham Young) established Fort Moroni, headquarters of the Moroni Cattle Company, seven miles to the northwest. The coming of the railroad established Flagstaff's reputation as a wide-open cattle town. In 1881 gold and silver bars worth $125,000 were stolen from a stagecoach outside Flagstaff; to foil holdup men, Wells Fargo had hidden them in two whiskey kegs. To this day, treasure hunters still comb the San Francisco Mountains looking for the loot, none of which was ever recovered.

An early resident, J. W. Weatherford, came from Texas in 1887; in 1897 he built the **Hotel Weatherford** (23 North Leroux Street), a fixture of downtown that has recently been restored. **Northern Arizona University** (Knoles Drive, 602–523–9011), located south of downtown, was opened as the Northern Arizona Normal School in 1899 in an unoccupied building that was built as a boys' reformatory. The first principal had to tour the northern part of the state by stagecoach and railroad to recruit the first twenty-three students. The school became Northern Arizona State Teachers College in 1925 and a state university in 1966.

Riordan State Historic Park

This immense (forty rooms, 13,000 square feet) log mansion, comprising two large wings connected by a common living area, was

An early photograph of one of the Arizona Lumber Company's mills in Flagstaff shows fifty-one men at work. This mill was built by D. M. Riordan in 1887.

built by brothers Michael and Timothy Riordan in 1904. They named it Kinlichi, Navajo for "red house." The Riordans' fortune came from the Arizona Lumber Company, the first major manufacturing company in northern Arizona, and they also built Flagstaff's first electric plant. The house, which was made a state park to save it from demolition by the expanding Northern Arizona University, is one of the finest examples of Craftsman-style architecture in Arizona. The original furnishings include a swinging settee suspended by chains from the ceiling, a Steinway grand piano, stained-glass windows, and an oval Mission-style dining-room table. The exterior of the mansion is done with log-slab siding, volcanic stone arches, and hand-split wooden shingles.

LOCATION: 1300 Riordan Ranch Road. HOURS: Mid-May through mid-September: 9–4 Daily; mid-September through mid-May: 1–4 Daily. FEE: Yes. TELEPHONE: 602–779–4395.

The **Pioneer Historical Museum** (Route 180, 602–774–6272) is located in an imposing stone building erected in 1908 as the Coconino
County Hospital for the Indigent. On display are old photographs,
logging tools, and other pioneer tools and artifacts, as well as the
photographs and equipment of Emery Kolb, who photographed the
Grand Canyon from 1902 to 1976.

The **Museum of Northern Arizona** (Route 180, three miles
north of Flagstaff, 602–774–5211) has exhibits of archaeology, eth-
nology, geology, and art that trace human development in the
Colorado Plateau. In addition to the displays of weavings, jewelry,
baskets, pottery, kachina dolls, and photographs, there is an orientation wall showing the settlement of the Colorado Plateau through
fourteen stages, from the paleo-Indians (15,000 to 8,000 B.C.)
through the Basket Maker, Sinagua, and Pueblo peoples to the contemporary Hopi and Navajo. The museum also has extensive
research collections, and changing exhibits include annual displays
of the work of contemporary Indian artists.

The **Lowell Observatory** (Mars Hill Road, off Santa Fe Avenue,
one mile west of Flagstaff, 602–774–3358) was founded in 1894 by
Dr. Percival Lowell of Massachusetts, who was attracted to Flagstaff
by its high altitude and clear mountain air. Lowell, who died in
1916, popularized the idea that the "canals" on Mars had been constructed by intelligent beings, a theory that has few supporters
today, and provided the calculations that led to the discovery in
1930 of the planet Pluto. The visitor center has exhibits including
Lowell's original globe of Mars and the blink comparator with which
Pluto was first viewed.

SUNSET CRATER
NATIONAL MONUMENT

Sunset Crater, the youngest of the more than 400 dormant volcanos
in the San Francisco volcanic field, was named by the explorer John
Wesley Powell, who led a U.S. surveying team there in 1885. He
wrote: "The contrast in the colors is so great that on viewing the
mountain from a distance the red cinders seem to be on fire. From
this circumstance the cone has been named Sunset Peak." The cone
rises 1,000 feet above the lava field at its base; the crater itself is 400

OPPOSITE: *Sunset Crater, formed in 1064 after a volcanic eruption blanketed more
than 800 square miles of central Arizona with ash and cinder.*

feet deep. Earthquakes preceding the eruption in 1064 may have warned the Sinagua to evacuate their dwellings, which may account for the scarcity of household items that have been excavated. Ash and cinders from the volcano covered more than 800 square miles and enriched the soil of the farmlands nearby. (The ruins of a prehistoric dwelling built and occupied by the Sinaguan farmers who returned to the area after the eruption can be seen at Wupatki National Monument.) The crater is important to the Hopi, who believe that the friendly Kana'a spirit lives there and that a wind god, Yaponcha, inhabits a fissure at the base of the cinder cone.

In 1928 local citizens learned that a Hollywood film company planned to dynamite the volcano's cinder slopes to create a landslide. Their protests led to federal protection of Sunset Crater as a national monument in 1930. A seismograph at the monument's visitor center monitors the earth's movements in the volcanic region. In order to protect the crater's fragile cinder surface it is no longer permitted to ascend the slopes. There is a self-guided Lava Flow Trail near its base.

LOCATION: Off Route 89, 15 miles northeast of Flagstaff. HOURS: 8–5 Daily. FEE: None. TELEPHONE: 602–527–7042.

WALNUT CANYON
NATIONAL MONUMENT

A steep trail descending 200 feet from the canyon rim leads past twenty-five cliff dwellings of the prehistoric people known as the Sinagua (Spanish for "without water"), who lived in this dramatic setting, formed by Walnut Creek cutting through the limestone and sandstone ledges, from about 1150 to 1250. The dwellings are all located under natural overhangs, which were closed off with stones and clay used as mortar. The Sinagua, who lived in clusters of family groups, farmed the land around the rim, hunted, and harvested edible wild plants such as wild grape, elderberry, and yucca, which still grow within the canyon. Why the Sinagua abandoned Walnut Canyon is uncertain; war, drought, depleted soil, and disease are all possibilities. It is also believed that the Sinagua were ancestors of the Hopi, whose earliest villages date from about 1300; some Hopi clans claim the Sinagua sites as their ancestral homes.

The Sinagua lived in Walnut Canyon for nearly 150 years before abandoning their cliff dwellings around 1250.

The canyon's existence did not become widely known until the transcontinental railroad reached Flagstaff in the 1880s. Looting, known as pot hunting, soon became epidemic, with some pot hunters even going so far as to dynamite the walls. Concerned citizens, including a Catholic priest from Flagstaff who preached that it was a desecration to vandalize the ruins, asked for federal protection, and in 1915, after the damage was already widespread, the canyon was made a national monument. In addition to the Island Trail, which descends into the canyon, the cliff dwellings are visible from afar from the Rim Trail, a level, two-thirds-mile loop that also passes two reconstructed surface dwellings. Sinagua pottery and artifacts are on display in the visitor center.

LOCATION: Off Route I-40, 3 miles south of exit 204, 7 miles east of Flagstaff. HOURS: 8–5 Daily. FEE: Yes. TELEPHONE: 602–526–3367.

WUPATKI NATIONAL MONUMENT

There are at least 2,500 prehistoric sites within this 35,693-acre monument. The Sinagua people had been living in the area for 400 years when the lava flows and ash falls from the eruption of Sunset Crater forced them to evacuate in A.D. 1064. The Sinagua, as well as some Kayenta Anasazi from the north, returned a few decades later, after they discovered that the layer of ash from the volcano made the land more fertile than before. Harold S. Colton, of the Museum of Northern Arizona, who surveyed the Wupatki area in the 1930s, speculated that the return amounted to a land rush, with Indians pouring into the area in large numbers. However, more recent evidence indicates that the population grew gradually after the eruption. The Indians' reasons for abandoning the area a second time—and permanently—between 1215 and 1225 are unknown. Disease, overfarming, and drought have all been suggested as causes. Pieces of pottery found in the excavations indicate that small groups of Hopi may have lived in Wupatki after the Sinagua left. The Hopi claim the ruin as the ancestral home of their Parrot Clan.

Captain Lorenzo Sitgreaves, seeking an overland route across northern New Mexico, was the first European-America to report on the deserted ruins at Wupatki: "all the prominent points occupied by the ruins of stone houses of considerable size, and in some instances, of three stories in height." In 1896 archaeologist Dr. Jesse W. Fewkes photographed, mapped, and described the ruins. He also gave them their Hopi names: Wupatki (Tall House), Wukoki (Big and Wide House), and others.

Four major sites are open to the public and accessible by self-guided trails, and a short trail leads up the crater known as Doney Mountain, named for the colorful prospector and pot hunter Ben Doney, who guided many archaeologists, including Dr. Fewkes, in the late nineteenth century. Doney spent many years looking for the Lost Padre Mine, a mercury deposit described by seventeenth-century Spanish explorers, which he firmly believed was located near Wupatki. From this vantage point, there is a splendid view of the Painted Desert and San Francisco Range.

Wupatki Ruin, the largest ruin in the monument, is reached by following a short trail behind the visitor center. Scholars estimate

OPPOSITE: *Petroglyphs near the Lomaki Ruin at Wupatki National Monument.*

that the Sinagua began building the pueblo about 1120. When it was at its peak, fifty years later, it was four stories tall, had up to 100 rooms, and housed about 125 people. Rooms were added as they were needed. A typical pueblo room had a small storage bin in the rear, a stone-lined fire pit in the center of the floor, and a T-shaped doorway. For warmth in the winter, a rug or an animal skin was hung over the door's upper opening, leaving the bottom free for ventilation. To the right of the trail is the circular depression known as the amphitheater. Although it resembles a kiva, or ceremonial chamber, it apparently never had a roof, so its precise function is still a matter of speculation. At the far end of the ruin, the oval ball court, enclosed by a banked stone wall, has been fully restored. (The rest of the site has been stabilized.) The ball court is similar to those found in Mexico and Central America. The game, as played with a rubber ball by the Aztec and Maya, was highly ritualized and had religious significance. The goal was to knock the ball—without using hands or feet—through a stone ring. Near the ball court is the blow hole, a fissure in the earth from which air rushes in or out, depending on the atmospheric conditions. Many prehistoric pueblos were built near blow holes, which seem to have had a special meaning for the inhabitants.

Situated prominently on an outcropping of Moenkopi sandstone, **Wukoki** is a three-story pueblo built entirely of finished blocks of the same material. Archaeologists are uncertain why the walls were so beautifully contructed if they were, as it is assumed, covered inside and out with plaster.

Located on a narrow butte nine miles by road northwest of the visitor center, the **Citadel,** as it is called because of its solid contruction and impregnable location, was once two stories tall, consisted of thirty rooms, and may have been inhabited by as many as sixty people. Despite its fortresslike appearance, there is no evidence that its inhabitants were warlike. Possibly this and other similarly sited pueblos were built so the inhabitants could watch over their fields or enjoy the view. The remains of terraced gardens are visible at the foot of the Citadel. The short footpath to this ruin passes the ten-room excavation known as the **Nalakihu Ruin;** the name means "house standing alone" in Hopi. When the Museum of Northern Arizona excavated the site in 1933 they found the bones of owls in burial pits and large storage jars that had been made near present-day Prescott, 150 miles away. The question of whether the jars are evidence of trade or of migration into Wupatki has never been answered. **Lomaki Ruin** bears a Hopi name meaning "beautiful house," a reference to the exquisite workmanship of its stone masonry. The pueblo is built near a collapsed earth crack that might have had special significance for prehistoric peoples. Ring dating of wooden beams indicates that the pueblo, which probably housed two to four families, was built about 1192.

> LOCATION: Between Flagstaff and Cameron off Route 89. HOURS: May through September: 7–7 Daily; October through April: 8–5 Daily. FEE: Yes. TELEPHONE: 602–527–7040.

KINGMAN

This small trading center, copper-mining town, and highway stopping-off place was originally a railroad camp named for Lewis Kingman, the civil engineer in charge of building what is now the Santa Fe Railroad. The town was established in 1882 after rails were laid to that point. The **Mohave Museum of History and Arts** (400 West Beale Street, 602–753–3195) tells, among other tales, the story of the building of nearby Hoover Dam. There are also re-created Mohave and Hualapai dwellings and examples of their crafts and art. Both tribes have reservations in the region. The **Bonelli House** (430 East Spring Street, 602–753–3195) was built of tufa stone in 1915 by one of Kingman's oldest families. It is one of the first permanent buildings in Kingman; the city restored it and furnished it with many original pieces as a Bicentennial project.

There are several ghost towns in the Kingman area. **Oatman,** located on old Route 66 and named for a pioneer family attacked by Apache near Gila Bend in 1851, was a gold-mining town that lasted from 1904 to the 1930s. In its heyday it had 12,000 citizens and twenty saloons, including a combination bar, soda fountain, and pharmacy called the Health Club. The **Oatman Hotel** (Main Street, 602–768–4408), built in 1923, is Mohave County's only two-story adobe building and houses the **Oatman Museum,** which displays photographs and artifacts depicting the town's history.

LAKE HAVASU CITY

Founded in 1964, this planned city and resort area became newsworthy when its founder, the late Robert McCulloch, purchased the **London Bridge** (Route 95) for almost $2.5 million and reassembled

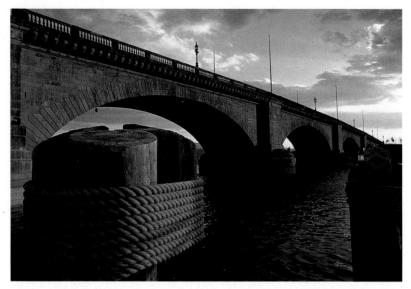

London Bridge started its second life in Lake Havasu City in 1971, 140 years after its original opening.

it here—all 10,276 granite blocks—where it connects an island in Lake Havasu with the main shore. The bridge, built in 1831, was dedicated in its new location in 1971; since then numerous other "English" attractions have opened nearby. The sight of the venerable span in the middle of the desert is a stellar example of the American flair for promotion.

PRESCOTT

Territorial Secretary Richard McCormick named Prescott for the popular historian William Hickling Prescott, chronicler of the Spanish conquistadors, shortly after the settlement was founded as the territorial capital by Governor John Goodwin in 1863. The first capitol was built of ponderosa pine logs from the nearby mountains. Goodwin lived in one wing, McCormick lived in the other, and the legislature met in the central room. (The building is now preserved as part of the Sharlot Hall Museum.) In 1867 the capital moved to Tucson, and Prescott stagnated for a few years until mining revived in the 1870s. The territorial government returned in 1877 but moved for the last time, to Phoenix, in 1889.

Prescott's **Roughrider Memorial Monument,** in front of the columned **Yavapai County Courthouse** (1917) on Montezuma Street, is a tribute to both the state's Spanish-American War volunteers and also to William Owen "Buckey" O'Neill, the city's most popular hero. Once described as "the most many-sided man Arizona ever produced," O'Neill was a lawman, editor, gambler (his nickname came from his habit of "bucking the tiger" in the game of faro), politician, and soldier. Soon after he was elected mayor of Prescott in 1898, the Spanish-American War broke out, and he helped recruit cowboys for a volunteer unit of Theodore Roosevelt's famous outfit, the Roughriders. He was killed by a sniper at the Battle of San Juan Hill. The monument was sculpted by Solon Borglum, the brother of Gutzon Borglum, the sculptor of Mount Rushmore.

Prescott's historic buildings include two operating hotels: the two-story Colonial Revival **Hotel Vendome** (230 South Cortez), which is little changed from when it was built in 1917, and the **Hassayampa Inn** (122 East Gurley Street), a three-story brick building completed in 1927, with a marvelous painted-and-stenciled Mission Revival lobby. The Neoclassical **Palace Hotel** (120 South Montezuma Street) was completed in 1901 and replaced an earlier building that burned in the fire of July 14, 1900, which destroyed most wooden buildings in town. As the fire approached, patrons carried the ornate back bar across the street to Courthouse Plaza and continued imbibing. The Palace is located on Prescott's once-infamous Whiskey Row, by the early 1900s a lively block-long stretch of saloons. It was once the custom for cowboys on a spree to start at one end of the row and work their way to the other, having one drink in every bar. Those who were still standing would then attempt the return trip. The 1895 **Prescott City Jail,** with its arched doorways and pressed-metal cornice, today houses the chamber of commerce (117 West Goodwin Street, 602–445–2000). The **Smoki Museum** (100 North Arizona Street, 602–445–1230), housed in a pueblo-style building, contains prehistoric Indian basketry and pottery and a reproduction of an Indian kiva, a round house used for Indian ceremonies.

Sharlot Hall Museum and Historical Society

This fine collection of historic buildings was begun by the Arizona historian and poet Sharlot Mabrith Hall, who came to Arizona from Kansas on horseback in 1882, when she was twelve years old. She was named Arizona's first territorial historian in 1909. In 1924 she received national attention when, as a publicity stunt to promote Arizona's mining industry, she wore a coat of copper mesh while representing the state in the electoral college in Washington, DC. The many museums she saw on this trip inspired her to achieve her dream of starting a museum of Arizona history; she leased the former territorial capitol grounds and restored the two-story log **Governor's Mansion** (the first capitol) to house it. Hall lived in the building until 1934, when she moved to what is now the stone exhibit building, where she lived until her death in 1943. The museum has since continued to expand under state ownership.

The clapboard **John C. Frémont House,** built in 1875, was rented by Frémont from 1878, when he was appointed Arizona's fifth territorial governor, to 1881, when his frequent absences and inattention to duty forced his resignation. The furnishings and decorative objects in the house date from the period 1875 to 1890. The house was moved to the museum grounds in 1972.

The late Victorian period is represented by the **William C. Bashford House,** built in 1877, which contains period rooms and a solarium. The main exhibit building, the **Sharlot Hall Building,** was constructed of native rock and pine by the Civil Works Administration in 1934 and houses exhibits of Prescott history and Indian art and artifacts. **Fort Misery,** one of the smaller buildings, was built as a general store in 1864. Later Judge John "Blinkey" Howard used the building as his courtroom, where he meted out "misery" in the name of justice. The **School House** is a replica of Prescott's first public school. The **Ranch House,** a log cabin built by Hall in the 1930s, contains a collection of branding irons and other cowboy paraphernalia.

Also on the grounds are a blacksmith shop, an operating windmill, an 1875 Porter locomotive, the **Pioneer Herb Garden,** and the **Memorial Rose Garden,** with more than 350 roses honoring Arizona's women. The first rosebush was brought to Prescott by Margaret McCormick, wife of the territorial secretary.

LOCATION: 415 West Gurley Street. HOURS: April through October: 10–5 Tuesday–Saturday, 1–5 Sunday; November through March: 10–4 Tuesday–Saturday, 1–5 Sunday. FEE: Yes. TELEPHONE: 602–445–3122.

Six miles north of town, **Prescott's Phippen Museum of Western Art**
(4701 Route 89 North, 602–778–1385) contains a collection of
paintings, sketches, and bronzes by Western artists past and present.
The museum was founded in 1984 by Prescott residents and named
in honor of George Phippen, a local Western artist who was one of
the founders of the Cowboy Artists of America, an organization of
contemporary Western artists.

JEROME

Although various prospectors had staked claims on the steep slopes
of Cleopatra Hill, not until Eugene Jerome, a New York financier,
invested $200,000 in the United Verde Mine in 1882 did the bonan-
za truly begin. (Jerome, who was the cousin of Winston Churchill's
American mother, Jennie Jerome, stipulated that the town be
named after him, although he never visited it.) The next year the
United Verde produced a modest quantity of silver, but high operating costs caused the company to fold after two years.

During the Great Depression, Jerome began to literally slide down the mountain.

In 1888 a Montana copper baron named William Andrews Clark purchased the United Verde for $300,000. In 1895 he ran a narrow-gauge railroad into Jerome, and between 1912 and 1915 he built a smelter in nearby Clarkdale. Jimmy "Rawhide" Douglas, the hard-living son of James Douglas of Bisbee, purchased the Little Daisy Mine at the foot of Cleopatra Hill in 1912, and two years later he hit a vein of copper five feet thick. The years 1914 to 1920 were the most prosperous yet, as World War I sent copper prices to new highs. During these years, Jerome's population reached 15,000.

Jerome grew up the side of the mountain despite three major fires between 1897 and 1899. Houses clung precariously to the side of the hill, one almost on top of the other. Residents boasted that every house had a view and that every occupant could lean out of the window and light a match on his neighbor's chimney. The town also developed a reputation for its saloons and houses of ill repute. During one of the conflagrations, the town's most prominent madam, Jennie Banters, is supposed to have promised free passes to a volunteer fire company if they would save her establishment from the flames. They did.

Prosperity in Jerome ended with the Crash of 1929; during the Depression, the town's population dropped to 5,000. In the meantime, underground dynamiting and other factors caused the geological fault under the town to shift, and Jerome began to slide—at the estimated rate of three-eighths of an inch a month—down the mountain. As a result, many of Jerome's buildings were torn down, banks refused to accept other buildings as collateral, and the town's famous **Sliding Jail** (Hull Avenue) ended up 225 feet from where it was built. Although mining picked up during World War II, the glory days were over, and the mines of Jerome closed for good in 1953. The town seemed to be headed for extinction, but retirees, tourists, artists, and others attracted to its location, architecture, and colorful past have promoted a revival. The surviving frame, brick, and stone buildings of downtown Jerome now make up the Jerome Historic District. On Main Street, the brick shell of the once-elegant **Bartlett Hotel** has been stabilized. Built for the United Verde Mine, it opened in 1902. The **Connor Hotel** (Jerome Avenue and Main Street), the first solid stone hotel in Jerome, was rebuilt twice after

OPPOSITE: *Copper was king in Jerome from World War I until the stock market crash in 1929, but the mines closed for good in 1953.*

being gutted by fire in the late 1890s. The **Jerome Historical Society Museum** (Jerome Avenue and Main Street, 602–634–5477), which contains a collection of photographs, mining tools, ore samples, and other odds and ends of mining history, is housed in one of the town's original fireproof buildings. The new structure, however, was damaged by the fire of 1899, which occurred before the fire doors were hung. The entrance is flanked by two halves of a four-ton flywheel from an early air compressor. On Douglas Road, leading to the Jerome State Historic Park, the privately owned **Powder Box Church** is visible on the left. The church's name comes from the dynamite boxes used to build it.

Jerome State Historic Park

This state museum and restoration is housed in the Douglas Mansion, built in 1916 by the colorful mining entrepreneur Jimmy "Rawhide" Douglas as a combination hotel and home for his family. (Douglas's nickname came from his inventive use of rawhide to reduce roller wear on a mining cable car.) When it was completed, the house had a wine cellar, a billiard room, steam heat, and a central vacuum system. There are splendid views of the town and the valley from the terraces outside the mansion. Here are displayed such early mining equipment as a stamp mill and large stone Chilean wheels that were once used to crush ore. At the foot of the hill are the two headframes of the Little Daisy Mine. Inside, the Douglas library and some of the living quarters have been restored. There are also old photographs from the Douglas family album, a video presentation on the history of Jerome, a reconstructed assay office, and a three-dimensional model of the town and the maze of mining tunnels beneath it.

> LOCATION: Douglas Road. HOURS: 8–5 Daily. FEE: Yes. TELEPHONE: 602–634–5381.

TUZIGOOT NATIONAL MONUMENT

When federal funds for archaeology became available during the Depression, the chamber of commerce of Yavapai County urged sci-

OPPOSITE: *The original Sinaguan pueblo at Tuzigoot had seventy-seven ground-floor rooms, entered through openings in the roofs.*

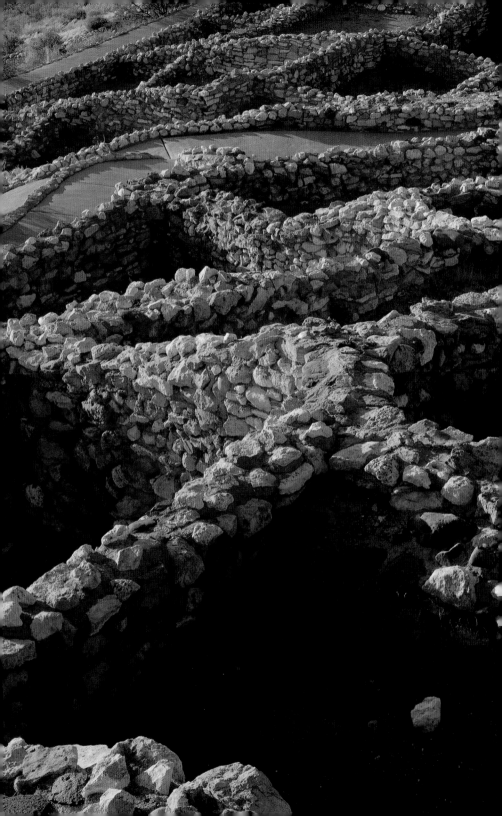

entists at the University of Arizona to find a ruin in the northern part of the Verde Valley to excavate to increase archaeological knowledge of the area and provide jobs for the unemployed. The site they chose was near the copper-smelting town of Clarkdale. Forty-eight men were hired for the project, and one of these, an Apache, suggested the name *tuzigoot* ("crooked water") for the ruin. Although the name actually described a nearby lake, the scholars liked the sound of it, and so it has remained to this day.

The ruin of the Sinaguan pueblo is splendidly situated and partly reconstructed on a limestone ridge 120 feet above the plain. The Sinagua are believed to have arrived from the north in the twelfth century, but the village did not begin to expand for another 100 years. In its heyday the one- to two-story village had 110 rooms and may have housed about 225 people. In about 1425, for unknown reasons, the Sinagua people left the settlement. Where they went remains a mystery. Trade ware (pottery) from pre-Hopi groups was found at Tuzigoot, and Hopi legend tells of an ancient people from the south joining them, so the Sinagua may be part of the Hopi ancestry. A quarter-mile trail leads through the ruin, and the lookout tower provides sweeping views of the Verde Valley. The visitor center has an excellent collection of prehistoric jewelry, tools, baskets, pottery, textiles, and religious objects. There is also a reconstruction of a pueblo room.

LOCATION: Alternate Route 89, between Cottonwood and Clarkdale. HOURS: June through August: 8–7 Daily; September: 8–6 Daily; October through May: 8–5 Daily. FEE: Yes. TELEPHONE: 602–634–5564.

MONTEZUMA
CASTLE NATIONAL MONUMENT

In 1864 an Indian fighter, after a foray into the Verde Valley, told a newspaper in Prescott that his party had seen "an immense spring or well with walled caves in the cliffs surrounding it. They were probably built by the Aztec. We gave the name of Montezuma to the well." The name stuck, but the man's assumption was incorrect; the cliff

OPPOSITE: *Montezuma Castle sits on a cliff 100 feet above Beaver Creek.*

dwellings were built by the Sinagua in the twelfth century, after drought or other causes had driven them here from Wupatki and Walnut Canyon. The sixteenth-century Aztec ruler Montezuma had never been anywhere near the ruin.

Montezuma Castle, a five-story structure of limestone blocks, is built into the cliffs about 100 feet above Beaver Creek. In places, the walls of the twenty-room dwelling are curved to conform to the shape of the cliffs. Building materials, including large sycamore beams, had to be hauled up ladders or along a narrow path to the site. The Sinagua were not a warlike people, but they must have picked the site for defense. In the 1880s Edgar Alexander Mearns, a surgeon stationed at nearby Fort Verde, extensively excavated the ruins, sending back "several thousand" artifacts to museums in the East. In a magazine article in 1890, he wrote: "The traveler in this region is quite certain of being entertained by exaggerated stories about gigantic human skeletons having been discovered in the ruined casas grandes; but if he be a good-sized man, and possessed of adipose tissue appertaining to the age of threescore years, he will become skeptical thereof when he comes to squeeze himself through the narrow portals of the ancient halls." The "castle" can be viewed from a paved pathway behind the visitor center, but the public is not allowed to climb up or enter it. The path continues to the foundations of another ruin, **Castle "A,"** at the base of the cliff, before returning to the visitor center. **Montezuma Well,** located eleven miles northeast of the Montezuma Castle, is also part of the monument. This natural sinkhole is 470 feet in diameter and 55 feet deep. Its flow of more than 1,000 gallons a minute has been used to irrigate the land since the first permanent inhabitants, the prehistoric Hohokam, moved here in the seventh century. A trail leads to pueblo ruins around the well, and a pithouse has been reconstructed on the road leading to it.

LOCATION: Off Route 17, 5 miles north of Camp Verde. HOURS: June through August: 8–7 Daily; September through May: 8–5 Daily. FEE: Yes. TELEPHONE: 602–567–3322.

FORT VERDE STATE HISTORIC PARK

The town of **Camp Verde,** at the junction of the Verde River and Clear Creek, was settled in 1865 by a small band of farmers from

Prescott who were attracted by the fertile soil of the Verde Valley. To protect the settlers from Indian attacks, a force of Arizona volunteers built a small fortification, which they called Camp Lincoln. The post was moved to its present location in 1871. In 1879 its name was changed to Fort Verde, although the post, consisting of twenty build-ings spaced around a parade ground, was never walled or fortified.

General George Crook conducted his winter campaign of 1872–1873 against the Apache from here. It ended when their lead-er, Cha-Lipun, rode into Camp Verde and surrendered. During the campaign Crook's well-trained and disciplined troops kept constant pressure on the Apache enemy; his use of friendly Apache as scouts also contributed to his success. Crook also understood and sympa-thized with his adversary. After the surrender Crook arranged for the Indians to be moved to a reservation near the fort, where they set about irrigating and farming the fertile land. However, after Crook was transferred in 1875, the Indians were moved from the valuable land to the San Carlos Indian Reservation to the southeast. On July 17, 1882, troops from Fort Verde ambushed a band of Apache north of Payson above the Mogollon Rim. Twenty-two Apache were killed and more captured in this, the Battle of Big Dry Wash, the last major conflict with the Apache in the territory. The fort was closed in 1891.

Four original buildings and part of the parade ground remain preserved in this ten-acre park: the administration building, the commanding officer's house, the bachelor officers' quarters, and the doctor's office. The buildings contain period furnishings and exhibits on army life and activities of the period.

LOCATION: Lane Street, 2 miles east of Route I-17, in Camp Verde. HOURS: 8–5 Daily. FEE: Yes. TELEPHONE: 602–567–3275.

For years **Payson** was one of the most isolated communities in Arizona; mail was delivered by horseback until 1914. The town was named as a political payoff for an Illinois congressman who never set foot in the settlement. In the distance rises the majestic escarp-ment the Mogollon Rim, also called the "backbone of Arizona," which marks the southern end of the Colorado Plateau. It was named for Juan Ignacio Flores Mogollon, New Mexico's governor from 1712 to 1715.

The writer Zane Grey, photographed in Tonto Basin with one of his favorite horses, Night. Grey's writings did much to publicize the great natural wonders of the American west.

Seventeen miles east of Payson on Route 260 is the turnoff to **Zane Grey's Lodge** (602–478–4243), which the famous Western writer built in 1920 as a hunting cabin. Today the lodge is a museum displaying original furniture, manuscripts, and first editions. Grey wrote several of his seventy-eight books during the nine years he visited the lodge. One of these, *To the Last Man,* is a fictionalized account of the Arizona's famous Graham-Tewksbury feud between farming families on the one hand and sheep and cattle ranchers on the other. At least nineteen people died in the conflict, which lasted from 1886 to 1892; historians still are not sure how the bloodshed started. The fighting took place in Pleasant Valley near the town of **Young,** southeast of Payson and accessible via Routes 260 and 288.

WHITERIVER

The military camp, four miles southwest of town, founded as Camp Ord in 1870 was, in 1879, renamed **Fort Apache** (Fort Apache Road, off Route 73, 602–338–4625), a legendary name in the history of Indian warfare. Troops from here participated in such famous forays against the Apache as General Crook's winter campaign of 1872–1873; the fight against the Apache chief Victorio in 1879; and the final effort to subdue Geronimo, which lasted from 1881 to 1886. In 1881 troops from Fort Apache were dispatched to Cibecue Creek to suppress an Apache faction that advocated the expulsion of whites. After the cult's prophet was killed in the fray, the army's Apache scouts joined an uprising against the army. (This was the only known instance of mutiny by the otherwise steadfast Apache scouts.) The Apache then attacked the fort, killing several soldiers, and placed it under siege. The prospects for the garrison's survival looked dim when a volunteer, Will C. Barnes, slipped out of the fort and eluded the Apache by, at one point, muffling his horse's hooves with pieces of his blanket. When Barnes reached Fort Thomas, almost due south on the Gila River, troops were sent to relieve Fort Apache. Barnes was awarded the Congressional Medal of Honor for his bravery.

There are many photographs of the army units and their Apache scouts in the **Fort Apache Museum** (Fort Apache Road, off Route 73, 602–338–4625). Fort Apache is located on the 1.6-million-acre Fort Apache Indian Reservation. In 1870 land in the White Mountains was set aside for a reservation with two administrative headquarters, one at Fort Apache, the other at San Carlos. In 1896 the White Mountain Reservation, as it was called, was divided into the Fort Apache and San Carlos (1.8 million acres) reservations.

The **Kinishba Ruins** (off Route 73 in the small town of Canyon Day, about three miles west of Fort Apache), once inhabited by the Mogollon, were first explored in the 1880s by the anthropologist Adolph Bandelier. Excavations in the 1930s uncovered a 200-room wing of the pueblo; experts estimate that the population might have reached 2,000 in the early 1300s. The site, which is administered by the Apache, is fenced off but may be viewed from outside the barrier.

NEVADA

OPPOSITE: *A nineteenth-century church in Paradise Valley, a former ranching community near the Santa Rosa Range in Northern Nevada.*

The election of 1864 was fast approaching, and President Abraham Lincoln was anxious that pro-reconstruction senators win the majority. To increase the odds in his favor, he decided to make Nevada a state; its three electoral votes would certainly go to the Republicans. But before he approved statehood for the mineral-rich territory, Lincoln insisted on seeing the constitution it had written for itself. To save time, the territorial governor took the unusual step of telegraphing it to the president—at a cost of $4,303.27, the longest ever sent. And so, a mere eight days before the election, Nevada became the thirty-sixth state to join the Union.

Nevada, which means "snow-covered" in Spanish, was still claimed by Spain in 1776; that country sent the first explorers into the region, seeking a route from New Mexico to California, but otherwise did not pay it much attention. It was Jedediah Smith, an American trapper seeking new sources of beaver, who in 1826–1827 first successfully crossed the region, which by then belonged to the newly independent Mexico. The explorer and soldier John C. Frémont led the first official U.S. exploring party into Nevada from Oregon in 1844. On that journey Frémont discovered Pyramid Lake, which he named after a curious rock formation that reminded him of the pyramids of Egypt. En route to California the next year, Frémont crossed Nevada east to west with an expedition that mapped such important geographical features as Walker Lake and the Humboldt and Truckee rivers.

Nevada became part of the United States by the Treaty of Guadalupe Hidalgo in 1848. The Compromise of 1850 put it under the jurisdiction of the Utah Territory, except for the southern tip, which fell to New Mexico. Nevada's first permanent white settlement was a Mormon trading post established at Genoa in the Carson Valley in western Nevada in 1851 to service wagon trains heading for California. Soon the lack of effective government, and their distance from Salt Lake City, began to rankle the settlers, and they began agitating for a separate territorial status. Nevada achieved this goal in 1861, after the southern states, which opposed the formation of any nonslave territories, had seceded.

Before the arrival of whites, Nevada was the home of nomadic Indian tribes such as the northern and southern Paiute, the Washoe, and the Shoshoni, who lived a marginal existence as hunters and gatherers in the territory's harsh climate. Despite numerous Indian raids on settlements and emigrant trains, Nevada only had one full-fledged Indian war. This occurred in May 1860,

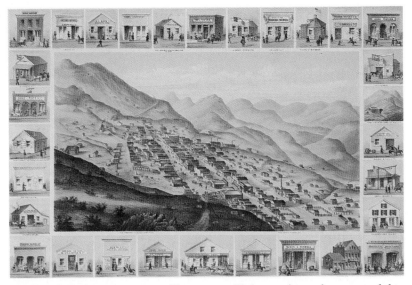

Pictures of Virginia City's principal business establishments form a frame around this 1861 panoramic view of the two-year-old town, which boomed with the discovery of the Comstock Lode.

when an ill-prepared posse of 105 whites rashly rode out to avenge a raid on a white settlement. Near Pyramid Lake, the would-be Indian fighters rode into an ambush in which 76 of them were killed. A second clash of the so-called Pyramid Lake War, or Paiute War, on May 31 went badly for the Indians. They were decisively defeated and dispersed by a force of 750 men.

Indian discontent partly resulted from the disruption of their way of life by the influx of miners after the discovery of gold on Mount Davidson in 1859. The strike was made by two miners, Peter O'Riley and Patrick McLaughlin, as they were attempting to clear a spring at the head of Six Mile Canyon. The men went into partnership with a boisterous prospector named Henry Tompkins Paige Comstock, whose claims about the find were justified, since it turned out to be one of the richest in history. Neither Comstock nor O'Riley nor McLaughlin became rich from the strike. Unlike the surface gold so easily scooped up by the forty-niners in California, the Comstock Lode ran deep beneath the earth. Extracting it required engineers with know-how, financiers with capital, and miners who would work for wages. Tunneling through the earth was expensive and dangerous, but the rewards to the mine owners were high.

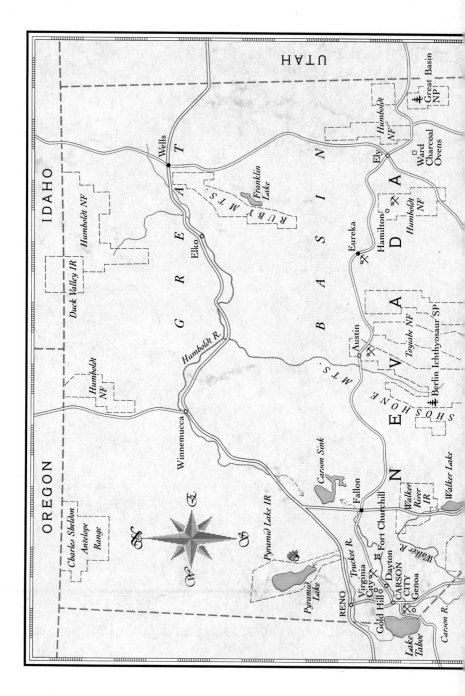

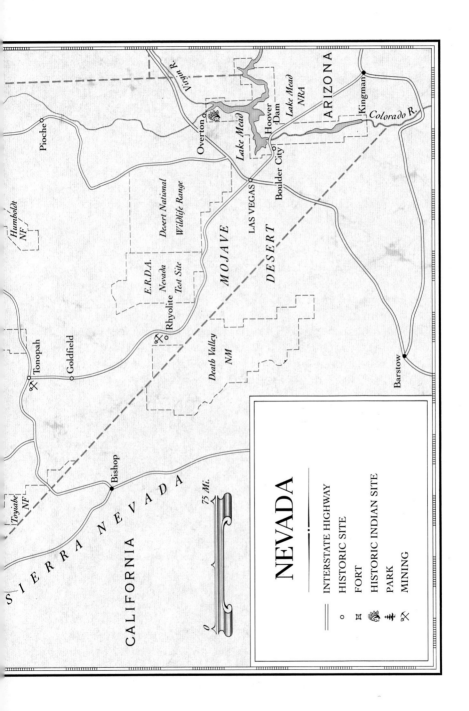

NEVADA

- INTERSTATE HIGHWAY
- HISTORIC SITE
- FORT
- HISTORIC INDIAN SITE
- PARK
- MINING

75 Mi.

0

ARIZONA

Kingman

Colorado R.

Lake Mead NRA

Hoover Dam

Lake Mead

Boulder City

Overton

Virgin R.

Pioche

Humboldt NF

Desert National Wildlife Range

LAS VEGAS

MOJAVE

DESERT

E.R.D.A. Nevada Test Site

Rhyolite

Death Valley NM

Tonopah

Goldfield

Barstow

Bishop

SIERRA NEVADA

CALIFORNIA

Toiyabe NF

Millionaires earned their piles on the Comstock. Minerals from the mines built hotels, banks, railroads, and several important American fortunes, and they helped finance the Union effort in the Civil War. In a few short years, Virginia City, a settlement on the Comstock, was transformed from a rowdy shanty town to an industrial city of considerable sophistication (albeit with a frontier flavor), with stock exchanges, stores, hotels, a railroad, and newspapers.

Engineers contributed as much to the success of the Comstock as did the financiers. For example, Almarin B. Paul is generally credited with developing an efficient ore-extracting technique known as the Washoe pan process, which led to a flurry of mill building in the area: nineteen mills in Virginia City by 1863, thirty-five between Gold Hill and Dayton to the south. To support the mines as they went deeper, a young German engineer, Philip Deidesheimer, devised sets of interlocking cubes, called square-set timbering, that propped up the mine tunnels and allowed them to be dug deeper and longer than ever before. Andrew S. Hallidie, designer of the San Francisco cable cars, invented a flat, woven-wire hoisting cable for use in the Comstock mines, and railroad engineers, with considerable ingenuity, brought the famous shortline railroad, the Virginia & Truckee, from Carson City to Virginia City, rising over 1,500 feet. In 1878 Adolph Sutro completed a 20,484-foot tunnel to drain and ventilate the Comstock and to facilitate the transportation of men, ore, and supplies. The Sutro Tunnel was completed too late to relieve the excessive heat and water that made working the Comstock hazardous to miners; by the time the tunnel was finished, the mines were on the verge of being played out. From its discovery in 1859 through 1880, the Comstock earned $308,894,721, or nearly three times as much as all other mining districts in Nevada combined. In those years control of the mines passed from individual mining companies, then to the Bank of California, and finally to an adventuresome partnership that dominated the lode after striking a munificent mineral deposit known as the Big Bonanza. And in those years, whoever controlled the Comstock also controlled the state politically.

With the Comstock in its last throes, Nevada entered into a period of economic depression that lasted twenty years, from 1880 to 1900. Many Nevadans blamed the reversal of fortune on the Coinage Act of 1873, which they called the Crime of '73, by which Congress demonetized silver and stopped coining silver dollars.

Silver became such a hot issue in the state that the Silver Party, formed to repeal the act, soon dominated state politics. In the meantime, a search for another mineral bonanza continued. So did the bad times. By the turn of the century, Nevada's population had dropped to 42,000, and there was talk in other parts of the country that it should be deprived of statehood.

A new era of prosperity began in May 1900, when a rancher named Jim Butler picked up a rock to throw at a balky mule and discovered it contained silver. Thus began the boom that built the towns of Tonopah, Goldfield, and Rhyolite and shifted political control of Nevada to men with ties to the mine fields in this part of the state, such as George Wingfield. Thanks to a government subsidy, the silver boom was long-lived, lasting until 1923. After that, copper, which had been discovered in eastern Nevada in 1900, became the mineral on which the state's well-being depended. By legalizing gambling in 1931, Nevada took the first step toward mining another bonanza, tourism. The gaming industry began to boom after World

An 1867 photograph by Timothy O'Sullivan, who accompanied the King Survey of the 40th parallel, shows one of the survey wagons—possibly containing his dark-room—making a lonely crossing of the sand dunes of Nevada's Carson Desert (detail).

A precarious remnant of the silver boom in the ghost town of Berlin, which was founded in the 1890s and largely abandoned in the first decade of the twentieth century.

War II, first in Reno, which had earlier established itself as the divorce capital of the country, and then in Las Vegas. Lax controls over this industry led to scandal and investigation; the Kefauver Crime Commission hearings in Las Vegas in 1951 revealed that the underworld had effectively penetrated the industry. Therefore, when Howard Hughes, Nevada's reclusive "first citizen," began buying casinos in 1967, the state gratefully waived such requirements as a recent photo and set of fingerprints. Hughes ushered in an era of corporate control of the gambling industry that continues to this day, although critics still assert that the influence of organized crime is widespread.

Today the vast majority of visitors to Nevada never leave the air-conditioned casinos and nightclubs of Las Vegas and Reno. But a growing number are coming to enjoy its historic sites, snow-capped mountains, or some of the most spectacular desert scenery anywhere. Nevada's wilderness is a fragile resource that has been under attack since the first miner drove a pick into the ground; in 1918 the naturalist John Muir called the mines of eastern Nevada "monuments of fraud and ignorance—sins against science." The placid desert and rugged mountains are still being raked over by strip miners. And there are other threats to the environment—gunnery ranges, supersonic aircraft, ammunition dumps, and nuclear waste.

In 1951 the Atomic Energy Commission conducted the first atmospheric test of an atomic weapon in the newly created Nevada Test Site, a 640-square-mile area carved out of the 5,400-square-mile military gunnery range in southern Nevada. The test site and the adjoining Nuclear Rocket Development Station have been an economic boon to the state. Since 1963, following a limited test-ban treaty with the Soviet Union, all tests have been conducted underground, but before that, in an age of nuclear innocence, many Nevadans would picnic along the highway to watch the blasts. As with the mining booms that preceded it, the nuclear age brought prosperity to Nevada but at a cost—in this case the beauty of its environment and the health of its citizenry.

With a population of only 963,000, primarily in Las Vegas and Reno, and an area of 109,889 square miles, Nevada is a state where the distances between settlements—and historic sites—are long and often lonely. But the state's lightly traveled roads lead through some of the most spectacular scenery in the West, often a breathtaking combination of desert falling away from mountain ranges. This tour of Nevada is divided into northern and southern sections.

NORTHERN NEVADA

WARD

Soon after silver, gold, and lead were discovered here in 1872 by Thomas F. Ward, the town grew into a substantial settlement with a post office, school, two breweries, two smelters, and a mill. By the end of the decade, the boom was over, and not long afterwards the town was deserted. All that remains today are six seemingly indestructible cone-shaped charcoal ovens, which rise in perfect alignment, like prehistoric ruins on the desert floor. Thirty feet high with walls twenty inches thick and a small hole in the top for ventilation, the ovens provided charcoal for the smelters. Each oven held about thirty-five cords of wood, which, after burning for twelve days, produced about fifty bushels of charcoal. The demand for wood stripped the hills of timber for a radius of about thirty-five miles.

Today the six ovens have been preserved as the **Ward Charcoal Ovens Historic State Monument,** located about seventeen miles southeast of Ely and accessible by a graded road off Route 6/50.

ELY

Some claim this town was named after Ely, Vermont, the hometown of a local miner. Another story attributes the name to John Ely, a colorful itinerant miner, investor, and one-time vigilante, who, after losing a fortune in an international mining venture, "proceeded to drown his sorrows and disappointments in liquid tumult." Yet another story names Smith Ely, who built the town's first smelting mill, as the source. Ely benefited from the gold, silver, and lead mining boom of the 1870s, although the actual mining was centered in nearby settlements such as Hamilton and Ward, now ghost towns. Then, in 1900, two young, nearly penniless miners named David Bartley and Edwin Gray bought the Ruth mining lode, a promising copper outcrop just west of town, that attracted the attention of Mark Requa, the son of a prominent Comstock miner. Requa consolidated the mines and built the Nevada Northern Railroad with headquarters in Ely. Requa was forced out by the Guggenheims, a New York family with worldwide copper holdings, to whom he had turned for financing to develop his mines. The Guggenheims' Nevada Consolidated Copper Company operated the mines until the Kennecott Copper Company took over in 1933. The mines closed in 1979. Many photographs and artifacts relating to the history of the town are displayed at the **White Pine Public Museum** (2000 Aultman Street, 702–289–4710), including material on the Liberty Pit at Ruth, once the largest open-pit copper mine in the world. (The pit is now closed to visitors for safety reasons.) Outside the museum are a pioneer's log cabin and two steam locomotives that did service on the Nevada Northern in the early twentieth century.

Nevada Northern Railway Museum

Although still in its infancy, this promising museum represents a complete railroad operation—that of the Nevada Northern—and includes rolling stock, depots, office furniture, files, and maintenance buildings and equipment. In this sense it is the most complete

OPPOSITE: *Charcoal produced in these cone-shaped ovens built in the 1870s was used to fuel smelters because it burns at a higher temperature than wood. They are now preserved in the Ward Charcoal Ovens Historic State Monument.*

railroad museum in the country. The Nevada Northern, the longest
short-haul railroad in the country, was founded to carry copper ore
from the mine at Ruth to the mill and smelter at McGill, and refined
blister copper 146 miles north to the Southern Pacific line at Cobre.
After the railroad closed in 1983, the Kennecott Copper Company
donated a substantial amount of equipment and other property to
the museum, including thirty-two miles of track, the East Ely Depot
and General Office Building, the sizable machine shop complex, and
rolling stock that includes three steam, six diesel, and two electric
locomotives; six passenger cars; and seventy freight cars dating from
1900 to 1917. On occasion Engine No. 40, a 1910 Baldwin steam
locomotive now called "The Ghost Train of Old Ely," takes an excur-
sion run from East Ely to the mining district at Keystone.

LOCATION: 1100 Avenue A, East Ely. HOURS: Memorial Day through
Labor Day: 8–4:30 Daily. FEE: Yes. TELEPHONE: 702–289–2085.

Established in 1986, **Great Basin National Park** (Route 488, near
Baker, 702–234–7331) contains such diverse natural attractions as

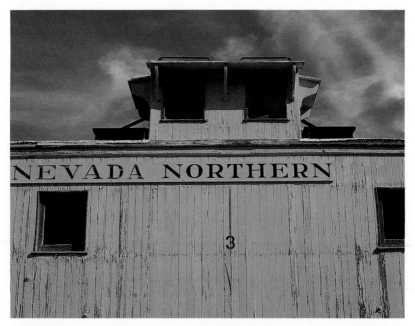

*A caboose at the Nevada Northern Railway Museum, which comprises one of the best
preserved short-haul railroads in the United States.*

a municipal election and had to tote a flour sack down Main Street. The sack was then auctioned off—for $350 in gold coin—with the high bidder donating it back to be resold and the money going to the Sanitary Fund, a Civil War relief organization and a forerunner of the American Red Cross. By auctioning the sack again and again, Gridley raised nearly $5,000 by the end of the day; his success inspired him to take the sack on a year-long nationwide tour that raised $275,000 for the Sanitary Fund. A dirt road at the south end of town leads to **Stokes Castle** (private), an architectural oddity that was built in 1897 of hand-hewn native granite for Anson Phelps Stokes. Fifty feet square at the base, the three-story tower is closed to the public, but the site commands a superb view of the Reese River valley. Stokes had railroad and mining interests in Austin.

Off Route 50 is the town of **Fallon,** the first community to benefit from irrigation provided by the Bureau of Reclamation's Newlands Project in the early 1900s. Photos of the dam's construction are on display at the **Churchill County Museum** (1050 South Maine Street, 702–423–3677), along with exhibits of period clothing, including Indian dresses made of sagebrush and rabbitskin, and period rooms depicting pioneer life. Also on display are a fine collection of quilts and antique firetrucks. The **Churchill County Courthouse** (10 West Williams Street), built in 1903, is perhaps the only wooden courthouse in Nevada. Near Grimes Point is **Petroglyph Park** (off Route 50), where vestiges of past civilizations may be seen.

FORT CHURCHILL
HISTORIC STATE MONUMENT

A period lithograph shows Fort Churchill as an unfortified settlement of one- and two-story wooden barracks, adobe buildings, tents, stables, and corrals built around a large parade ground. Today only ruins of the adobe buildings remain, although the desolate desert setting has changed little over the years. Fort Churchill was built after the conflict known as the Paiute War or Pyramid Lake War of 1860, Nevada's only Indian war. After Indians attacked a trading post about twenty-five miles east of Carson City, a volunteer force of miners took off in hasty pursuit but were ambushed and badly defeated by a band of southern Paiute under a chief named Numaga at the Big Bend of the Truckee River (near present-day Wadsworth). In the aftermath of defeat, Captain Joseph Stewart and

The ruins of Fort Churchill, established in the mid-nineteenth century to protect white settlers attracted to the Comstock Lode from attacks by the Paiute, are preserved in a state of arrested decay.

a former Texas ranger named Colonel Jack Hays organized a force of 750 volunteers and defeated the Indians at Pinnacle Mountain. Stewart established Fort Churchill. The fort was strengthened during the Civil War in response to the secessionist movement among southern-born miners in Virginia City and Carson City, but its duties consisted mainly of guarding overland routes and protecting settlements from Indian attacks. Fort Churchill was a major Pony Express station, since it was also the terminus of the telegraph to California. It was abandoned in 1869 and its buildings auctioned off in 1871 for $750. Now a state historic park, Fort Churchill is more of a military ghost town than a reconstructed fort. Park rangers have located the sites of the buildings that did not survive, however, and have begun limited restoration of the adobe ruins. There is a model of the original fort in the visitor center.

LOCATION: 8.5 miles south of Silver Spring off Route 95A. HOURS: *Visitor Center:* March through October: 8–4:30 Daily. *Park:* Always open. Fee: None. TELEPHONE: 702–577–2345.

DAYTON

The discovery of gold near here in 1849 led to the strikes on the Comstock a decade later. In 1853 Dayton became the site of the first marriage and divorce in Nevada, when a 14-year-old girl married a prospector and then divorced him almost immediately afterwards to rejoin her irate father. (If the story is to be believed, then Nevada's divorce laws must have been even more liberal in 1853 than they were earlier in this century when fast divorces became an important industry.) The town, which had prosperous mills during the early years of the Comstock, then fell into doldrums until a brief respite in 1960 when Marilyn Monroe, Clark Gable, and other members of the cast of the film *The Misfits* came to town to film rodeo scenes. Most of Dayton was destroyed in two big fires in 1866 and 1870, but otherwise the town has remained relatively untouched despite being so near Route 50. Gold Creek, near where gold was discovered in 1849, runs under the street near **Odeon Hall** and the old **firehouse.** James "Old Virginny" Finney (or Fennimore), the bibulous prospector who named Virginia City, is buried in the **Dayton Cemetery,** one of the oldest (1851) continuously maintained cemeteries in the state. The wagon road to the Comstock passed directly in front of it.

VIRGINIA CITY

The rush to the slopes of Mount Davidson began in 1859 after two Irish miners, Peter O'Riley and Patrick McLaughlin, discovered gold in some sand they had excavated, which turned out to be the edge of a fabulously rich lode. After some legal wrangling, the pair became the reluctant partners of Henry Tompkins Paige Comstock, a lazy loudmouth whom one historian has described as "a gaunt Canadian fraud." Comstock bragged so much about the strike that the lode, one of the richest in history, eventually took his name. The name of Virginia City, the so-called "Queen of the Comstock," had an even less auspicious origin. A chronically besotted miner named James "Old Virginny" Finney (or Fennimore) spilled his whiskey one night and christened the place of the mishap "Virginia," either after his birthplace, the source of the whiskey, or both. Or so that story goes. Within a year Virginia City was well on its way to becoming a boom town, and the discovery of silver 900 feet beneath the earth in the

This panoramic photograph of Virginia City was taken after the city was rebuilt following a disastrous fire in 1875, which consumed most of its buildings. The town,

Crown Point mine only accelerated the rush. J. Ross Browne, a well-known traveler and reporter of the day, described "the wondrous city of Virginia": "On a slope of mountain speckled with snow, sagebrushes, and mounds of earth, without any apparent beginning or end. . . . Frame shanties, pitched together as if by accident; tents of canvas, or blankets, of brush, of potato-sacks and old shirts, with empty whiskey barrels for chimneys." And all this on a mountainside so high and desolate that it had previously been considered uninhabitable. "A more barren-looking and forbidding spot could scarcely be found elsewhere on the face of the earth," Browne wrote in dismay.

Within a few years, however, Virginia City was unequaled by any metropolis between Denver and San Francisco. By the mid-1870s there were 110 saloons, over 50 dry goods stores, 4 major banks, 20 laundries, 7 churches, 5 newspapers, and a railroad, the famed Virginia & Truckee, that made thirty-two trips in and out of town a

established after the discovery of the Comstock Lode in the late 1850s, never regained its former importance after the fire.

day. Samuel Clemens first used his pen name, Mark Twain, while reporting for Virginia City's *Territorial Enterprise.* His colleague William Wright (pseudonym, Dan De Quille) worked for the same paper and in 1876 produced the standard reference work on the Comstock, *The History of the Big Bonanza.* Virginia City was also the home of Nevada's best-known artist of the era, Cyrenius B. McClellan, much of whose work was destroyed in a fire in 1875. That fire, which burned nearly three-quarters of the city, was halted just before spreading to the mine tunnels themselves. But the city rebuilt, in brick this time, and most of the interesting architecture that has survived postdates the fire. By 1878, however, Virginia City was in decline, and by 1880 its glory days were over for good. Mining continued, however; in 1899, its mines earned $400,000, a mere pittance by Comstock standards. The mines closed in 1942, when the government declared gold and silver not essential to the war effort.

After World War II, Virginia City began attracting tourists in a modest way. This fledgling industry received a boost—and publicity—after Lucius Beebe, the flamboyant newspaper society columnist, railroad buff, writer, and bon vivant, moved to Virginia City in 1950. Beebe named one of his private railroad cars "Virginia City" and revived the *Territorial Enterprise*. Shortly thereafter, the "Bonanza" television series set its plot in Virginia City, somewhat inaccurately since it revolved about a family of cattlemen and Virginia City's history is strictly centered on mining. Today tourists cram Virginia City. But to those preservation purists who decry the commercialization, the garish atmosphere, and the "hokum," David W. Toll writes: "In its glory Virginia City was one of the great hokum capitals of the world, as crude and as brash a city as ever rooted itself to a western mountainside." He points out that a visiting journalist, in 1863, wrote of the "inordinate passion of the inhabitants for advertising . . . the streets and hillsides are pasted all over with flaming bills. . . . All is life, excitement, avarice, lust, deviltry, and

The Mark Twain Museum, in Virginia City's Territorial Enterprise *Building, is devoted to the history of the paper where the young Samuel Clemens fist used the pseudonym "Mark Twain." Featured is a portrait of Lucius Beebe, who revived the paper in 1952.*

The 1860 Mackay Mansion was originally constructed by the Gould and Curry Mining Company as a residence and mining office. It was later the home of John W. Mackay, a proprietor of the Big Bonanza mine.

enterprise. Despite the commercial atmosphere, Virginia City has retained a wealth of historic buildings, many of them restored and in prime condition. The imposing, Second Empire-style **Fourth Ward School** (537 South C Street), a three-story building with a granite block base, was paid for mainly by contributions from the miners. The last class graduated in 1936, and it now houses a visitor center and a history museum. On D Street, one block down the slope, are three distinguished mansions that served simultaneously as mining offices and residences. Near the Fourth Ward School, the **Chollar Mansion** (565 South D Street, 702–847–9777) was originally built, between 1861 and 1863, on top of the Chollar Mine, one of the Comstock's leading producers. The house, now a bed-and-breakfast, was moved to its present location in 1871 when the mine began to sink and the mansion with it. It features a three-level cantilevered staircase, a paymaster's booth, and a 164-square-foot arched vault, used to store bullion. The **Mackay Mansion** (129 South D Street, 702–847–0173) was built in 1860 and was lived in first by George Hearst, father of William Randolph Hearst. It survived the devastating fire of 1875 and became the home of John W. Mackay, the rich-

est man in Comstock. It is notable architecturally for its "hanging" stairs and colonnaded verandah from which the superintendent could observe the mining operation directly below the house. The mansion, which has original furnishings and gold and silver artifacts, is open for tours.The three-story Second Empire-style **Savage Mansion** (146 South D Street, private) was built by the Savage Mining Company in 1861. The ground floor was the mining office, while the superintendent and his family occupied the upper two floors. Since its renovation, many of its original furnishings have been returned; a walk-in safe in the office, a seven-foot copper bathtub, and the faux-wood detailing on the walls and staircase are some of the highlights of the interior. Former president Ulysses S. Grant spoke from the front porch—with its intricately turned railings—during a tour of Virginia City in 1879.

Virginia City's railroading past came alive again when the famous shortline railroad the **Virginia & Truckee** (702–847–0380) was put back in operation as a tourist line over a short stretch of the original track. The two-car train pulled by a steam locomotive makes the half-hour run ten times a day in summer. When it first opened in January 1870, the line, designed by Isaac James, was an engineering marvel. To make the twenty-one-mile trip from the Comstock to the mills on the Carson River, the railroad negotiated a 1,575-foot drop through an ingenious series of tunnels, trestles, and curves. Remains of the V & T's passenger and freight depots can be seen at E and Sutton streets. The V & T, which was extended from Carson City to Reno in 1871, did not finally go out of business until 1950.

Also on the east side of town is Virginia City's largest church, the Gothic Revival **Saint Mary's in the Mountains** (E and Taylor streets). When the fire of 1875 was raging out of control, John W. Mackay promised to rebuild the church if the parishioners would help him save his mine instead. He was true to his word, and the silver bell from the original church, which survived the fire, hangs in the belfry today. Behind it is the small wooden **Saint Paul's Episcopal Church** (1135 12th Street), which was also rebuilt after the fire. Both have fine interiors. The oldest church in town, the exquisite Carpenter Gothic **Presbyterian Church** on the south end of C Street, was built in 1867 and managed to survive the fire.

Another C Street landmark is the *Territorial Enterprise* **Building**

OPPOSITE: *The interior of Saint Mary's in the Mountains, rebuilt after the fire of 1875, contains beautiful redwood columns, trusses, and arches.*

(C Street between Union and Taylor streets), where the young Mark Twain worked as a reporter. The paper spread the word of the Comstock silver strike to the rest of the world. The building houses the **Mark Twain Museum** (702–847–0525), a collection of antique printing presses, type fonts, desks, and other memorabilia. C Street's brick-fronted **Old Washoe Club** (C and Taylor streets) claims to be the oldest saloon in town. It numbered most of the Comstock's movers and shakers among its members during the days of the Big Bonanza. On the northern end of C Street, the low-slung wooden building with an old ore wagon and other pieces of mining equipment in the front yard is **The Way It Was Museum** (702–847–0766), which is devoted to mining history. Included among its artifacts, photographs, and other exhibits is a model of the northern end of the Comstock Lode, the 250 miles of tunnels directly below Virginia City. It shows all the principal mine shafts, cross cuts (horizontal underground passages that intersect a vein), and drifts (passages that run parallel to a vein), as well as the square-set timbering supporting the mine, the all-important technical advance that allowed the Comstock to be developed.

Virginia City's most distinguished public buildings are grouped together on B Street at the head of Union Street. The **Miner's Union Hall,** built after the original building was lost in the 1875 fire, contained a library and ballroom when it was finished. The building is flanked by two other postfire buildings, the **Knights of Pythias Hall** and the **Moran Building. Piper's Opera House** is the third building of that name built in the town and the second one on this site. Its six arched entrances are matched by the arched windows above it. The **Storey County Court House,** also a replacement after the fire, has a life-size zinc-painted-gold figure of Justice, who is not wearing a blindfold, over the main entrance. The graceful Italianate building with its double windows separated by slender Corinthian columns was completed in February 1877 at a cost of $117,000. Farther south on B Street is the elegant Victorian mansion known as **The Castle** (70 South B Street, 702–847–0275). Built in 1868 by Robert N. Graves, superintendent of the Empire Mine, the three-story mansion is perched on the side of Mount Davidson, its front terrace supported by sandstone blocks and edged by an elaborately turned railing. Once referred to as "the House of the Silver

OPPOSITE: *The Virginia City Cemetery originally comprised twenty-two separate burying grounds devoted to different religions, fraternal orders, or tradesmens' groups.*

Doorknobs," virtually all its furnishings, which are original to the house, are from Europe and include cut rock crystal chandeliers from Czechoslovakia, fireplaces of Carrara marble surmounted by large, French, gold-leaf mirrors, and a massive front door carved from black walnut from Germany. "To insure the continental flavor, the workmen and artisans were likewise imported from Europe," says the brochure. It could be true, although San Francisco had already produced a generation of craftsmen working in these styles.

On Nevada Route 342, in the canyon south of Virginia City, the town of **Gold Hill** grew into a thriving community of almost 10,000 around the original strike on the Comstock Lode, then shrunk to its present diminutive size. Still visible are the **Virginia & Truckee Railroad Depot,** scheduled to be restored, the **Bank of California Building,** a privately owned brick-and-stone building constructed in 1862, and the remains of the **Yellow Jacket Headframe** at the entrance of one of the Comstock's leading mines. The headframe is on the hill behind the **Gold Hill Hotel** (702–847–0575), the oldest hotel in the state. Built in 1859 as a Comstock boardinghouse, the hotel was renovated once, as the Veasey House, in 1863 and again in 1987

GENOA

A charming settlement in the fertile Carson Valley, Genoa (pronounced Jen-NO-ah) was the first permanent white settlement in the state. In June 1849 Hampton S. Beatie established a profitable trading post here catering to travelers on their way to California. Beatie sold out that fall, returned to Salt Lake City, and went to work in a general store owned by a Mormon named John Reese. Inspired by Beatie's accounts, Reese left for Carson Valley the next spring with seventeen other men and ten wagons of goods. Reese built a permanent cabin and stockade, which soon became the center of a thriving community. Originally called Reese Station, then Mormon Station, the town was renamed Genoa in 1855 by Orson Hyde, a Mormon apostle and probate judge, who had been sent there by Brigham Young to administer the recently created Carson County. (The mountains reminded him of Genoa, Italy, where he had been a missionary.) When Brigham Young recalled Mormon settlers in 1857 to defend against a threatened federal invasion, Hyde and

OPPOSITE: *The headframe of the Yellow Jacket Mine at Gold Hill. Despite the town's name, it was a silver mining center.*

most of the other Mormons returned to Salt Lake City, and their property was taken over without payment by non-Mormons. Hyde later tried to extract $20,000 from the Gentiles (as Mormons call non-Mormons) who had taken over his sawmill but was unsuccessful even after he threatened them, in an open letter he read before the Utah legislature, "with thunder and with earthquakes and with famine until your names are not known among men." During the brief run of the Pony Express—from April 1860 to October 1861—Genoa was the station between Lake Tahoe and Carson City.

A fire in 1910, supposedly set by a resident of the poorhouse who was trying to fumigate his mattress, destroyed Reese's trading post and about half of downtown Genoa. (The possibility that this and other calamities were somehow connected to Hyde's malediction occurred to many residents.) The town never fully rebuilt after the fire, as Carson City had become the commercial and population center of the region because of its proximity to the Comstock. **Mormon Station** (Main Street, 702–782–2590) has been rebuilt and is now administered as a historical park. The replica of the Reese store and stockade, set amid a grove of black locusts, now contains a small museum with pioneer furniture, tools, and artifacts such as a

The Mormon Station in Genoa, originally established as a trading post in the early 1850s, re-creates what may have been the earliest cabin built in Nevada.

Pony Express Bible carried by the riders. Across the street from the state park is the former county courthouse, a graceful red-brick building with a white wooden balcony trimmed with dentil molding. Built in 1865, it is the oldest surviving courthouse in Nevada. After the county seat moved to nearby Minden in 1916, the building became a school and then, in 1969, the **Genoa Courthouse Museum** (702–782–2476), operated by the Carson Valley Historical Society. Inside, the courtroom retains some original oak furnishings, and the jail is complete with a steel-enclosed privy. The collection includes a pioneer kitchen, a replica of an early blacksmith shop, agricultural implements such as a fence puller and stretcher, and a display on a famous local character, John A. "Snowshoe" Thompson, a Norwegian immigrant who in the 1860s attained a degree of fame by delivering mail on skis for prodigious distances over the mountains.

There are over thirty historic houses in the Genoa Historic District. The **John Reese House** (Genoa Lane and Main Street, private), built for the founder of Genoa in 1855, is also known as the Pink House; the verandah with the turned railings was added in 1904. The **Genoa Bar** (Main Street), which bills itself as "Nevada's Oldest Thirst Parlor," is in an 1850s brick building and is a veritable museum with its long wooden bar, potbelly stove, pool table, and memorabilia on the walls. A **marker** at the corner of Main Street and Genoa Lane commemorates the founding of the famous Nevada newspaper the *Territorial Enterprise* in 1858. The plaque notes that "Mark Twain began his career as a writer on its staff" but fails to mention that this happened after the paper moved to Virginia City.

BERLIN

Sited on the western slope of the Shoshone Mountains, and best reached by Route 50, Berlin existed from the late 1890s to about 1909, when its silver mines played out. It owes its existence today—in a state of "arrested decay"—to Dr. Charles Camp's discovery in 1954 of a fossilized giant ichthyosaur, a sixty-foot sea creature from the Upper Triassic period (about 180 million years ago), when much of Nevada was covered by an inland sea. The town and the fossil remains of the nineteen ichthyosaurs have come under the protection of the state as the **Berlin Ichthyosaur State Park** (Route 884, 23 miles east of Gabbs). Three large ichthyosaurs are displayed under cover in the Fossil Shelter in **Union Canyon,** about two miles from Berlin, where park rangers give talks on the area's geology, his-

tory, and natural history. The buildings of Berlin (open for special tours) include residences, the assay office, a stage station, machine shop, mill, clubhouse, and hoist shack near the entrance to the mine. Markers on the houses contain colorful comments by Firmin Bruner, an old-timer who lived in the town as a youth. The notes on one building recall a Fourth of July celebration in 1906 that took place within the bachelors' quarters: "Again and again someone appeared at the open door to empty a six-shooter into the air thereby accentuating the merrymaking within." The ruin of a miner's dugout on a hillside above the town bears this reminiscence about its two occupants: "On summer evenings they often sat in the doorway singing songs accompanied by the mellow notes of an accordion, which indicated that their shelter, however humble, was full of cheer and contentment."

CARSON CITY

Many of those who first settled Eagle Valley in 1851 were Mormons. After Brigham Young recalled them to Salt Lake City in 1857, the richest part of the valley was purchased by Abraham Curry and three business partners, who established the town site in 1858. With the discovery of the Comstock Lode the next year, Carson City began to boom and rapidly outgrew nearby Genoa, Nevada's original settlement. The shipments of precious ore and currency to and from the Comstock were a bonanza for highwaymen, particularly for an alert saloonkeeper named Jack Harris, who would overhear loose talk about lucrative freights that he would then hold up and rob. As long as he worked alone, nobody suspected him; he was caught when he took on an accomplice. Carson City became the territorial capital in 1861 and the state capital in 1864. The county in which it is situated was named for Major William Ormsby, who was killed leading the ill-fated expedition against the Paiute in the Pyramid Lake War. In 1869 the U.S. Mint opened in Carson City to produce coins from the minerals coming from the Comstock Lode, more than $50 million worth by the time it closed in 1893. Carson City became a railroad center when the Virginia & Truckee Railroad was completed from Virginia City to Carson City in 1870; it was extended to Reno, where it connected with the Central Pacific in 1872. (The immense buildings housing the V & T Repair Shops, on

OPPOSITE: *The Berlin Knickerbocker 30 Stamp Mill, which ceased operations in 1909, is now part of Berlin Ichthyosaur State Park.*

Stewart Street south of its intersection with Route 50, are still standing.) In 1969 Carson City became an independent municipality when Ormsby County was disolved.

Most of the historic public buildings and homes are within close distance of the **State Capitol** (Main Street, 702–885–5670), which was built in 1870–1871 and designed by a California architect, Joseph Gosling. Although enlarged after the turn of the century, critics have pointed out that the building looks like an "oversized courthouse." It has an hexagonal cupola, round-headed paired windows, a columned portico, and prominent quoins. The senate and assembly chambers are on each end of the second floor, although those legislative bodies have moved to a nearby building. Since 1909, Nevada's chief executives have lived in the **Governor's Mansion** (606 North Mountain Street, 702–885–5670), a two-story, Classical Revival frame building with a wraparound porch. In keep-

The Nevada Governor's Mansion was completed in 1909 to the designs of the Reno architect M.J. Curtis. The side porches were added in the late 1960s.

ing with the architectural theme, the reception room is furnished with reproductions of eighteenth-century furniture; the drawing room is finished in ivory.

Nevada State Museum

The Nevada State Museum is housed in the former U.S. Mint of 1869. On exhibit is a coin press weighing six tons that arrived at the Carson City mint in 1869 and a set of Carson City Morgan dollars, all bearing the distinguishing "CC" mark of the mint. Another display devoted to gambling has a faro dealer's board and a chemin de fer pallette. A photograph of early Indian advocate, writer, and teacher Sarah Winnemucca Hopkins is among the portraits of notable Nevadans displayed in the Women's Gallery. The weapons collection includes a gleaming brass-plated Gatling gun (1885) that was once used on the guard tower of the state prison. On its two floors, there is

The entry hall of the Nevada Governor's Mansion has an Italian marble floor. The drawing room features a portrait of Abraham Lincoln, president when Nevada achieved statehood.

also a button collection, a butterfly display, and the silver service from the battleship USS *Nevada,* made from 5,000 ounces of silver from the Tonopah mines and lined with gold from Goldfield. The establishment of the museum in the U.S. Mint in 1939 was made possible by a gift from Max Fleischmann, a principal benefactor of worthy causes in Nevada, who was the son of the founder of the Ohio yeast company that became Standard Brands.

> LOCATION: 600 North Carson Street. HOURS: 8:30–4:30 Daily. FEE: Yes. TELEPHONE: 702–885–4810.

Among several smaller museums in Carson City is the **Warren Engine Company Museum** (Curry and Musser streets, 702-887-2200), which houses the collection of the oldest volunteer fire company in the country, founded in 1863. The collection includes a 1912 chain-driven Seagraves fire truck, early uniforms, alarm systems, and early firefighting paraphernalia. The **Nevada State Railroad Museum** (South Carson Street at Fairview Drive, 702–885–4810) holds the Virginia & Truckee's collection of historic equipment including locomotives and twenty-six freight and passenger cars. On occasion the museum operates a steam-powered V & T train over a mile-long loop of track. A restored Southern Pacific station relocated from Wabuska serves as the start/return point for the rides. The **Stewart Indian Museum** (5366 Snyder Avenue, about a mile east of Route 395, 702–882–1808) is located on the campus of the former Stewart Indian Boarding School, a complex of fifty handsome stone buildings built between 1923 and 1957 by students working with stonemasons. The intertribal school, which opened in 1890 and closed in 1980, was originally known as the Carson Indian Training School; it was renamed for Senator William Morris Stewart, who obtained federal funding for the institution. The museum offers changing exhibitions of memorabilia from the school, western Indian baskets, photogravures of Indians by Edward S. Curtis, and other artifacts.

A local-history museum is inside the **James D. Roberts House** (1217 North Carson, 702–883–7921), a wood frame structure with elaborate gable trim. Possibly the oldest house in Carson City, it was built in Washoe City in 1859 and moved here in 1873. The area west

OPPOSITE: *An undated photograph of Sarah Winnemucca Hopkins, granddaughter of Paiute Chief Truckee, whose command of the English language made her the leading spokesperson for her tribe.*

of North Carson Street holds a rich collection of old Carson City houses, many built by individuals prominent in Nevada history. Starting on the north end, highlights include the fifteen-room **Bliss House** (710 West Robertson, private), with six marble fireplaces, was built by the owner of the lumber mill in Lake Tahoe and owner of the narrow-gauge Lake Tahoe Railroad, which hauled lumber to the top of the Sierra Nevada, where it was floated by a V-flume into Carson City. The sandstone **Stewart-Nye House** (108 North Minnesota, private), distinguished by its bay and dormer windows, was built about 1860 by attorney William Morris Stewart, who sold it to Territorial Governor James W. Nye. After statehood, Stewart and Nye were the first U.S. senators from Nevada. Two blocks south is the brick **Ormsby-Rosser House** (305 South Minnesota, private), built in 1862–1863 by Margaret Ormsby, the widow of the Nevada pioneer William Ormsby, who was killed in 1860 leading an expedition against the Paiute Indians in the Pyramid Lake War.

On North Division Street are several historic properties, including the **Orion Clemens House** (502 North Division Street, private), built in 1864 by Orion Clemens, the first and only territorial secretary of Nevada. His brother, Samuel Clemens, frequently visited him during his time as a fledgling reporter for the *Territorial Enterprise* in Virginia City. The house, originally sided with wood, was covered with stucco in the 1940s. The **Yerington House** (512 North Division Street, private) was built in 1863 and purchased by Henry M. Yerington in 1869. Yerington was a lumber and mining figure and general manager of the Virginia & Truckee Railroad. His additions to the house include a solarium with arched windows, probably designed to look like a railroad car. Two of Carson City's oldest churches are also on North Division: the 1865 **First United Methodist Church** (Division and Musser streets), which was built of sandstone quarried at the Nevada State Prison, and **Saint Peter's Episcopal Church and Rectory** (314 and 302 North Division Street). Saint Peter's, a white frame building with a tall narrow steeple, has the look of a New England church. One of the founders of Carson City built the **Abe Curry House** (406 North Nevada, private) in 1871 from Nevada State Prison sandstone.

BOWERS MANSION

Sandy Bowers, the builder of this extraordinary granite mansion, was one of the few prospectors to strike it rich on the Comstock.

(The mining companies bought up most of the claims before they started paying off.) He built this house, north of Carson City, on the outskirts of what was once Washoe City, for his wife, Eilley, who owned the adjoining claim. An Italianate townhouse, completed in 1864, it is symmetrical, with brackets, round-headed windows, an octagonal cupola, and three matching balustrades on the front porch, the second-floor deck, and the roof. The Bowerses traveled to Europe to acquire furnishings; in all, the project is locally said to have cost more than $200,000, a very large sum in those days. Sandy Bowers died of silicosis in 1868, and Mrs. Bowers, who had begun to turn the house into a hotel, lost the property in a civil suit in 1875. She ended her days as a fortune teller in San Francisco.

LOCATION: Washoe Valley, 10 miles north of Carson City on Route 395. HOURS: May through October: 11–4:30 Daily. FEE: Yes. TELE-PHONE: 702–849–0201.

RENO

In 1927 an iron arch was erected across Virginia Street at the railroad tracks and emblazoned with the words "RENO—the Biggest Little

Crowds surround several craps tables and a roulette wheel in the Bank Club, a Reno casino, in this 1931 photograph.

City In the World." The motto survived and still adequately describes the financial center and hotel, gambling, and entertainment complex that Reno has become. In the beginning—1859—Reno was a river crossing, but a lucrative one, and its second owner, Myron C. Lake, was able to acquire substantial land holdings in the vicinity. This put him in a good bargaining position when the Central Pacific Railroad came through in 1868; Lake donated the land north of the Truckee River for a town, and in return the railroad put a station there. The railroad named the new settlement after a deceased Union general, Jesse L. Reno. As a freighter depot, the city was a major supplier for the Comstock (the main street is called Virginia Street, as this was the path the teamsters took to Virginia City), a position strengthened when the Virginia & Truckee Railroad was extended from Carson City to Reno in 1872.

The city also benefited from the state's second bonanza, the mineral discoveries in Goldfield and Tonopah in 1900, but a more significant source of profit came from Nevada's liberal divorce laws and six-month residency requirement. Many were attracted by the well-publicized 1906 divorce of Laura and William Corey, he being the president of U.S. Steel. In 1910 the Goldfield promoter Tex Rickard staged a heavyweight fight between Jim Jeffries and Jack Johnson, and the news coverage brought Reno and its quick divorces to national attention. In 1920 Mary Pickford, "America's Sweetheart," went to Nevada to shed her husband so she could marry Douglas Fairbanks, and in 1927 the Nevada residency requirement was cut in half, to three months. It was said that newly divorced women would emerge from the courthouse, walk to the Virginia Street Bridge, and toss their wedding rings into the Truckee River. After the boom in Goldfield and Tonopah ended about 1915, George Wingfield, the so-called "Proprietor of Nevada," moved to Reno. From here he controlled the state until his empire went bankrupt in the early years of the Depression, whereupon political control passed to Patrick McCarran, U.S. senator from Nevada for twenty years. In 1931 Nevada legalized the gambling that had actually been flourishing despite its ban in 1910 and, at the same time, reduced the residency requirement for divorce to six weeks. The credit for bringing tourists to gamble in Reno is generally given

OPPOSITE: *The Mackay School of Mines at the University of Nevada—Reno was named after John W. Mackay, the Virginia City miner who struck it rich with the Big Bonanza mine. The statue is by Gutzon Borglum, the sculptor of Mount Rushmore.*

JOHN WILLIAM MACKAY

1831–1902

to Raymond I. "Pappy" Smith, founder of Harold's Club, and William
Harrah of Harrah's Hotels, both of whom came to Reno in the mid-
1930s. Smith was particularly clever; he set up a roulette game that
used mice instead of balls and was the first to employ women as
blackjack dealers. But most important was his innovative promotion-
al campaign—"Harold's or Bust" signs were posted, and photographed, as far away as Siberia, Africa, and the Asia, citing the
number of miles to Reno.

The **University of Nevada** (9th and North Virginia streets,
702–784–4865) was established first at Elko and then moved to Reno
in 1888. Among the buildings at the beautiful campus is **Morrill
Hall,** a three-story brick building with a central bell tower, and the
Mackay School of Mines Museum, which has exhibits relating to the
history of mining in Nevada. The **Nevada Historical Society** (1650
North Virginia Street, 702–789–0190) has exhibits on Nevada history
from prehistoric times to the present, including Native Americans,
exploration, mining, ranching, and gaming with such specific items
as stone knives, baskets, a miner's bathtub, a model stamp, and prehistoric duck decoys. In addition, the society's library houses the

*The Italianate Lake Mansion, constructed in 1877 in what is now downtown Reno,
was moved five miles from the center of town in 1975 when it was threatened with
demolition due to urban growth.*

state's largest collection of materials relating to Nevada and the Great Basin, including manuscript collections, maps, photographs, and ephemera.

The two-story frame Italianate **Lake Mansion** (4690 South Virginia Street, 702–323–5608) is the house that Myron C. Lake, one of the city's founders, purchased in 1879, two years after it was built. Originally located near Lake's trading post, it was moved to its present site in 1975. The restored house is now a museum maintained by Washoe Landmark Preservation. Inside are the original cantilevered staircase and such decorative touches as ornamental plaster and hand-etched glass in the front doors. The **Glendale School,** which was also moved to its current location (next to the Lake Mansion), was the first educational institution in the Truckee Meadow. The **Nevada Museum of Art** (702–329–3333) has a permanent collection of paintings and sculpture relating to the art and history of the Great Basin, as well as rotating exhibits. It has two locations, one in one of the great residences of Reno, the Georgian Revival **Hawkins House** (549 Court Street), the other at 160 West Liberty. Moved from its former location in nearby Sparks, the William F. Harrah Foundation **National Automobile Museum** (Lake and Mill streets, 702–333–9300) has vintage, classic, and special-interest cars on display. Life-size street scenes depict the facades, autos, and artifacts in style in each quarter of the twentieth century.

PYRAMID LAKE

In 1844 John C. Frémont happened upon Pyramid Lake and named it for an unusual tufa rock formation on the eastern shore that reminded him of the great pyramid of Cheops. The lake, located in the Pyramid Lake Indian Reservation, was a part of prehistoric Lake Lahontan, which covered much of northwest Nevada and part of northeast California. In his journal Frémont described the lake as "a sheet of green water, some twenty miles broad . . . set like a gem in the mountains, which, from our position seemed to enclose it entirely." In 1859 groups of Paiute and their allies, the Bannock, gathered at Pyramid Lake to discuss the influx of whites to the Comstock region, which was disrupting their hunting and gathering. While at the conference, the Indians received word of the Bannock attack on Williams Station, a white trading post, on May 7. The attack, in which several whites were killed, led to the Paiute, or Pyramid Lake, War of 1860. A historical **marker** on Route 447, seven miles south of Nixon, commemorates the conflict. Visitor centers at the **Pyramid Lake Fisheries** (Star Route, off Route 445, in Sutcliffe, 702–673–6335; and off Route 447 between Nixon and Wadsworth, 702–789–1081) display photographs and information on the land, lake, and people.

In the town of **Lovelock** is the **Pershing County Courthouse,** a round courthouse patterned after the Pantheon in Rome. Completed in 1921, it is perhaps the only round courthouse in the country.

WINNEMUCCA

In the 1850s trappers established a trading post at this site on the Humboldt River. When it came time officially to name the town post office in the early 1860s, Winnemucca was selected over French Ford, as the settlement was originally known, in commemoration of a principal Paiute chief. One of the town's earliest settlers, a Frenchman named Joseph Ginacca, promoted an ambitious scheme in the 1860s to build a canal to divert water from the Humboldt River near Golgonda to reduction mills ninety miles to the west. The project was never completed. One obstacle was the sandy terrain west of Winnemucca, which could not hold water. Traces of the French Canal can be seen east of town.

On September 19, 1900, more than $32,000 was stolen from the First National Bank by, some claim, Butch Cassidy and his gang. A photograph of bandits dressed in business suits that Cassidy supposedly sent the bank president from San Antonio hangs in the bank today. George Nixon, a part owner of the bank who witnessed the holdup, suspected that the robbers were actually local men. Nixon went on to become the partner of George Wingfield; together they controlled most of the mines around Tonopah and Goldfield. In addition to a collection of local artifacts, pioneer items, and a country store, the **Humboldt Museum** (Jungo Road and Maple Avenue, 702–623–2912) displays a flapper-style beaded dress worn by Edna Purviance in the 1917 film *The Adventurer.* Purviance, born in 1896 in northern Humboldt County, went on to Hollywood to become Charlie Chaplin's co-star in thirty-five films and his inamorata for many years, although they never married.

ELKO

Elko is an interesting combination of cowtown, railhead, and center for Basque sheepmen. The Central Pacific arrived there at the end of

1868. The town prospered as a freight terminus serving the region's mines, and in 1874 it was selected as the seat for the state university, which opened the following year with seven students. The town's population began to dwindle, however, and the school soon moved to Reno. In the 1940s several important casinos featuring name entertainers thrived in Elko. Between 1943 and 1952, Bing Crosby purchased in different pieces a large ranch north of town, which he described as "a functioning cow-and-calf operation with nothing dudey about it." The Ruby Valley Pony Express Station, built in 1860, has been moved to the grounds of Elko's **Northeastern Nevada Museum** (1515 Idaho Street, 702–738–3418), one of the best-endowed regional museums in the state. Many of the items, including the pioneer vehicles, have been donated by the community. For the right to exhibit the old bar from the Halleck Saloon, however, the museum must pay rent: one bottle of gin per year.

A formal portrait of Butch Cassidy (seated at right) and his gang, taken in Fort Worth, Texas, in 1901. Local tradition holds that Cassidy sent this photograph as a joke to the president of a Winnemucca bank he had recently robbed. OVERLEAF: *A distinctive tufa pyramid inspired the name of Pyramid Lake, discovered by the explorer John C. Frémont in 1844.*

SOUTHERN NEVADA

TONOPAH

Silver was discovered in Tonopah on May 19, 1900, by Jim Butler, a Nevada prospector, rancher, and lawyer. According to a story Butler liked to tell, he was prospecting in the San Antonio Mountains when he picked up a rock to throw at a stubborn mule and found it filled with silver. Another version has the mule running off in a storm, leaving Butler to take shelter under a rocky ledge. The ledge contained silver. For the first few years of its existence, the town was officially known as Butler, but Tonopah, an Indian word for "brush springs," was the name that stuck. Butler became partners with Tasker L. Oddie, an easterner employed by Anson Phelps Stokes, who later went on to become governor and U.S. senator from the state. Control soon passed to the Brock family of Philadelphia, who owned the most important mines and the two railroads in Nevada. Next to the Comstock, the Tonopah strike was the largest in the state's history and revived the mining industry in Nevada.

Unlike many towns of the era, Tonopah did not simply die when the boom came to an end in 1907, indeed, the mines continued to produce silver profitably until 1923, and today the hills that hedge in the town still contain working mines. Tonopah's architectural gem is the fifty-six-room **Mizpah Hotel** (100 Main Street, 702–482–3559), built in 1907; its brick-and-sandstone exterior and Victorian interior were recently refurbished. The facade of the domed **Nye County Courthouse** (1 Frankee Street, 702–482–8127), which sits on a knoll overlooking the town, is still handsome despite the addition of two cinder-block wings. The **Central Nevada Museum** (Logan Field Road, 702–482–9676), just east of town, offers a diverse collection of artifacts from the region, including a replica of an assay office, a barber's chair from the Goldfield Hotel, an organ from the Tonopah Presbyterian church, and a dry washer for placer ore. Jack Dempsey won one of his first professional fights in Tonopah, when he defeated a decision over an experienced heavyweight, Johnny Sudenberg, on June 13, 1915. Dempsey returned to Tonopah in 1950 on the town's fiftieth anniversary.

GOLDFIELD

Now almost a ghost town, Goldfield was once the largest city in Nevada and the most cosmopolitan city between Denver and San

Francisco; its main hostelry, the still-standing **Goldfield Hotel,** was a paragon of opulence. After gold was discovered here in 1902, the control of the mines was soon consolidated by George Wingfield and his partner, the banker George Nixon. Wingfield went on to become so powerful in the state that a national magazine once referred to him as the Proprietor of Nevada. The flamboyant fight promoter Tex Rickard also got his start in Goldfield; in 1904 he staged a lightweight championship fight between Oscar "Battling" Nelson and Joe Gans, which lasted a record forty-two rounds. With a typical flair for promotion, Rickard drummed up interest in the fight by displaying the prize money, $32,000 in gold pieces, in the window of his saloon. Rickard went on to promote many of Jack Dempsey's fights; his brick home, still privately owned, is at the corner of Crook and Franklin streets.

In 1907 the radical International Workers of the World (IWW) made Goldfield a target of its union activities. A strike called in

Goldfield's Main Street in 1905. The city, which had been founded in 1902, quickly, and briefly, became the largest settlement in Nevada. OVERLEAF: *Goldfield's cemetery has plain wooden crosses and indigenous Joshua trees.*

November was provoked in part by the miners' refusal to accept company scrip as wages and their objection to the changing rooms where they were watched as they donned street clothes to prevent them from stealing valuable ore, a practice known as high-grading. At the request of the governor, President Theodore Roosevelt sent in federal troops to preserve order, although public safety was never threatened. Still, the arrival of troops ended the strike and broke the back of the union movement in Nevada.

By the time the Goldfield Hotel opened in 1908, Goldfield had three stock exchanges, a theater—the **Lyric,** still standing—and five newspapers. According to a local story, the bricks to build the hotel were sent to Goldfield by parcel post; because of an idiosyncrasy in the rates it turned out to be cheaper that way than by regular freight. The hotel with its lavish appointments—Belgian carpets, Venetian chandeliers, ceilings leafed in gold, and one of the first passenger elevators west of the Mississippi—cost a half million dollars. The mining boom in Goldfield ended about 1918, and the hotel closed in 1936, then reopened temporarily to house Air Force personnel during World War II.

RHYOLITE

In its desolation, with the stately facade of a bank building still standing on Golden Street, Rhyolite is a poignant reminder of early-twentieth-century mining booms that created major settlements overnight and, when they ended with the Panic of 1907, left them without a reason to exist. The town, named for a volcanic rock found in the area, serviced the Bullfrog Mining District; in its heyday it had two railroads, three newspapers, and by some estimates 6,000 people. By 1920 its population numbered a mere fourteen.

Rhyolite, one of the most accessible of Nevada's ghost towns, is reached by a graded gravel road off Route 374, four miles west of Beatty. The elaborate, privately owned **Las Vegas and Tonopah Railroad Depot** at the upper end of town has been the object of much care and restoration. The **Rhyolite bottle house,** built during the boom but restored in the 1920s, is typical of many early settlers' houses, which were ingeniously constructed from any available material. On the exterior walls, the bottle ends make geometric pat-

OPPOSITE: *The ruins of the once prosperous town of Rhyolite, which in the first decade of the twentieth century had hotels, office buildings, banks, bars, churches, a school, a jail, and a power company.*

terns like small cobblestones. Farther down the slope toward the highway, a side road leads to the site of the smaller town of **Bullfrog,** where the ruin of the town icehouse and a hand-lettered sign reading "Bull Frog Bank was here" remain.

LAS VEGAS

Spaniards and Mexicans using the Old Spanish Trail between Santa Fe and southern California christened this stopping place Las Vegas, meaning "the meadows," which George W. Bean, a Mormon settler, described in 1855 as "a nice patch of grass about a half a mile wide and two or three miles long." The expedition of the Mexican trader Antonio Armijo, the first to have reached Los Angeles from New Mexico, camped nearby in the winter of 1829–1830, and American explorer John C. Frémont passed through in 1844. The Mormons arrived in 1855, primarily to convert the Indians (which they did with some success), but also to farm and set up a trading post on the trail. The Mormons' goal was self-sufficiency; to this end they grew a variety of crops, including cotton, and mined for lead at nearby Potosi. But their mission was plagued by crop failures, Indian attacks, and problems with the lead-mining operation, and by early 1857 most of the Mormon colonists had left.

The town of Las Vegas came into being when the San Pedro, Los Angeles, & Salt Lake Railroad, later the Union Pacific, purchased a town site and in 1905 auctioned off building sites. The first structures in town were tents; even the thirty-room Hotel Las Vegas was a frame covered with sections of canvas. Two years later, the Las Vegas & Tonopah linked the town with the gold mines and mills to the north. Las Vegas's promising future as a railroad town suffered a setback, however, when floods in 1907 and 1910 washed out the lines, and the Panic of 1907 all but closed the mines around Rhyolite, Bullfrog, and Goldfield. A new era of prosperity opened when Black Canyon, thirty-one miles away, was chosen as the site of the Boulder Dam across the Colorado. By the time construction began in 1931, the town's population had soared to over 10,000 people. That was also the year Nevada legalized gambling. A few small gambling joints opened on Fremont Street, but Las Vegas's future did not begin to take shape until Bugsy Siegel, "the hood who invented Las Vegas," opened the flashy Flamingo Casino in 1946. Siegel was slain gangland-style in Los Angeles a year later, but other mobsters followed in his footsteps. In 1967 the eccentric billionaire industrialist Howard Hughes gave gambling a more businesslike image when he began to purchase casinos

A Corinthian portico invites visitors to "Enter Caesars World" at Caesars Palace, one of the most lavish casinos in Las Vegas.

and hotels. Not long afterwards, major corporations, with at least the facade of respectability, entered the gaming business. In 1974 daily gambling revenues topped $1 million for the first time. Today, for pure, unadulterated phantasmagoria, Las Vegas has no equal. "The Strip," with its hotels, casinos, and unbroken vistas of signs—"Armageddon in neon"—has even gained a measure of respectability in architectural circles as an example, unlikely to be surpassed, of the style known as "commercial vernacular." Not surprisingly, not much of the city's early history or architecture has survived the onslaught of development in the name of pleasure. The adobe **Las Vegas Mormon Fort** (908 Las Vegas Boulevard, 702–386–6510) is a small part of the complex that the Mormons built in 1855. After they left two years later, it was headquarters for the ranch that later became the city of Las Vegas.

The **Nevada State Museum and Historical Society** (Lorenzi Park, 702–486–5205) focuses on the history of southern Nevada from about 12,000 B.C. to 1950 in its Regional History Hall. Anasazi pottery and baskets, an old slot machine, and a prospector's pan for washing gold are among the many artifacts on display. The Biological Science Hall features plant and animal life of southern Nevada and holds the world's smallest pygmy blue butterfly, about an inch wide. Two galleries have changing exhibits of folk art, paintings, sculpture, photography, and other arts, concentrating on western and southwestern subjects. The **Las Vegas Museum of Natural History** (3700 Las Vegas Boulevard S., 702–798–7757) houses dinosaur and wildlife exhibits and an art gallery containing paintings, prints, bronze and marble sculptures, and woodcarving on wildlife subjects by artists from all over the country. The **University of Nevada/Las Vegas** (4505 Maryland Parkway), established in 1957, has on its campus a thirty-four-ton steel flashlight sculpted by Claes Oldenburg, who was commissioned to create a work symbolizing the university. The significance of the work, entitled *The Beacon of Knowledge,* remains open to interpretation, but it has become a popular if eccentric landmark.

A room at the Las Vegas Mormon Fort, which was established in 1855 under orders from Brigham Young, who directed thirty men to "go to Las Vegas, build a fort there to protect immigrants and the United States mail from the Indians, and to teach the latter how to raise corn, wheat, potatoes, squash, and melons."

BOULDER CITY

For a traveler through Nevada, Boulder City is likely to come as a visual shock. With its neat suburban tracts, planned streets, well-kept homes, and manicured lawns and gardens, it is unique in a state whose towns and cities—more often than not wedged between the slag heaps of mines—seem permanently scarred by the boom-or-bust mentality that built them. Boulder City was built as a railhead for materials going to Hoover Dam and as a model community for its workers. At the time, Las Vegas wanted to be that railhead and even tried to further its cause by closing the saloons and sweeping the prostitutes off the street when Ray Lyman Wilbur of the Bureau of Reclamation in Washington, DC, came to town to look over the area. But Wilbur decided instead to create Boulder City, declaring, according to a newspaperman of the day, that "Las Vegas was no place for people to live." Boulder City was a federal reservation until 1960, and even today, as a chartered Nevada city, there is no gambling. The **Boulder Dam Hotel** (1305 Arizona Street, 702–293–1808) was built in 1933 to house important visitors to the dam. Recently restored, it is reminiscent of a New England country inn, with its comfortable lobby and colonnaded front porch. The nearby **visitor center** (1228 Arizona Street, 702–293–1081) shows the construction of Hoover Dam through historic film footage. The huge (fourteen feet in diameter), round metal object in the town park is a turbine runner, used to convert falling water into energy, from one of the generators at Hoover Dam.

HOOVER DAM

If all the materials that went into building Hoover Dam were put into one freight train, it would stretch from Boulder City, Nevada, to Kansas City, Missouri. There is as much steel in the structure as there is in the Empire State Building and enough concrete to lay a highway twenty feet wide from California to Florida. Other statistics are equally mind-boggling: 9 million tons of rock excavated, 840 miles of steel pipe installed, 3.25 million cubic yards of concrete poured. Work began in April 1931 and ended in March 1936; President Franklin D. Roosevelt dedicated the dam in September 1935. On that occasion Roosevelt called it Boulder Dam, and so it was generally called until Congress switched the name back to Hoover in 1947.

Herbert Hoover, an engineer, had good claim to the name. As secretary of commerce, he negotiated the Colorado River Compact

of 1922, which divided the water among the seven states it served, and when he was president, he participated in decisions on the dam's design and location. Before the dam was built, the Colorado River overflowed regularly; in 1905 it changed course and flooded California's Imperial Valley. Its irregular flow also made using its waters for irrigation difficult. Hoover Dam, when completed, was the largest ever built: 726 feet high, 1,244 feet long at its crest, 660 feet thick at bottom, and 45 feet thick at top. The dam permanently changed the character of the river. Across the Colorado River it created Lake Mead, 110 miles long with a 822-mile shoreline. Water from Lake Mead irrigates some of the country's richest farmlands, provides water to such major cities as Los Angeles and San Diego, and delivers hydroelectric power to Nevada, Arizona, and southern California. Today Hoover Dam and Lake Mead are part of the Lake Mead National Recreation Area.

> LOCATION: Via Route 93, 8 miles east of Boulder City, in Black Canyon between Nevada and Arizona. HOURS: June through August: 8–6:45 Daily; September through May: 9–4:15 Daily. FEE: Yes (for tours). TELEPHONE: 702–293–8321.

OVERTON

Mormon colonists sent from Utah to settle the Muddy Valley founded the towns of Saint Thomas, Saint Joseph, and in 1869, Overton. Although the settlers succeeded in draining the land and farming it, they had to contend with marauding Indians, drought, insects, and heat so intense that one pioneer reported watering his carrots in the morning and harvesting them fully cooked at noon. Indeed, he might have only stretched the truth slightly; the highest temperature ever recorded in the state was at Overton: 122 degrees Fahrenheit in June 1954. The Mormon colony lasted until 1870, when a survey determined that this section was part of Nevada, not Arizona as the settlers claimed. When the state of Nevada insisted on collecting back taxes, more than 600 Mormons packed up and left, leaving behind farms, fields, and an irrigation system valued at $100,000.

Archaeological digs beginning in the early 1920s uncovered the prehistoric site of Lost City, otherwise known as Pueblo Grande de Nevada, an Anasazi community of 10,000 to 20,000 people that existed along the banks of the Muddy River. Most of the ruins, pithouses, mines, shelters, and artifacts date from about 300 B.C. to A.D. 1500.

OPPOSITE: *The Hoover Dam on the Colorado River near Boulder City has a profound effect on the water supply of three states—Nevada, Arizona, and California.*

Lost City became the focus of national attention in about 1930 when it was revealed that the waters of Lake Mead rising behind Hoover Dam would inundate a part of the area. The site was extensively excavated, and in the 1930s the Civilian Conservation Corps built the **Lost City Museum** (721 South Highway 169, 702–397–2193). It stands on a restored portion of the pueblo as a repository for the pottery, baskets, beads, and pendants—many made of turquoise mined by the Anasazi—and other artifacts.

PIOCHE

This once wild and woolly frontier mining town was named for a genteel, French-born San Francisco financier, François Louis Alfred Pioche, who never visited the mining district he financed. A Mormon missionary, William Hamblin, discovered silver in the area in 1864, but Pioche did not start to boom until mines in Hamilton—100 or so miles to the north but still the nearest settlement of any size—began to decline about 1870. It then developed a reputation of being, according to the *Territorial Enterprise,* "overrun with as desperate class of scoundrels as probably ever afflicted any mining town on this coast." A local legend claims that the first seventy-five men buried in the local cemetery all died of unnatural causes; the gunfighter John Levy got his start in Pioche when he shot a man—for a $5,000 reward—and then finished him off by beating him over the head with his gun. Today the town is best known for the **Million Dollar Courthouse** (Lacour Street, 702–962–5182), a two-story structure built of low-grade ore-bearing stone in 1871. The initial cost of $88,000 (three times the estimate) was financed and continually refinanced by bonds that were not paid off until 1937, by which time the debt amounted to nearly $1 million. It now houses a museum of local history.

Over 600 million years ago, shifting of the earth's plates, combined with later erosion and mineral oxidation, created the spectacular sandstone formations of **Valley of Fire State Park** (off Route 15, 702-397-2088). Within the 34,880-acre park are intriguing petroglyphs of the Anasazi and Paiute peoples that may have served as maps, clan records, or even a lost language. A segment of the Arrowhead Trail blazed by ·Jedediah Smith and Kit Carson in the 1840s lies near the western boundary.

OPPOSITE: *Elephant Rock, one of many spectacular rock formations in Nevada's Valley of Fire State Park.*

NORTHERN UTAH

OPPOSITE: *The interior of the Utah State Capitol in Salt Lake City features monolithic Ionic columns made of gray Georgia marble. From the center of the dome hangs a 6,000-pound chandelier on a 7,000-pound chain.*

Before he led the Mormon pioneers to Utah in 1847, Brigham Young expressed a yearning for a land that "nobody else wanted," where members of the Church of Jesus Christ of Latter-day Saints would find sanctuary from persecution and could build the true Church of Christ. Young had read a report that was entirely to his liking by the western explorer John C. Frémont, who described a region with fertile areas, isolated from the rest of the world, that was arid, desolate, and deserted. The Ute Indians, who hunted and fought in the Great Basin, did not occupy it in permanent settlements like those of the Pueblo Indians farther south. The desert Brigham Young chose to settle and cultivate is part of the Great Basin, a region of prehistoric dry lake beds, rugged peaks and valleys, and seemingly endless salt flats that run westward from the mountains. The Great Basin drains into itself, a phenomenon that Frémont described as "new and strange, unknown and unsuspect, and discredited when related." Northern Utah's two major mountain ranges, the Wasatch, through which the Mormons passed before descending into the Salt Lake valley, and the unusual, east–west Uinta, are offshoots of the Rocky Mountains. This land legally still belonged to Mexico when the Mormons began to settle it in 1847; it became American the next year with the Treaty of Guadalupe Hildago.

Before the Mormons arrived, a succession of hardy mountainmen passed through northern Utah in search of furs: Jim Bridger, who discovered the Great Salt Lake in 1824; the Hudson's Bay Company's Peter Skene Ogden ("the terror of the Indians and the delight of all gay fellows") in 1825; the literate and pious Jedediah S. Smith in 1826. After the fur trade died, a trapper-turned-trader named Miles Goodyear established Fort Buenaventura, the first permanent white settlement in the territory, in 1846. Goodyear's "fort" was no more than a few cabins over thirty miles north of Salt Lake City, but this was too many and too close for Brigham Young, who wanted no Gentiles, as the Mormons call non-Mormons, in the region. Accordingly, he wasted no time in buying out Goodyear and establishing a Mormon community at the site.

The territory mapped out by Young was immense, encompassing all of Utah, most of Nevada and Arizona, parts of present-day Oregon, Idaho, Wyoming, Colorado, New Mexico, and even California, where Young wanted to establish a seaport. Young called this empire Deseret, a word from the *Book of Mormon* meaning hon-

Between 1856 and 1860, thousands of Mormon immigrants, unable to afford wagons and oxen, walked the Mormon Pioneer Trail from Iowa to Utah, hauling all their earthly possessions in hand carts. This view was painted by Carl Christian Anton Christensen, a Mormon artist who made the 1,300 mile journey in 1857 (detail).

eybees, and within a few years, Mormons had been "called" to colonize much of it. In 1849 the Mormon John M. Bernhisel was sent to Washington, DC, to petition Congress for statehood. Two years later Congress denied the petition but made Utah, its boundaries diminished but larger than they are now, a territory with Brigham Young its governor. Unlike other settlers of the West, the Mormons lived in relative peace with the Indians. Young took the practical approach that it was "cheaper to feed them than to fight them." The Mormons also believed that the Indians were brothers—"through the loins of Joseph and Manassah"—who had fallen from grace, hence the dark color of their skin. For their part, the Indians regarded the Mormons, whom they called "Mormonee," as a race distinct from other white Americans—"Mericats." After the Walker War of 1853, an armed conflict with the Ute led by the bellicose warrior Chief Walkara, or Walker, Brigham Young himself participated in the peace

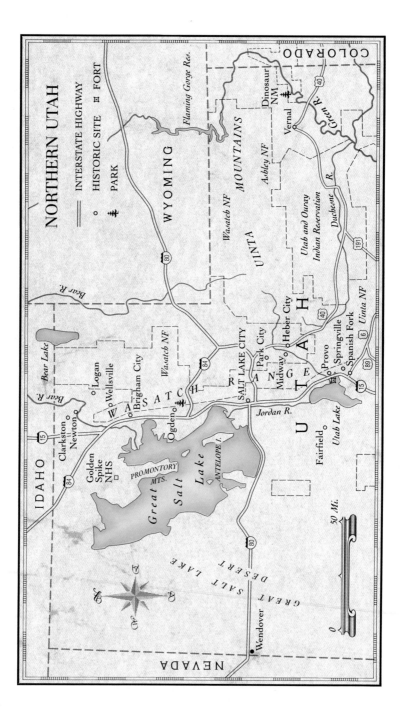

NORTHERN UTAH

— INTERSTATE HIGHWAY
○ HISTORIC SITE ⊞ FORT
⚓ PARK

parley, smoked a peace pipe, and laid his hands on the ailing chief in an attempt to cure him. Afterward, Young stepped up efforts to convert the Indians and sent missionaries all over the territory to "learn their language . . . feed them, clothe them, and teach them."

In the early 1850s, Mormons poured into the territory in great numbers; in the first five years of the decade, the population grew from 10,000 to 60,000. As the numbers increased, so did suspicion of the Mormons in distant Washington, DC. In 1852 apostle Orson Pratt, one of the governing body of the church, widened the breach by announcing publicly that polygamy was a fundamental tenet of the Mormon church. Polygamy was practiced in biblical times, said Pratt, citing the Old Testament, as well as by four-fifths of the world's people. When Indians massacred a party of federal surveyors in 1854, President Franklin Pierce, suspecting the Mormons of the crime, sent Lieutenant Colonel Edward J. Steptoe with a detachment of more than 350 military and civilian personnel to investigate the incident and to replace Young as territorial governor. Although alarmed by the federal intrusion, Young was diplomatic, and Steptoe soon became convinced of the Mormons' innocence in the massacre. On Steptoe's recommendation, Pierce reappointed Young to another four-year term.

But Young's victory was temporary. Anti-Mormonism in the east was being preached by such figures as the ambitious Illinois senator Stephen A. Douglas, who campaigned vociferously against the "twin relics of barbarism": slavery and polygamy. The exploits of the militant Mormon secret society, the Sons of Dan, or Danites, also contributed to the anti-Mormon sentiment. The society was formed in 1838 to counteract—with bloodshed—the violence the Mormons encountered in Missouri, and it continued its clandestine activities after the Mormons reached Utah. Its name came from the book of Genesis: "Dan shall be a serpent by the way, an adder in the path, that biteth the horse heels, so that his rider shall fall backward." Although the Mormons sometimes dealt harshly with their enemies, it is unclear how violent the Danites actually were, since their deeds were exaggerated by the anti-Mormon press and other anti-Mormons. The most notorious Danite was Orrin Porter Rockwell, the so-called Destroying Angel, who served occasionally as bodyguard for Joseph Smith, the founder of the church, and for Brigham Young. Although he was never convicted, Rockwell was implicated in several murders, including the decapitation, in Utah in 1850, of a

In the rush to complete the transcontinental railroad, both the Union Pacific and the Central Pacific worked up to 300 miles ahead, which caused them to build parallel lines for some 200 miles. This trestle near Promontory, built hurriedly by the Union Pacific, was used only briefly. The parallel Central Pacific track, laid on fill only a few hundred feet away, was ultimately used.

Missourian who was said to have been a member of the mob that had killed Joseph Smith in Carthage, Illinois, on June 27, 1844.

In 1857 President James Buchanan declared that the Mormons were in a state of open rebellion and dispatched a federal force to Utah, the opening act in the bloodless conflict known as the Utah War. This time Young reacted less diplomatically, calling the president "a stink in the nostrils of every honorable person throughout the nation." Young also alerted the territorial militia, recalled settlers from distant parts, and gave thought to moving elsewhere, to another land that "nobody else wanted."

In an attempt to settle the Utah War, Young agreed to accept a federal governor in return for amnesty for any treasonable acts the Mormons might have committed, but he refused to allow federal troops within forty miles of Salt Lake City. A tense period followed. As the federal troops, under the command of General Albert Sidney Johnston, approached in June 1858, Young ordered Salt Lake City abandoned. The only Mormons left to greet the soldiers were scattered individuals under orders to torch the city if the army tried to occupy it. Johnston, however, marched his men through and set up Camp Floyd, just over forty miles south.

Although he was no longer governor, Young remained *the* power in Utah. After Horace Greeley passed through, he called the federal presence—military, gubernatorial, and judicial—"three transparent shams—three egregious farces." Camp Floyd, the largest concentration of troops in the country, was dismantled at the onset of the Civil War. In 1862 its troops were replaced by a smaller unit of California volunteers commanded by Colonel Patrick E. Connor, an Irish immigrant with an obsessive hatred of Mormons. Connor had a dual mission: to guard the Overland mail route and to keep an eye on the Mormons. The colonel installed his men on the bluffs above the city, where he kept a cannon aimed at Brigham Young's home, and in another provocative move, named the encampment Fort Douglas after the anti-Mormon senator.

After Abraham Lincoln was elected, he expressed sympathy for the Mormons but kept Connor in place to deal with the Indians. (A visit from Mormon representatives was the occasion for one of Lincoln's famous stories. When he found a log on his farm that was impossible to move, "we plowed around it," the president explained. "That's what I intend to do with the Mormons.") Connor, in the meantime, sent his men out to prospect for precious minerals. If they made a major strike, he reasoned, the news would bring non-Mormons in great numbers to Utah and weaken the hold of the Latter-day Saints over the territory. Connor never got the big strike he wanted, but he did establish the first mining district in Utah, spread the word about the area's mining potential, and set the stage for the rushes that would follow.

It took the driving of the golden spike upon completion of the transcontinental railroad at Promontory Summit on May 10, 1869, to bring large numbers of non-Mormons to Utah. The railroad spelled the end of the western frontier; it also spelled the end of the nearly exclusive rule of the Mormons. By 1880 Mormon presence in Utah had been whittled down to 85 percent. Railroad towns such as Ogden developed large and ethnically diverse non-Mormon populations, and the rail lines provided the needed muscle to develop the mines. During the 1870s mines at Alta, Ophir, and Silver Reef attracted labor and capital from outside Utah, and Alta's fabulously rich

Emma mine was exploited through a stock manipulation scheme that ended in international scandal. Although a few Mormons later became rich from mining, the industry was dominated by non-Mormons. As long as he lived, Brigham Young maintained that mining was a godless pursuit, unfit for his followers.

Between 1856 and 1887 the Utah Territory petitioned Congress for statehood five times. The stumbling block was polygamy, which had become entrenched in Utah despite the passage of an 1862 law banning it in the territories. In 1874 the church, confident that polygamy was protected by the First Amendment, tested the antipolygamy laws in a suit before the Supreme Court. A decision was still pending when Brigham Young died in 1877, leaving at least sixteen wives and forty-four children. Two years later the Supreme Court ruled against polygamy. After this decision, more antipolygamy legislation was passed, including one law that disenfranchised practitioners of plural marriages. To avoid arrest, prominent Mormons, including John Taylor, Young's successor as president, went into hiding. Amid the hysteria, the Mormon church was badly misrepresented in the lurid stories circulating throughout the country. In truth, only about one-tenth of Mormon males living in Utah had more than one wife. During the 1880s more than 1,000 Mormon men were imprisoned for polygamy. As pressure grew, the Edmunds-Tucker Act of 1887 disincorporated the church, federal judges began refusing to naturalize Mormon immigrants, and a bill was introduced in Congress to disenfranchise all Mormons regardless of marital status. The situation was resolved in 1890, when the church suddenly renounced polygamy, after President Wilford Woodruff, Taylor's successor, said that he had received a revelation from God ordering Mormons to comply with the law. A period of reconciliation and good feeling followed, and in 1896 Utah became the forty-fifth state. From time to time, Mormonism became an issue again; in 1907 anti-Mormons tried without success to oust Reed Smoot from his seat in the U.S. Senate on the grounds that his loyalty to the church conflicted with his allegiance to the country. But Utah's story in the twentieth century is largely one of assimilation.

Following statehood, Utahans fought loyally in the Spanish-American War and in all wars that followed. Utah politics, previously split between Mormon and non-Mormon camps, formed along national lines. After two decades of economic depression, World War II brought industry and prosperity to the state, and the

More than 1,000 Mormon polygamists were convicted under a number of federal anti-polygamy laws, greatly increasing the population of the Utah Territorial Prison, shown in an 1880s photograph by Charles R. Savage.

Mormon church entered the economic mainstream and became an institution of immense economic power. The discovery of uranium in 1952 touched off a boom reminiscent of the silver bonanza in the 1870s, and the space industry created jobs and prestige for the state. Today only 65 percent of the people of the state are Mormons, but Utah remains a place apart, a "near nation," as one sociologist recently described it, not quite like the rest of the country. The state was founded by strong, determined men and women who came in search of isolation and endured incredible hardship for the privilege of being left alone.

This chapter begins in the north with Logan and meanders through the Cache Valley, near the Idaho border, to Wellsville. It then proceeds south through Brigham City, Ogden, and Salt Lake City. The route next moves from Provo north to Park City before turning east to Dinosaur National Monument.

LOGAN

Logan's altitude (4,535 feet), cold winters, and distance from Salt Lake City (seventy-nine miles north) kept Mormon settlers away until about 1859, when they began to arrive in substantial numbers to irrigate and farm the fertile Cache Valley. The town, located on the eastern edge of the valley, takes its name from the Logan River, which in turn was named for Ephraim Logan, a local fur trapper in the 1820s. Between 1823 and 1824 the famous scout and fur trader Jim Bridger and members of the Rocky Mountain Fur Company worked the region. Because they hid—or cached, from the French *cacher*, meaning to hide—their furs in underground caves, the valley, which extends into Idaho, became known as the Cache Valley.

In 1923 two events occurred that have endured in folklore: a sheepherder shot Old Ephraim, a gigantic marauding grizzly bear; and a student at Utah State discovered what is believed to be the oldest and largest juniper tree in the world. **Old Ephraim's Grave** (off Route 89 in Logan Canyon, about sixteen miles from town) is

The Logan LDS Temple, completed in 1884, is constructed of locally-quarried quartzite. The wooden details were milled from local timber at a sawmill built specially for this project.

marked by an eleven-foot shaft, the same height as the bear; the bear's skull is on display at Utah State University. **Old Jardine Juniper** (about one mile off Route 89 in Logan Canyon), located on a limestone ledge, is forty-five feet high and twenty-seven feet in circumference and is estimated to be 3,500 years old. It is named for Utah State alumnus William J. Jardine, secretary of agriculture under Herbert Hoover. Both the grave and the tree are located in the **Cache National Forest.**

At the mouth of Logan Canyon, **Utah State University** (University Hill, 801–750–1710) overlooks the Cache Valley. The institution was founded in 1888 as the Agricultural College of Utah; its landmark building, **Old Main,** was built between 1889 and 1902. The pyramid-topped tower nearly doubles the height of the three-and-a-half-story building, which was restored after a fire caused extensive damage in 1983. On another bluff overlooking the city, the **Logan LDS Temple** (175 North 300 East) was the third Mormon temple erected in Utah. Truman O. Angell, architect of the Salt Lake Temple, designed this fortresslike building with crenelated battlements and massive buttresses and oversaw its construction from 1877 to 1884. During this period 25,000 people worked on the structure. Two square towers, 165 and 170 feet tall, at each end are flanked by octagonal towers 100 feet tall at each corner. The Logan Temple is one of seven in Utah where LDS baptism, marriage, and sealing ceremonies are performed. As elsewhere, the temple is open only to Mormons in good standing, but visitors are welcome to view the grounds and the exterior.

On an open, parklike block on Main Street in the center of town, the **Logan LDS Tabernacle** (between Center and 1st North) was started in 1865 after 175 individuals pledged more than $26,000, but it was not completed until 1891. Built of locally quarried quartzite, the tabernacle, or meetinghouse, for LDS and public functions seats 1,500 people. The engaged central tower, with a round window with a Star of David motif, is topped by a wooden lantern with a gold dome. The quoins, arches, and buttresses of white limestone stand out vividly against the dark stone walls. The building has recently been restored. Unlike the temples, LDS tabernacles are open to the non-Mormon public. Across 1st North, the Gothic-style **Saint John's Episcopal Church** (85 East 100 North) is one of the outstanding examples of non-LDS church architecture in the state. Built in 1909 from light-colored brick, it has buttresses and segmental arched windows. Also downtown, the **Cache County Courthouse** (179

North Main Street), with its domed tower and central balcony, is probably the oldest courthouse used for that purpose in the state.

There are many private homes in Logan's historic district dating from the late nineteenth and early twentieth centuries. Some of the most notable belonged to the Thatchers, Eccles, and Nibleys, the town's leading families. The spacious brick Victorian **G. W. Thatcher House** (165 East Center, private) was purchased by George W. Thatcher, a grandson of Brigham Young, about 1920. George and his brother, Brigham Guy Thatcher, had extensive holdings in mining, milling, banking, and other enterprises in the region. The **Moses Thatcher, Jr., House** (95 South 1st West, private), a two-and-a-half-story brick building with a wraparound porch and detailed woodworking, was built in 1892 by the Mormon apostle Moses Thatcher as a wedding present for his son.

Many old farm towns and villages in the Cache Valley still have buildings from the pioneer era. **Clarkston,** northwest of Logan near the Idaho border, is the burial place of Martin Harris, the only one of the three original witnesses to the book of Mormon to reach Utah. Harris came to Clarkston when he was 88 and died in 1875 at the age of 93. An eighteen-foot-high granite shaft marks his grave in the local cemetery. To the southeast, **Newton** was settled as a "new town" by settlers from Clarkston in 1869–1870. It is an example of how an early Mormon farming community was organized: Families lived on large lots in town and farmed the outlying areas. When the earth-and-rock Newton Dam was completed in 1886 it was the first reservoir in the country used to store water for irrigation. It was replaced by the present dam in the 1940s.

WELLSVILLE

At the southern end of the Cache Valley, Wellsville was settled in 1856 by a party led by Peter Maughan. The town, known as Maughan's Fort until 1913, is the oldest in the valley, and Maughan was its first pioneer. The Wellsville **cemetery** contains the graves of several former slaves and their children who settled in the area. There are also a number of interesting buildings dating from the town's earliest days.

OPPOSITE: *The 1875 farmhouse and 1867 summer kitchen, now at the Jensen Living History Farm in Cache Valley, were used by Mormon farm families until the 1950s. The log construction is typical of the region, which was settled by German, Swiss, and Scandinavian immigrants.*

Ronald V. Jensen Living Historical Farm

This re-creation of a Mormon family farm from about 1917 has nearly 120 acres of fields, meadows, orchards, and gardens. Livestock includes work horses, dairy cows, sheep, hogs, and poultry. Numerous farm artifacts—vintage tractors, threshing machines, wagons, plows, and household items—are on display. There is a granary, smokehouse, root cellar, lambing shed, barn, hay derrick, 1875 farmhouse, and 1867 summer kitchen. Many special events occur throughout the year, including a ca. 1917 baseball game; a threshing bee; and demonstrations of traditional crafts, among them sauerkraut making, blacksmithing, weaving, and water dowsing.

LOCATION: Route 89/91. HOURS: June through August: 10–4 Tuesday–Saturday. FEE: Yes. TELEPHONE: 801–245–4064.

The engineers of the Central Pacific's Jupiter, at left, and the Union Pacific's No. 119, at right, are poised to christen each other's locomotive with champagne after the last spike was driven in the first transcontinental railroad at Promontory Summit on May 10, 1869. General Grenville Dodge, chief engineer of the Union Pacific, shakes hands with Samuel Montague, chief engineer for the Central Pacific.

An exact replica of the Central Pacific steam locomotive Jupiter, *which met the Union Pacific's No. 119 at Promontory Summit, operates during the summer months at Golden Spike National Historic Site.*

GOLDEN SPIKE NATIONAL HISTORIC SITE

The great race to build the transcontinental railroad that ended here on May 10, 1869, began officially when the Central Pacific broke ground in January 1863 in Sacramento, California, and started pushing eastward over the Sierra Nevada. The Union Pacific began laying track west from Omaha in December 1863, but the race between the two companies did not heat up until the Civil War ended and money, materials, and manpower became available. At stake in the epic competition were generous federal subsidies for each mile of track and land grants along the route. Each company employed about 10,000 men. The Central Pacific imported large numbers of Chinese for the task, and the Union Pacific hired a volatile mix of drifters, Civil War veterans, former slaves, and European immigrants. When fully trained to work with military precision, the crews could lay an astounding two to five miles of track a day on flat ground—two rails more than four feet apart, with each thirty-foot section of rail weighing 560 pounds.

An act of Congress in 1864 permitted the graders of each company to work up to 300 miles in advance of its end-of-track, and so the two grades actually overlapped and ran parallel for over 200 miles, until Congress on April 10, 1869, decreed that Promontory Summit would be the meeting place. The ceremony, originally scheduled for May 8, was delayed two days when irate workers demanding back pay chained the private railroad car carrying Union Pacific vice president Thomas C. Durant to the rail in Wyoming until he came up with the money. At noon on May 10, two engines—the Union Pacific's *Number 119* and the Central Pacific's *Jupiter*—drew up to the gap in the rails. A polished railroad tie made from laurel was put in place, and UP's Durant and CP president Leland Stanford slid four spikes—two gold, one silver, and one, a gift from Arizona, "ribbed with iron, clad in silver, and crowned with gold"—into precut holes and tapped them into place with a silver sledgehammer. When it came time for Durant and Stanford to drive the last spike, an ordinary iron one, both men missed. Nevertheless, at exactly 12:47 P.M. the word went out by telegraph to the nation: "The last spike is driven. The Pacific railroad is finished." The news set off a tumultuous country-wide celebration, but few that day could foresee how profoundly the railroad would change the country. Crossing the continent would now take days, rather than months. Within a few years, the frontier disappeared, the West became an integral part of the country, and the Indians were driven from the plains onto reservations. The railroad also brought large numbers of non-Mormons into Utah and loosened the hold of the Mormons on that region.

After the driving of the last spike, the hastily erected railroad settlement of Promontory declined quickly. Early in 1870 the terminus (where passengers had to change from one line to the other) was moved to Ogden. Then, in 1903, Promontory was bypassed entirely when the Lucin Cutoff was built across the Great Salt Lake. In 1919, on the fiftieth anniversary of the event, the Southern Pacific Railroad placed a monument at Promontory. Congress created the Golden Spike National Historic Site in 1965. The visitor center opened in time for the centennial celebration in

1969, which was attended by more than 30,000 people. Today fifteen miles of the original railroad right-of-way lie within the historic site's 2,200 acres. In 1979 working replicas of Engine *Number 119* and *Jupiter* were completed and brought to Promontory. Roads within the site offer views of parallel grades and other rock cuts, fills, grades, and box culverts. To the west a sign marks the completion of "ten miles in one day," a record set by the Central Pacific crew on April 28, 1869. East is a path to the Last Cut, one of several passes through the Promontory Mountains that the Union Pacific had to blast during the last days of construction. The driving of the last spike is re-enacted every year on May 10.

LOCATION: Promontory Summit, 32 miles west of Brigham City. HOURS: May through September: 8–6 Daily. FEE: Yes. TELEPHONE: 801–471–2209.

The Box Elder Tabernacle in Brigham City as rebuilt after it was severely damaged in a 1896 fire caused by a malfunctioning furnace. A local newspaper claimed "What on the day of the Great Fire appeared a calamity, will tomorrow be looked upon as a great blessing—there is really no comparison between the old and the new."

BRIGHAM CITY

Settled in 1851 as Box Elder, this fruit-growing community in the shadow of the rugged Wasatch Range changed its name to Brigham in 1856. Its namesake, Brigham Young, delivered his last speech here in 1877. In 1864 Lorenzo Snow, who became a noted Mormon leader, organized the Brigham City Mercantile and Manufacturing Association, a successful communal enterprise that included a retail store, mills, farms, and other local enterprises. In 1874 the association became part of Brigham Young's United Order, an attempt to organize Mormon communities along communal lines. The **First Security Bank Building** (Main and Forest streets) was built in 1891 as a co-op store, but by that time the association was on its last legs. Architecturally, the city is known for the **Box Elder Tabernacle** (251 South Main Street), a distinguished example of Mormon architecture. The tabernacle was begun in 1865, completed in 1890, and partially destroyed by fire in 1896. The present building, with its Gothic Revival tower and sixteen side steeples atop brick buttresses, dates from 1897. Renovation of the building was completed in 1987.

OGDEN

A major city with the air of a small town, Ogden was named for Peter Skene Ogden, a trapper active in the area in the 1820s, but its founder was Miles Goodyear, a Connecticut-born trapper-turned-trader, who in 1846 established Fort Buenaventura, a trading post, as the first permanent white settlement in Utah. In 1847 the Mormons arrived in Salt Lake City, and Brigham Young sent James Brown to buy out Goodyear for $1,950, which he did and then renamed it Brownsville. On a visit in 1849, Brigham Young renamed it Ogden and the next year sent 100 families to settle there. The coming of the transcontinental railroad in 1869 secured Ogden's future. Less than a year after the line was completed, Ogden became the junction city where passengers and freight transferred between the Union Pacific and Central Pacific. The railroad brought in many non-Mormons, and a struggle for control of the town began. When, in 1889, non-Mormons won every seat on the Ogden city council, the headline in the *Utah Daily Union* read: "Ogden Americanized."

OPPOSITE: *The pulpit in the 1897 Box Elder Tabernacle is surrounded by seating for the choir. An organ decorated with Gothic ornamentation echos the building's style.*

Fort Buenaventura, originally built by the trapper and trader Miles Goodyear in 1846, has been carefully reconstructed using nineteenth-century construction techniques, including wooden pegs and mortise and tenon joints. There are no nails in the structure.

Fort Buenaventura State Park

After an extensive archaeological excavation of the site of Miles Goodyear's trading post revealed the original post holes, Fort Buenaventura was reconstructed in 1980 by the Utah Division of Parks and Recreation. The fort, which is staffed by interpreters in period dress, consists of three primitive log cabins within the log stockade and a garden similar to the one planted by Goodyear. Nearby is the sand hill that Brigham Young climbed in 1849 "to view out a location for a town." The fort, located on low ground on the banks of the Weber River, had been flooded the previous year.

LOCATION: 2450 A Avenue. HOURS: March through November: 8–Dusk Daily. FEE: None. TELEPHONE: 801–621–4808.

Ogden Union Station

This Spanish Colonial Revival railway station with a red-tile roof was built in 1924 after a fire destroyed an earlier depot on the same site. Inside, the main lobby is a soaring open space with giant wrought-iron chandeliers, inlaid decorative brick, and mosaic tiles. The Ogden-born writer and historian Bernard De Voto called the station "a deliberate triumph of hideousness," but today the building is seen in a kinder light. The station was given to the city in 1977 by the Union Pacific and Southern Pacific railroads and is still used for limited rail service. Northern Utah made the restoration of the station its major Bicentennial project, and it was opened to the public in 1978 as a museum and cultural center featuring firearms and railroad museums. The **John B. Browning Firearms Museum** displays weapons invented by the famed Ogden-born gunsmith John Moses Browning, who achieved many breakthroughs with firearms, most notably the Browning automatic rifle. There are also old photographs of his early Ogden workshops. The **Wattis-Dumke Model Railroad** at the north end of the station displays model train layouts depicting different parts of the original transcontinental route, including the Lucin Cutoff across the Great Salt Lake. The **Browning-Kimball Classic Car** collection includes eight exquisitely restored classic American cars, among them a 1931 Pierce Arrow equipped with a built-in gun holster, once owned by a Chicago gangster. The **Spencer S. and Hope F. Eccles Railroad Center** displays some of the world's largest locomotives and railcars.

LOCATION: 2501 Wall Avenue. HOURS: 10–6 Monday–Saturday; June through August: 1–5 Sunday. FEE: Yes. TELEPHONE: 801–629–8444.

During the early days of the railroad, the lower end of 25th Street was a colorful amalgam of hotels, boardinghouses, and immigrant-run cafes and restaurants, animated by street vendors. To the rear of the street, once known as "Two Bit Avenue," ran Electric Alley, both the red-light district and the home of the many Chinese who came to Ogden with the railroad. Although 25th Street declined with the railroad after World War II, many of the early commercial buildings have been restored as the **25th Street Historic District.** The two-story brick former **Murphy Building and Windsor Hotel**

(101–109 25th Street) was built in three sections between 1887 and 1890 and still has its original windows and brick, corbeled cornice. One of the current tenants, the Curio Shop, has been there since 1892. One of the oldest buildings in the district is the ca. 1883 **London Ice Cream Parlor Building** (252–254 25th Street), with an Italianate facade and bracketed cornice. The upper floors once housed a boardinghouse, then a brothel. The three-story Victorian–style commercial **Gomer A. Nicholas Building** (202–204 25th Street), once simultaneously housed a boardinghouse on the second and third floors, a grocery store on the ground floor, and a tobacco shop in the basement.

In the vicinity, the Episcopal **Church of the Good Shepherd** (2374 Grant Avenue) was built in the Carpenter Gothic style by a New Yorker in 1874 in memory of his daughter, who died passing through Ogden. At 2439 Washington Boulevard, Ogden's main street, **Peery's Egyptian Theater** is an outstanding example of the Egyptian Revival style popularly used for movie theaters in the

Ogden's Daughters of Utah Pioneers Museum features portraits of Mormon pioneers who arrived in Utah before the completion of the transcontinental railroad in 1869.

Peery's Egyptian Theater opened in Ogden in 1924. Another Egyptian movie palace was built in Park City in 1926.

1920s. When the theater opened in 1924, the program referred to the building as "one of the few pure Egyptian structures of the western hemisphere." The facade is decorated with lotus columns, winged serpent scarabs, and life-size pharaohs. The theater, which has been closed since 1980, is being restored.

The **Daughters of Utah Pioneers Museum** (2158 Grant Avenue, 801–393–4460) is housed in the brick Gothic Revival building that was built in 1902 as the Relief Society Stake Hall of the Mormon Church. The DUP museum, one of several around the state, contains a collection of pioneer artifacts donated by local Mormons. One room is set up as a pioneer kitchen, another as a bedroom. Also displayed are such curiosities as a set of brass knuckles belonging to the first police chief and Brigham Young's cane, with a compass on its head. At the rear of the museum is the **Miles Goodyear Cabin,** built from cottonwood logs in 1846 by Utah's first settler. The cabin was moved several times from its original location on the banks of the Weber River, and arrived at this address in 1928.

S A L T   L A K E   C I T Y

In 1851 Mormon president Brigham Young decided to move the capital of Utah from Salt Lake City to Fillmore, the geographic center of the new territory. The Mormon leader had a genius for locating new towns and cities, but Fillmore was one of his mistakes. The territorial legislature met there a few times for appearance's sake but soon retired to Salt Lake City to conduct its real business. The lesson was clear: Salt Lake City was the heart, the hub, the nerve center of Utah. And so it has remained. Within a few days after reaching Great Salt Lake in July 1847, the Mormons, under Brigham Young's direction, were hard at work plowing fields and building a road to bring out timber, a fort for protection from the Indians, and a leafy bower for Sunday services. On July 28 Young marked with his cane the spot where the Mormon temple would be built as if to affirm that Great Salt Lake City (as it was called until 1868) was to be a city of God as well as men. The city itself was laid out according to the "Plat of the City of Zion," drawn up by the church founder,

A panoramic view of Salt Lake City, drawn in 1891 by Henry Wellge. The city's square grid was laid out in the four cardinal compass directions, in the manner pre-

Joseph Smith, in 1833. Streets 132 feet wide were to run true to the compass—east, west, north, and south—with Temple Square at the center. Each block would be ten acres. Water, so desperately needed for irrigation, would be communally owned. Lots would be parceled out according to need; men with more than one wife would receive a lot for each family.

Great Salt Lake City grew phenomenally fast; one month after the Mormons arrived, nearly thirty log-and-adobe cabins had been built. By October 2,000 additional settlers had arrived. Within a year there were 4,000, and by 1850 that number had doubled. The settlers barely survived their first two years in the valley. In June, the second year's crops were first hit by a late frost and then, "to make the disaster complete," by a plague of crickets. Their salvation was a large flock of gulls with a taste for insects. At the time one diarist wrote: "It seems the hand of the Lord is in our favor." Prospectors passing through on their way to the gold fields of California— between 20,000 and 30,000 in 1849 and 1850—brought prosperity to Salt Lake City. Brigham Young urged the Mormons to charge

scribed by Joseph Smith in 1833. OVERLEAF: *The civic, religious, and economic monuments of Salt Lake City illuminated at night.*

the prospectors whatever the market would bear, no matter how inflated the prices, for much-needed supplies and livestock. In 1850 the city's business district, not a part of Joseph Smith's vision, slowly began to take shape on the west side of Main Street.

The transcontinental railroad, completed in 1869, made it possible to develop Utah's mineral resources, but the mines were a mixed blessing to the Mormons. Mining profits helped build Salt Lake City, especially its finer residences and its fledgling business district, but they also gave non-Mormons, whose numbers were growing rapidly, power and influence. In 1868, in a move against non-Mormon businessmen, church authorities organized the Deseret National Bank and the Zion Cooperative Mercantile Institution (ZCMI), whose motto was Holiness to the Lord. These enterprises prospered, but so did their competitors. As the city's population grew, more than doubling in the 1880s, the business communities polarized; the Mormons concentrated north of South Second Street; the non-Mormons, to the south. The Mormon–non-Mormon split spilled over into politics, with the non-Mormon Liberal Party controlling the city government from 1890–1893 and again from 1906–1911.

The city's population growth slowed after the depression of 1893 and then boomed again in the early twentieth century. With World War II came industry and an end to the economic doldrums produced by the Great Depression. Although the city's population remained relatively stable during the postwar era, the number of people in the region more than tripled between 1950 and 1970. The postwar building boom destroyed much of the city's architectural heritage, but enough remains—commercial, governmental, residential, and ecclesiastical—to attract Mormons from around the world and others with historical interests.

CAPITOL HILL

The Capitol Hill district extends from North Temple Street on the south, to Ensign Peak on the north, and from Second West to City Creek Canyon, boundaries that also include the charming Marmalade Historic District. The **State Capitol** (head of State Street, 801-538-3000), built in 1915, sits on a bluff of the Wasatch

OPPOSITE: *The Utah State Capitol, completed in 1915, was financed using a windfall—nearly $800,000 in inheritance taxes paid to the state by E.H. Harriman's widow—with additional funds raised with a $1 million bond issue.*

Mountains to the north, which gives it a splendid view of the city but disrupts the city's geometric plan. The capitol was designed by Richard K. A. Kletting, Utah's foremost architect, and completed at a cost of almost $3 million. The design is based on the U.S. Capitol, although here the House of Representatives is located in the west wing, the Senate in the center, and the State Supreme Court in the east wing (somewhat like the original plan of the U.S. Capitol). The 285-foot-high dome is covered with Utah copper. The interior is lavishly decorated with marble, and in the arches leading to the dome are four murals depicting early historical figures—members of the Domínguez-Escalante expedition, trapper Peter Skene Ogden, John C. Frémont, and Brigham Young. Before the capitol stands a bronze replica of the **statue** of Massasoit that Utah sculptor Cyrus E. Dallin erected at Plymouth Bay, Massachusetts. When the capitol was completed, a plaster cast of the same statue occupied a place of honor under the dome. To the southeast of the capitol is the granite **Mormon Battalion Monument,** completed by the Chicago sculptor Gilbert Riswold in 1927 to honor Mormons who enlisted to fight for the United States in the Mexican War of 1846.

The square red-sandstone building with white wood trim and a cupola, **Council Hall** (801–538–1030), was completed in 1866 to serve as the Salt Lake City Hall and the seat of the territorial legislature. The architect was William Folsom, who built the city's Mormon Tabernacle, the Salt Lake Theater, and the temple in Manti. Council Hall was dismantled in 1960–1962 and moved to its present location, across Third North from the capitol. It now houses the Utah Travel Council and a travel information center for visitors. A historical display on the ground floor includes Brigham Young's copy of the territorial code and a bust made from his death mask.

The **White Memorial Chapel** (East Capitol and 300 North Street) is a reconstruction of the LDS Eighteenth Ward Chapel, built in 1883 in the Gothic Revival style with pointed-arch windows and buttresses. The chapel was torn down in 1973 and later rebuilt with the original bricks on Capitol Hill; it is now used for community functions. The chapel was designed by the San Francisco architect Obed Taylor. On the approach to Capitol Hill, the **McCune Mansion** (200 North Main, 801–533–0858), one of the city's grandest, was

OPPOSITE: *A bronze figure of an infantryman is the focal point of the Mormon Battalion Monument, on the grounds of the Utah State Capitol, which commemorates the company of Mormons who fought for the United States in the Mexican War of 1846.*

built by Alfred W. McCune, a wealthy railroad builder. McCune wanted a large bungalow with "stately or gorgeous pretensions not to be tolerated"; he ended up importing tiles from Holland, mahogany from South America, and oak from England. The house may be viewed by appointment, arranged with the Utah Heritage Foundation.

Pioneer Memorial Museum

This collection of pioneer crafts and artifacts represents the period from the Mormon arrival in 1847 to the turn of the century and is maintained by the Daughters of Utah Pioneers, which operates smaller museums around the state. The Classic Revival building, built in 1905, is a replica of the Old Salt Lake Theater, built in 1862 and long since gone, which was the theatrical center of the pioneer West. There are displays from prominent Utah families, including the wardrobe of Utah's Silver Queen, Susanna Bransford Emery Holmes, Utah's wealthiest woman at the turn of the century. The eagle that topped Eagle Gate, the entrance to Brigham Young's estate, is in the basement. Antique carriages, a mule-drawn streetcar, a steam-powered fire engine, antique farm machinery, and Brigham Young's wagon are among the early vehicles displayed in the nearby **Carriage House.**

LOCATION: 300 North Main Street. HOURS: 9–5 Monday–Saturday; June through August: 1–5 Sunday. FEE: Yes. TELEPHONE: 801–538–1050.

Marmalade District

This diverse collection of early homes squeezed into a triangle formed by Quince Street, 300 North, and Center Street, on the side of Capitol Hill, is named for the fruit trees that the earliest residents planted there and the names of its streets—Quince, Apricot, and Plum. Although the district is now neighbor to high-rises, it remains remarkably intact, and many homes have been restored with meticulous care. The **John Platts Home** (364 Quince Street, private) is one of the oldest residences in the district. Platts, an English immigrant and fruit grower who was Brigham Young's carriage keeper, chose the location because he thought peach trees would do well there. He used apricot pits to bind the mortar in the original building in

1858. In about 1860, he added a second story of brick and a clap-board addition in the rear. The district contains many elegant Victorian homes. However, one of the finest, the **Thomas Quayle House** (355 Quince Street, 801–533–1858), was moved here in 1975. The Carpenter Gothic structure, built in 1884 with steep gables, wooden quoins, and decorative bargeboard, is the headquarters for the Utah Heritage Foundation. The **Richard Vaughen Morris House** (314 Quince Street, private) is a stucco-over-adobe home completed in 1866. Morris, a member of the Nauvoo Legion Cavalry and presi-dent of the Utah Soap Factory, was a polygamist, which leads to speculation that the second-story door over the porch was put there to give his upstairs wife a front door of her own, even though it led nowhere. The Russian-style **Nineteenth Ward Chapel** (168 West 5th North Street), with its onion dome and onion-topped pillars, was built in 1890, when the Mormon church had become less rigid about the style of its buildings. The adjacent **Relief Society Hall** was built in 1908 about two blocks away and moved to its present loca-tion. The nineteenth ward was one of the original nineteen wards organized in Salt Lake City.

TEMPLE SQUARE

Surrounded by a fifteen-foot wall, this ten-acre center of the Mormon faith might seem at first forbidding to the non-Mormon, but the reality is quite different. Inside these confines, Temple Square is both an architectural fantasyland and a garden sanctuary from the rush of the city outside. Walks, shaded by gigantic elms, crisscross lush green lawns that seem in summertime to be constant-ly watered and pass exquisite beds of flowers planted according to season. The Mormon **Temple,** its six spires rising from the east-cen-tral part of the square, was envisioned by Brigham Young even before the Mormons left Illinois. Ground was broken in 1853, and the temple took forty years to the day to complete. During the Mormon War of 1857, work was halted and the foundation filled in to protect the sacred site from federal invaders. Aesthetically, the gray-granite temple is less pleasing than smaller temples at Manti and Logan, but the building's impressive size—186.5 feet long, 118 feet wide, with towers rising as high as 210 feet—represents well the spiritual and temporal dominion that the Mormons came to Utah to establish. The Temple was designed by the architect Truman O. Angell, who was Brigham Young's brother-in-law. Its granite blocks

were hauled by teams of oxen from a quarry at Little Cottonwood Canyon twenty miles to the south. Atop the highest spire is a gold-leafed statue of the angel Moroni, who delivered to Joseph Smith the golden tablets on which the *Book of Mormon* was written. It was sculpted by Cyrus Dallin, a well-known Utah-born sculptor. Like all Mormon temples, this one is open only to Mormons in good standing and is used for sacred ceremonies such as marriages, baptisms, and sealing ceremonies.

At the southwest corner of the square, **Assembly Hall** is a small gem of a rough-cut granite building topped and flanked by gleaming white spires. Brigham Young proposed its construction in August 1877, less than three weeks before he died, and the building was dedicated in January 1882. It replaced two structures built shortly after the Mormons arrived in Salt Lake City: the Bowery, which a contemporary newspaper described as a series of poles and braces supporting "an immense quantity of leafy branches of trees, which composed the roof and served to shelter the congregation of earnest worshippers from the rays of the summer sun"; and the original adobe tabernacle. Assembly Hall was designed by Obed Taylor. It was thoroughly restored from 1979 to 1981 and is used for church services and community functions. The **Seagull Monument** in front of Assembly Hall was sculpted in 1912–1913 by Mahonri Young, Brigham Young's grandson. On top of the spire, two sea gulls are gracefully alighting on a sphere. Bronze bas-reliefs on the base illustrate the famous story of how gulls saved the harvest of 1848, the Mormons' second year in the valley, from a plague of crickets.

The **Tabernacle** and its marvelous acoustics have been made famous by the 325-voice Mormon Tabernacle Choir, which has sung here since the structure was built in 1867. The building is an engineering wonder; its huge oval auditorium—250 long and 150 feet wide, seating 7,000 people—has no supporting columns. The design, attributed to Brigham Young, was executed by William Folsom and by Henry Grow, a Pennsylvania bridge builder responsible for the wooden lattice truss construction. The Tabernacle's great pipe organ at the west end of the auditorium has been greatly enlarged since it was first built in 1867, although some of the original pipes, made of southern Utah pine, still play. The Mormon church maintains large **visitor centers** (801–240–2534) at the north

OPPOSITE: *The spires of the Mormon Tabernacle in Salt Lake City, with the golden image of Moroni, the angel who delivered the* Book of Mormon *to Jospeph Smith.*

and south gates to Temple Square. Both have displays and literature on church history and doctrine.

At the intersection of Main and South Temple streets, the **Brigham Young Monument** is a twenty-five-foot-tall bronze statue of the Mormon leader on a granite base. A plaque on the north side lists the names of the main body of pioneers who arrived here with Young on July 24, 1847. The work by the Paris-trained Cyrus E. Dallin, a Springville, Utah, native, was commissioned for the Utah Jubilee in 1897. On the northeast corner of Main and South Temple stands Salt Lake City's once-grand hotel, the white terra-cotta brick **Hotel Utah,** closed by its owner, the Mormon church, in 1987. The elegant hotel, which had been at the heart of the city's social life since it was built in 1911, will be converted into church offices.

On the west side of Temple Square, the modern five-story **Family History Library** (35 North West Temple, 801–240–2331) is the largest facility of its kind in the world and is open free of charge to Mormons and non-Mormons alike. The Mormon emphasis on genealogy is a result of the belief that the family unit, including all ancestors, remains together after death. Between the library and the Museum of Church History and Art is the evocative **Deuel Log Cabin,** a one-room pioneer home with period furnishings. The cabin is surrounded by meticulously researched plantings from the pioneer era. The cabin is the oldest house in Salt Lake City; it was moved to its present location in 1985.

Museum of Church History and Art

This modern 63,500-square-foot facility, which opened in 1984, is the heir of the "useful and attractive museum" that Brigham Young advocated in 1847 when he urged his flock to donate "all kinds of mathematical and philosophical instruments, together with all rare specimens of natural curiosities and works of art . . . from which, the rising generation can receive instruction." The original Deseret Museum opened in 1869; in 1919 it became the LDS Church Museum and moved to Temple Square. The museum's collection consists of over 60,000 items, including displays connected with important moments in Mormon history, such as the murder of the church founder, Joseph Smith; artifacts related to prominent Mormons; church documents; Indian artifacts; and photographs from the church archives. A new installation traces the entire history of the church. Also displayed are works by such important Mormon artists as C. C. A. Christensen, John Hafen, Le Conte Stewart, and Minerva Teichert. Teichert, Utah's most notable woman artist, studied at the Art Students League in New York City, where she performed roping acts at a western circus to earn money on the side. She became a protégé of Robert Henri, who urged her to return home and paint the "great Mormon story." Many of her paintings depict the trek west and the early days of settlement in Utah.

> LOCATION: 45 North West Temple Street. HOURS: April through December: 9–9 Monday–Friday, 10–7 Saturday–Sunday; January through March: 10–7 Tuesday, Thursday–Sunday, 10–9 Monday and Wednesday. FEE: None. TELEPHONE: 801–240–3310.

Just east of the Hotel Utah, the **Lion House** (63 East South Temple, 801–240–2977) takes its name from the carved stone lion over the first-floor portico. The house with its many gables was built in 1856 to house some of Brigham Young's many wives and children. The architect was Truman O. Angell, designer of the Salt Lake Temple and the brother of one of Brigham Young's wives. The house is open to the public for social functions.

Beehive House

The wooden beehive, a Mormon symbol of industriousness, atop the cupola of this two-story adobe house supplies its name. From the time it was built in 1854, the house served as Brigham Young's home and his official residence as the territorial governor of Utah. The house, with its New England–style widow's walk and its double porch supported by six columns, was designed by Truman O. Angell and William Ward. Angell's sister, Mary Ann, Brigham Young's senior wife, was the only one of the patriarch's many wives to live there while he was alive. Between 1893 and 1918, it was the official residence of church presidents Lorenzo Snow and Joseph F. Smith. The house has been thoroughly restored with period furnishings and includes Young's bedroom, the second-floor Long Room where distinguished visitors such as President Ulysses S. Grant, General William T. Sherman, and Samuel Clemens were received, and the commissary from which Young's large family ordered supplies. Between the Lion House and the Beehive House is **Brigham Young's**

An 1851 portrait of Brigham Young, his first wife Mary Ann Angell, and their six children, painted by William Warner Major, shows the Mormon leader's family in an idealized setting. OPPOSITE: *Lion House, designed by Mary Ann Angell's brother, Truman, was constructed in 1856 to house an unspecified number of Brigham Young's wives.*

Office, which Angell built for the church president in 1852. Today it is the visitor reception area for the Beehive House.

LOCATION: 67 East South Temple Street. HOURS: 9:30–4:30 Monday–Saturday, 10–1 Sunday. FEE: None. TELEPHONE: 801–240–2671.

Another Salt Lake City landmark, the **Eagle Gate,** spanning North State Street at South Temple, is today more of an arch, seventy-six feet across, than a gate. The original Eagle Gate was twenty-two feet wide and guarded the entrance to Brigham Young's estate. It was replaced with the present model in 1890 to make way for streetcars. The original eagle, carved by Ralph Ramsey, is in the Pioneer Memorial Museum. Brigham Young is buried in the **Mormon Pioneer Memorial** (half a block east of State Street on First Avenue) along with several of his wives and children. The small shaded park, now closed in by tall buildings, was once part of Young's estate.

There he was buried as he wished, on September 3, 1877: "Take my remains on a bier and repair to the little burying ground which I have reserved on my lot east of the White House on the hill, and in the southeast corner of this lot . . . there let my earthly house or tabernacle rest in peace." His grave is marked by a bust sculpted in 1974 by Edward J. Fraughton.

South Temple Street

This thoroughfare runs east from the French Renaissance–style **Union Pacific Depot** (400 West South Temple). Before it became Salt Lake City's first fashionable residential street, it was lined with simple adobe structures, pastures, and orchards. The depot, with its massive mansard roof, was completed in 1909 by the Oregon Short Line; its domed waiting room with marble floor and murals depicting scenes from Utah history is open to the public. Nearby, the **Devereaux House** (334 West South Temple, private), orignally a two-story Gothic Revival cottage built in 1857, was extensively remodelled in 1868 by William Jennings, Utah's first millionaire. The Queen Anne–style house was built of brick, which was then stuccoed and scored to look like stone. In 1858 this house became the temporary headquarters of the new territorial governor, Alfred Cumming. Brigham Young met here with him to devise the compromise that avoided bloodshed in the Utah War.

The Romanesque Revival **Cathedral of the Madeleine** (331 East South Temple Street), with a Gothic Revival interior, is an architectural landmark that was built by Lawrence Scanlan, the first Catholic bishop of Utah, with money donated by wealthy Catholic mining families. The cathedral, which was completed in 1909, is particularly noted for its stained glass, most of which came from Munich, Germany. The **First Presbyterian Church** (347 South Temple Street), built in 1906 in the Gothic Revival style by a local architect, W. E. Ware, has a square tower and three arched entrance doors. The construction of both churches just after the turn of the century indicates the growing influence of non-Mormon groups within the city.

The **Keith Brown House** (529 East South Temple Street, private) was built in 1909 in the Renaissance Revival style with a colonnaded entrance for David Keith, part owner of the Silver King Mines in

OPPOSITE: *Salt Lake City's Devereaux House, built in 1868, is constructed of stuccoed brick scored to resemble stone.*

Park City. Keith's partner in the Silver King built the French Renaissance–style **Thomas Kearns House** (603 East South Temple Street, 801–538–1005) in 1902. The two men also purchased the *Salt Lake Tribune* in 1901, and Kearns went on to become a U.S. senator from Utah. The three-story house is built from cream-colored oolite limestone and originally had thirty-six rooms, including a bowling alley. The house served as the Utah governor's mansion from 1937 to 1957 and, after a thorough restoration, from 1980 to the present. On the same block, just east of the Kearns mansion, the **James Glendinning Home** (617 East South Temple Street, 801–533–5895) was built in 1883 of painted brick with stone quoins and columned porches and balconies by mining engineer J. W. Epley and purchased in 1884 by the tenth mayor of Salt Lake City. In 1975 the house was taken over and restored by the Utah Arts Council. Its art gallery is open to the public.

The **East Bench,** a table of land in the Wasatch foothills overlooking Salt Lake City, is the location of the **University of Utah,** the state's oldest institution of higher learning; Fort Douglas, where federal troops were stationed during the Civil War; and Pioneer Trail State Park, at the mouth of Emigration Canyon, which preserves the route Brigham Young and the first Mormon pioneers took into the valley in 1847. The university opened in 1850 as the University of Deseret but closed the next year for want of funds; it became the University of Utah in 1892. The **John R. Park Building** (1912) is named for the university president who reorganized the school after it had been closed. The university includes the **State Arboretum of Utah,** more than 7,000 trees planted in groups around the campus; the **Utah Museum of Fine Arts** (801–581–7049), built in 1970 and part of the university's impressive Art and Architecture Center; and the **Utah Museum of Natural History.**

FORT DOUGLAS

Although the adobe infantry barracks in which the **Fort Douglas Military Museum** is housed was not constructed until 1875, the post itself was established in 1862 by Colonel Patrick E. Connor, a virulent anti-Mormon who once characterized the Mormons as "a community

OPPOSITE: *The Utah Governor's Mansion was built in 1904 by silver millionaire Thomas Kearns three years after he was elected to the U.S. Senate. It was given to the state by his widow in the 1930s.*

of traitors, murderers, fanatics and whores." Connor named the fort for the recently deceased senator Stephen Douglas, also known for his anti-Mormon views. Connor's stated mission was to guard the Overland Express mail route, but he was also there to prevent the Mormons from seceding from the Union, as many in the federal government feared they would do. Connor's troops killed more than 250 Shoshoni at Bear River in the northern Cache Valley in January 1863, but never clashed with the Mormons, despite much tension and name calling. The colonel also encouraged his men to prospect for minerals in hopes that a major strike would attract non-Mormons to Utah and thereby undermine Mormon control. Connor's men made the initial strikes at Park City and Alta, Utah. The post, hemmed in today by the university and a medical research center, is much smaller than it was in its heyday. The **Post Cemetery** is the only part of the fort that dates from 1863; Connor is buried there, as are the twenty-three men killed at Bear River. The museum has a collection of uniforms, weapons, and photographs from Utah's military past, which spans from 1857 through the war in Vietnam. Although the other buildings are closed to the public, the grounds are open.

LOCATION: Building 32, Potter Street, off South Campus Drive. HOURS: 10–12 and 1–4 Tuesday–Saturday. FEE: None. TELEPHONE: 801–524–4154.

PIONEER TRAIL STATE PARK

Located at the mouth of Emigration Canyon, through which Brigham Young and the first Mormon pioneers passed before descending to Salt Lake valley, this 450-acre park commemorates the arrival of the Mormons in 1847. When they reached the canyon, Brigham Young was so sick from Colorado tick fever that he had to be helped from his wagon to survey the valley. He was nonetheless pleased by what he saw—a land desolate and barren, a guarantee, he felt, that his flock would be left alone in their new home. His words, "It is enough. This is the right place. Drive on," have been immortalized by Mormon chroniclers and provided the inspiration for the **This Is the Place Monument,** which was sculpted for the 1947 centennial of the pioneers' arrival by Mahonri Young, Brigham's grandson. Eighty-six feet long and sixty feet high, the monument

Mahonri Young's sculptural monument commemorates the 1847 arrival in Utah of his grandfather, Brigham Young, with the first Mormon pioneers.

consists of life-size bronze figures that stand atop massive granite towers. They represent the white explorers and settlers of the region—the Domínguez-Escalante expedition of 1776, the trappers and fur traders, and the Mormons, depicted by statues of leaders Young, Heber C. Kimball, and Wilford Woodruff. The monument marks the western terminus of the Mormon Pioneer Trail, which begins in Nauvoo, Illinois, and winds west for 1,300 miles through Iowa, Nebraska, Wyoming, and Utah.

At the information center just north of the monument a large mural depicts in vivid colors and meticulous detail the Mormons' westward trek. The mural was completed in 1959 by Lynn Fausett, the noted Utah-born artist who painted the historical murals in the municipal building in Price, Utah. Also in the park is **Old Deseret,** a reconstructed pioneer village that presents a picture of life in Utah in the years 1847–1869. The farms, shops, homes, and public buildings are a mix of authentic and replica structures, and costumed guides inhabit the village. Dominating the village is the **Brigham Young Forest Farmhouse,** which the Mormon leader built in the

1850s on an experimental farm where he cultivated the first alfalfa grown in the region. The farmhouse, which is furnished with Victorian antiques, is open for tours.

> LOCATION: 2601 Sunnyside Avenue. HOURS: *Park:* Mid-September through mid-May: 8–5 Daily; mid-May through mid-September: 8–8 Daily. *Visitor Center:* Mid-September through mid-May: 9–4:30 Daily; mid-May through mid-September: 10–6 Daily. *Old Deseret:* Memorial Day through Labor Day: 12–5 Daily. FEE: Yes, for Old Deseret. TELEPHONE: 801–533–5881.

THE AVENUES HISTORIC DISTRICT

This historic district, which spreads over a hillside north of South Temple and east of State Street, contains more than 2,000 buildings, mostly private homes visible from the street, representing a variety of styles, including Gothic Revival, Italianate, Queen Anne, Craftsman, and Prairie. Although the neighborhood was surveyed in 1850, it was not extensively developed until water became available in the 1880s. Most of the first property owners in the Avenues were Mormons, some of them polygamists. The houses at **379** and **385 Fifth Avenue,** for example, were built about 1884 for the Woolley sisters, who were both married to the same man. Non-Mormon businessmen, who appreciated the district's proximity to downtown and the fine views of the valley, began to purchase property toward the end of the century. Houses in the Avenues also represent the work of some of the city's best architects. One of the earliest, H. H. Anderson, a Danish immigrant who arrived in Salt Lake City in 1881, built the house at **73 G Street** in 1894, as well as his own home, a Victorian cottage with Eastlake detailing at **207 Canyon Road,** on the fringe of the district. The designer of the Utah state capitol, the German-born Richard K. A. Kletting, did a number of homes in the district, including the home at **36 H Street,** built in 1902 for George H. Dern, a mining magnate who became governor of Utah and secretary of war under President Franklin D. Roosevelt. The architect W. E. Ware built his own home at **1184 First Avenue,** a two-story Dutch Colonial Revival house with a large gambrel roof, in 1905. Ware was the son of Elijah Ware, inventor of a steam-driven carriage that is considered a forerunner of the automobile. With his partner, the M.I.T.–trained Alberto O. Treganza, Ware designed the Prairie-style two-story house at **206 Eighth Avenue** with the hip roof and broad eaves, built in 1902.

BUSINESS DISTRICT

Despite the destruction and alteration of many of the turn-of-the-century buildings in downtown Salt Lake City, the area still contains a number of fine examples of commercial architecture. Even a few buildings erected before 1880 remain: The **Eagle Emporium** (102 South Main Street), the oldest commercial building in the downtown area, was completed in 1864 by the merchant William Jennings, Utah's first millionaire. The original building was a one-story brick structure; the upper stories were added in the mid-1880s; and the present Classic Revival facade, in 1916. The building has been occupied by the Zion's First National Bank since 1890. The distinguished New York architect Richard Upjohn designed the other important pre-1880 building, the **First National Bank Building** (161 South Main), which today has the oldest-known cast-iron front in the transmontane West.

At 15 South Main stands the cast-iron **ZCMI Storefront,** a handsome architectural relic that in 1901 was attached to a new addition of the ZCMI (Zion Cooperative Mercantile Institution) store. When the addition was demolished, the storefront was dismantled,

Salt Lake City's Renaissance Revival Commercial Club was built in 1908 as an inducement to increase commerce in Utah.

restored, and altered to fit the front of the new ZCMI shopping mall. ZCMI was an LDS-church-run operation designed to monopolize merchandising in the territory. Brigham Young, who said, "It is our duty to bring goods here and sell them as low as they possibly can be sold," was ZCMI's first president. The facade was designed by William Folsom and Obed Taylor. The **McIntyre Building** (68 South Main), built in 1909, is an early skyscraper designed by Richard K. A. Kletting in the style of Louis Sullivan. Kletting also designed the Richardsonian Romanesque **Utah Commercial and Savings Bank** (20 East First South), built in 1890, with the red-sandstone front and steep triangular center facade. The **Old Clock** at 1st South and Main streets is one of the few remaining historic street fixtures in the city. The four-faced timepiece was built by the Seth Thomas Clock Company of Connecticut in 1873. The **Walker Bank Building** (171 South Main) was completed in 1912. The boxlike building with classical detailing was built for the first bank in the Utah Territory by the Walker brothers, who originally came to Salt Lake City to sell goods to Johnston's army stationed at Camp Floyd.

Exchange Place, the narrow, one-block street now known as the **Exchange Place Historic District,** was developed between 1903 and 1917 at the south end of the business area by Samuel Newhouse. Newhouse, who made his fortune from copper mining in Utah and Colorado, wanted Exchange Place to resemble New York's Wall Street, with its tall buildings on either side, and to serve as the center of non-Mormon business activities. The street runs east–west, connecting Main and State streets between Third and Fourth South streets. Newhouse gave his name to the **Newhouse Building** (2–16 Exchange Place), completed in 1909 along with its twin, the **Boston Building** (9 Exchange Place), named for Newhouse's mining company, Boston Consolidated. Both buildings were designed by Henry Ives Cobb. Newhouse donated the land for the **Commercial Club** (32 Exchange Place), built in 1908 for the organization, which was founded a few years earlier to attract out-of-state businessmen to Utah. The handsome Renaissance Revival building was modeled on the New York City Athletic Club by the architects W. E. Ware and Alberto O. Treganza. Newhouse was one of the most important figures in the development of the Utah copper-mining industry. His company pioneered the techniques of open-pit mining, including the use of steam shovels to gouge out huge amounts of low-grade ore.

The **Capitol Theater** (50 West Second South, 801–534–6398) was built from 1912–1913. Originally called the Orpheum, the theater was designed in the Renaissance Revival style with an ornate facade in brick and polychrome terra-cotta by the San Francisco architect G. Albert Lansburgh, who studied at the Ecole des Beaux-Arts in Paris. When it was completed in 1910, the **Denver & Rio Grande Railroad Station** (Third South and Rio Grande streets, 801–364–8562) included a "men's smoking room and women's retiring room." The railroad was formed and the station built to lure passengers away from the Union Pacific. The railroad sold the building to the state for one dollar in 1977, and it has since been restored as the home of the Utah State Historical Society. The main waiting room, which is lighted by six twenty-eight-by-thirty-foot-high windows, is used for exhibits on Utah and western history.

On the fringe of the downtown area, the **Salt Lake City and County Building** (451 Washington Square, between 4th and 5th South, State, and 2d East) was built between 1891 and 1894 at a cost of almost $1 million. The ornate many-turreted Richardson Romanesque building, which was modeled after the City Hall of London, has over 100 rooms and a central tower that rises more than 300 feet. The elaborately sculpted ornament on the exterior depicts many figures from Utah history, including members of the Domínguez-Escalante expedition; Jedidiah M. Grant, who was Salt Lake's first mayor; Chiefs Jospeh and Wakara; and the mountainman Jim Bridger. **Trolley Square** (between Sixth and Seventh East and Fifth and Sixth South, 801–521–9877) is a private development, decorated with old city lights and Victorian architectural elements, of shops, restaurants, and theaters located in the Mission-style car barns that once housed the city's early trolleys and buses. The entrance is on 7th East. Nearby, the **Garden of Gilgal** (749 East Fifth South) is an unobtrusive but interesting collection of folk sculpture carved and constructed between 1945 and 1963 by Mormon bishop Thomas B. Child as a shrine expressing thanks for the deliverance to Utah, the Mormons' promised land. At the gate a circle of twelve stones representing the twelve tribes of Israel surround a heavenly messenger, a sword-bearing figure with an unhewn rock as a head. The most unusual sculpture is an Egyptian sphinx, symbolizing spiritual darkness, with the head of Joseph Smith, the founder of the Mormon church and the dispeller of such darkness.

N O R T H E R N   U T A H
PROVO

When the Domínguez-Escalante expedition entered the Utah Valley in 1776, Father Silvestre Vélez de Escalante noted "large plains of good land for planting . . . plenty . . . if irrigated, for two or even three large villages." Provo today is Utah's third-largest city. The city was named for the French-Canadian explorer Etienne Provost, who entered the valley in 1825. Only three days after the main group of Mormons reached Salt Lake City in July 1847, apostle Orson Pratt scouted the site, and in March 1849 John S. Higbee and thirty families were sent to Provo to fish Lake Utah, to farm, and for the purpose of "instructing the Indians in cultivating the earth and teaching them civilization." The settlers built the first Fort Utah on the south bank of the Provo River and soon had over 200 acres under cultivation. In September Brigham Young ordered the fort moved east to higher ground. The Mormon policy of befriending and aiding the Indians paid off during the Walker War of 1853, when the friendly Ute warrior chief Sowiette moved his braves inside the fort and successfully discouraged an attack by Chief Walker. The site of the second Fort Utah has been preserved as **North Park** (500 West and 600 North, 801–379–6600). On the grounds the **Pioneer Memorial Building** (801–379–6609) contains pioneer and Indian artifacts. North of the building is a replica of an early pioneer cabin furnished with furniture of the period. A replica of **Old Fort Utah** (801–379–6600), the pioneer's first fort of 1849, stands at 200 North 2050 West (Geneva Road).

Brigham Young University

Today Provo's largest industry, Brigham Young University began as Brigham Young Academy in 1875, when the Mormon church "called" schoolmaster Karl G. Maeser to the job. Although the school was flourishing by the turn of the century, its growth accelerated after World War II. Now, with more than 30,000 students, it is the largest church-sponsored university in the world. Its motto—The Glory of God is Intelligence—comes from the sayings of Joseph Smith, founder of the Mormon church. Between 1884 and 1912, the university was housed in six large brick buildings trimmed with stone embellishments, a complex known as the **Lower BYU Campus** (500 North and University). The present campus, located on a bluff over-

An 1891 building at Provo's Brigham Young University, founded in 1875 as Brigham Young Academy, still bears the inscription "B. Y. Academy."

looking the city and Utah Lake, is a diverse collection of architecture, which includes the **Franklin S. Harris Fine Arts Center,** a massive complex designed by the contemporary architect William Pereira. The **Harold B. Lee Library** holds nearly 2 million volumes. The university is sometimes called the "Y," perhaps in reference to the 320-foot-high letter made from whitewashed stone blocks precariously located 2,000 feet above the campus on the steepest part of the Wasatch Range. Students using pack horses put the letter in place in 1906. The Y is the second such hillside letter in the country and more than four times the height of the first, the Big C (1905) at the University of California at Berkeley. The hillside letter craze then spread to colleges and universities throughout the west.

LOCATION: University Avenue (Route 189) and 800 North Street. TELEPHONE: 801–378–4678.

Dominating the city center, the red-brick **Provo LDS Tabernacle** (50 South University Avenue), with a towering steeple and arched windows, was completed about 1885. The tabernacle's other tower, which made the building unsafe, was removed in 1920. The distinctive three-story brick-and-stone building called the **Knight Block** (20–24 North University) was built in 1900 by Jesse Knight, a

Mormon mining millionaire, who established, in the words of the writer Wallace Stegner, a string of "drinkless and smokeless and whoreless mining camps" and spent his last years as a benefactor of Brigham Young University. Another leading citizen, Reed Smoot, lived in the imposing Queen Anne–style **Reed Smoot Home** (183 East 1st South, private). The Mormon apostle and U.S. senator was coauthor of the 1930 protectionist Smoot-Hawley Tariff Act, which imposed the highest U.S. tariffs in history on manufactured products. After he was elected to the U.S. Senate in 1902, Smoot's connection with the Mormon church was scrutinized in a lengthy series of sensational hearings that turned up no conflict of interests. After they were over, Smoot was whimsically described by a fellow senator as "a polygamist who doesn't polyg."

The Utah War and the founding of Camp Floyd, the largest army post in the United States, in 1858 turned the small farming community of **Fairfield** into the third-largest town in Utah. The year before, General Albert Sidney Johnston, commanding about 2,500 troops, had been sent to Utah to quell what Washington perceived as a Mormon threat to federal authority, and Johnston set up camp here to avoid a clash with Brigham Young. Fairfield prospered while the soldiers stayed. In 1861, however, at the start of the Civil War, the camp closed and the town all but disappeared.

CAMP FLOYD AND STAGECOACH INN STATE PARK

Nothing remains of the 400-odd buildings that once made up Camp Floyd except the **Camp Floyd Military Cemetery,** where eighty-four soldiers are buried, and the rebuilt **Commissary Building.** The restored **Stagecoach Inn** was built after the arrival of troops by Fairfield's original white settler, John Carson, a Mormon whose inn has been described as "an island of decency" during the boisterous army occupation. The L-shaped two-story building of wood and adobe has a porch and gallery on the south side. In addition to the kitchen and dining room on the ground floor, there is a large recreation room, which was built as a dance hall for Mormon youth to keep them from less-desirable elements in town. General Johnston frequently stayed in the upstairs bedroom off the porch, as did

OPPOSITE: *Utah Senator Reed Smoot, co-author of the Smoot-Hawley Tariff Act, lived in this eclectic Queen Anne style house with Richardsonian Romanesque touches.*

Orrin Porter Rockwell and Bill Hickman, reputed leaders of the Mormon vigilantes, the Sons of Dan. The inn was a stagecoach stop for many years.

> LOCATION: Off Route 73 at North and West streets. HOURS: *Park:* 8–10 Daily. *Inn:* 11–5 Daily. FEE: Yes. TELEPHONE: 801–768–8932.

The Spanish explorers and Franciscan priests Silvestre Vélez de Escalante and Francisco Atanasio Domínguez were the first white men to pass through **Spanish Fork** in the Utah Valley on September 23, 1776. In the city park, a **statue** by the Utah sculptor Avaard Fairbanks commemorates the Domínguez-Escalante expedition. The town was settled by Mormons in 1850 and chartered in 1855. During the next five years Mormon converts from Iceland established the first permanent Icelandic community in the United States. The **Icelandic Monument** (895 East 300 South, 801–798–6264), a lighthouse-shaped tower, commemorates the settlement.

SPRINGVILLE

Settled by Mormons in 1850, Springville was the location of the bartering incident that began the Indian conflict known as the Walker War. On July 17, 1853, a Mormon woman traded an Indian squaw three pints of flour for three large trout; the Indians' dissatisfaction with the deal led to the conflict. The **William Bringhurst Home** (306 South 200 West, private), was built in 1856 of rock, adobe, and native pine with walls eighteen inches thick. Brigham Young usually slept here on his way from Salt Lake City to Saint George, where he had a winter home. The noted sculptor Cyrus Dallin built the house at **253 South 300 East** (private) for his mother; he was born in 1861 in a log cabin, no longer standing, on the corner. Dallin, who studied in Boston and Paris, is best known for his sympathetic studies of Indians. He returned to Boston in 1900.

Springville Museum of Art

This important collection began in 1903 when a Springville native, the painter John Hafen, presented the local high school with one of his paintings. The Mormon church sent Hafen and several other Utah artists to study in Paris in 1890 to prepare them to paint the murals for the Mormon temple in Salt Lake City. (In Paris, Hafen met Cyrus Dallin and a veritable colony of Utah artists. "Evenings we study anatomy," Hafen wrote home. "None of the Utah artists knows how to draw the big toe.") The Springville High School Art Gallery opened in 1907 with works by Hafen, Dallin, and other Utah artists, including Brigham Young's grandson, the sculptor Mahonri Young. The museum also has a collection of works by the non-Utah artist Rockwell Kent and a painting, *The Open Sea,* by the Provincetown-based seascapist Frederick Judd Waugh. The museum's spacious Mediterranean-style building was built by the WPA during the Depression.

> LOCATION: 126 East 400 South. HOURS: 10–5 Tuesday, Thursday–Saturday, 10–9 Wednesday, 2–5 Sunday. FEE: None. TELEPHONE: 801–489–9434.

PARK CITY

Soon after the discovery of silver in 1869 by three soldiers under the command of Colonel Patrick E. Connor, Park City became a booming, wide-open mining town in staid Mormon Utah; in 1884 the local editor complained of "too much promiscuous shooting on streets at night." George Hearst, father of William Randolph Hearst, was one of several well-known figures who started his career in Park City. In 1898 the town was virtually destroyed by fire, but the business district was quickly rebuilt. The old part of the city, businesses and residences alike, has been almost entirely restored and renovated. In the **Main Street Historic District,** the old city hall, first built in 1885 and rebuilt after the fire of 1898, is now the **Park City Museum** (528 Main Street, 801–649–0375). The museum includes a replica of a newspaper office with a linotype and printing press. The large cell of the territorial jail in the basement is where members of the Industrial Workers of the World were jailed in 1916 while trying to organize miners. The IWW symbol made with candle smoke is still on the wall. The narrow, two-story brick building at **434 Main Street** was designed by the noted Utah architect Richard K. A. Kletting for the Rocky Mountain Bell Telephone Company in 1898, when service began in Park City. The **Egyptian Theatre** (328 Main Street) opened on Christmas Eve in 1926 with the Zane Grey movie *Man of the Forest.* The Egyptian Revival building was modeled after Warner's

OVERLEAF: *The Wasatch Mountains extend north and south across the center of Utah, terminating near the middle of the state.*

Egyptian Theater in Pasadena, California. The **Alamo Saloon** (447 Main Street, 801–649–2380), a Mission-style building, has ornate decorative brickwork on the facade and an unusual brick vaulted ceiling inside. It was built in 1903 to house the Utah Independent Telephone Company, competitor of Rocky Mountain Bell.

The **Miners Hospital/Park City Library** (1354 Park Avenue, 801–649–8118), a large two-and-a-half-story brick Victorian building, was built in 1904 as Park City's first hospital. Before that time, injured miners and those suffering from consumption, the lung condition caused by breathing granular dust in the mines, had to go to Salt Lake City, thirty miles away. The miners' union raised the money for the building, and the miners donated their labor. The building was moved to its present location, restored, and converted into the town library in 1982.

There are no millionaires' mansions in Park City; those who made their fortunes from mining soon left to escape the noise and pollution of the city's smelters and stamp mills. The grandest Victorian house in town is the **Raddon House** (325 Park Avenue, private), a two-and-a-half-story frame home with a double porch and truncated hip roof. It was built in 1901 by Sam Raddon, the outspoken editor and publisher of the *Park Record*. **Saint Mary's of the Assumption Catholic Church** (121 Park Avenue) and the adjoining school building were built of stone blocks in 1884 after fire destroyed the original structures; the simple twin buildings with gable roofs sit side by side above the street on a plot held back by a stone retaining wall. Because the first miners were predominantly Irish, the Catholic church was the first to hold services in the camp. Here Mormons, in the minority, were victims of discrimination.

The neighboring towns of Heber City and Midway are located in the scenic Heber Valley, known locally as the Switzerland of America, both for its mountain scenery and for the large numbers of Swiss who settled here. **Heber City,** which is named for Heber Kimball, a counselor to Brigham Young, was settled in 1859. The **Wasatch Stake Tabernacle,** in a park on Main Street, was dedicated as a Mormon church in 1889. The sandstone structure with a central bell tower and cupola has been converted into Heber's city offices. The **Heber Amusement Hall** (90 North 100 West, 801–654–4920) is part of the tabernacle complex. The T-shaped sandstone structure, built in 1906, with a spring-mounted dance floor inside, has been converted into the Wasatch County Senior Citizen Center. On the road to Midway, **Pioneer Village** is a complex of pioneer-era buildings reconstructed for commercial use. The village's main attraction, the **Heber Creeper** (600 West 100 South, 801–654–2900), a recreational steam railroad, takes passengers on a thirty-two-mile round trip to Vivian Park in Provo Canyon. In **Midway,** the **Homestead Resort** (700 North Homestead Drive, 801–654–1102), still one of Utah's most popular and venerable resorts, was founded in 1886 as Schneitter's Hot Pots, a spa offering baths in the waters from the limestone springs found in the area. In town, the **Watkins-Coleman Home** (5 East Main Street, 801–654–1697), a house built in 1869 of hand-pressed adobe brick and decorated with hand-cut lacy bargeboard, was built by the Mormon bishop John Watkins, an architect and builder from England.

VERNAL

Before it was officially named Vernal in 1893, this town was known, among other names, as Ashley Center, for General William H. Ashley, who passed through on an exploring trip on the nearby Green River. John Wesley Powell made two surveying trips to the area in 1869 and 1871, and in 1873 settlers entered the valley to raise livestock. In 1879, after the Meeker Massacre in Colorado, a fort was built here for protection against the Indians.

In 1909 the bones of an apatosaurus were discovered in rock formations east of Vernal, an area now protected as Dinosaur National Monument. In Vernal, the **Utah Field House of Natural History State Park** (235 East Main Street, 801–789–3799) houses an excellent collection of fossils, models, and reconstructions of dinosaurs, as well as displays on prehistoric cultures and the Ute Indians. Fourteen life-size models of dinosaurs by Utah sculptor Elbert Porter are in the adjacent **Dinosaur Gardens.**

The **Daughters of Utah Pioneers Museum** (500 West and 200 South, 801–789–0288) is housed in a building attached to the former Uintah Stake Tithing Office. The stone building, built in 1887, was moved to its present location in 1960. In its well-displayed collection is an array of nearly 3,000 pioneer artifacts, including a variety of household items such as old oil lamps, butter churns, cooking stoves, clocks, glassware, crocks, clothing, dolls, large farm equipment, tools, and saddles. Also featured are the instruments and medicine cabinet of a pioneer doctor and undertaker, an early machine for making

Among the Fremont Indian petroglyphs in the Island Park section of Dinosaur National Monument is this figure of a man carrying a shield decorated with concentric circles.

ice-cream bars, and several hundred photographs. Across the street is the **Uintah Stake Tabernacle** (500 West 200 South), a handsome Colonial Revival brick building with an octagonal cupola. Construction began in 1900, and the building was finally paid for and dedicated in 1907 as a Mormon meetinghouse. The Daughters of Utah Pioneers also maintain the **Old Ashley Post Office** (2000 North 1365 West, 801–789–0288), a log cabin built in 1879 by Wilbur C. Britt, the first postmaster in the region. The cabin is constructed with wooden pegs and square nails. Once a week, carriers riding horseback or walking with the aid of snowshoes delivered the mail over the Uinta Mountains to and from Green River, Wyoming.

The **Bank of Vernal Building** (3 West Main Street) is also known as the Parcel Post Bank, because it was built in 1916 out of forty tons of individually wrapped bricks mailed by parcel post from Salt Lake City. Parcel post rates at the time were less than half of freight rates.

Until the rates were finally changed, farmers also took advantage of this discrepancy and often mailed farm products to market.

DINOSAUR NATIONAL MONUMENT

In 1909 Andrew Carnegie sent Dr. Earl Douglass to Utah because he wanted "something big" to put in the new wing of the Carnegie Museum in Pittsburgh. Douglass found an almost complete skeleton of an apatosaurus in a ledge near the Green River, and in the next fifteen years the Carnegie Museum removed over 350 tons of fossil bones from this quarry. To protect his finds, Douglass tried to stake a mining claim; when this failed, he succeeded in 1915 in having eighty acres declared a national monument. (In 1938 the monument was enlarged to more than 200,000 acres). The quarry face, where work continues to this day, is covered by the glass walls of the **Quarry Visitor Center.** The monument also has many examples of rock art created by the Fremont Indians, who occupied the area over 1,000 years ago. The **Cub Creek Archaeological Area** is particularly rich in petroglyphs, made by carving through the so-called desert varnish (magnesium oxide) covering the rock face. The distinctive trapezoidal figures have come to be known as the Vernal style.

The area of the Great Basin that now comprises the monument was first explored in 1825 by General William Ashley, a trapper and trader. John Wesley Powell, the renowned explorer and surveyor of the West, extensively investigated the area from 1869 to 1871 during his 900-mile expedition down the Green and Colorado rivers, which ultimately led to the Grand Canyon. By the turn of the century, ranchers and traders enticed by the beautiful scenery and clean water had established settlements in the region. A number of their homestead and ranch buildings still stand at the monument, including the log **Josie Morris Cabin.** Morris lived and ranched in the monument area from 1914 until her death in 1964. Also within the monument is Echo Park, which lies at the confluence of the Green and Yampa rivers; the park draws its name from the echoes that can be produced near the massive Steamboat Rock. More than half the monument is in the state of Colorado.

LOCATION: Route 149, 7 miles north of Jensen. HOURS: *Monument:* Always open. *Quarry Visitor Center:* June through August: 8–7 Daily; September through May: 8–4:30 Daily. FEE: Yes. TELEPHONE: 801–789–2115.

SOUTHERN UTAH

OPPOSITE: *West Mitten, one of the most distinctive buttes in Monument Valley.*

Brigham Young asserted that farming should be the primary Mormon occupation, but he also wanted the Deseret empire to be self-sufficient. So in 1851 he sent the Iron Mission, a contingent of experienced miners from Scotland and Wales, 250 miles south to Cedar City to tap the rich deposits in the area. Although they lacked the technical skill to succeed in this venture, the Mormons managed to establish a foothold in southern Utah. Saint George, the other major mission in the area (known as Utah's Dixie because of its short, mild winters) was established in 1861 when 250 families were sent there to grow cotton and raise silkworms. Although Brigham Young liked the town's climate so much he built a winter home there, the earliest settlers were less than charmed with the heat and the wind. One disillusioned poet wrote: "The wind like fury here does blow / That when we plant or sow, sir, / We place one foot upon the seed / And hold it till it grows, sir." Like their brethren in the north, the southern Mormons had to put up with Gentile—their name for nonbelievers—miners seeking precious minerals. After the strike at Silver Reef, that community grew overnight into the third-largest town in the Utah Territory. The Mormons generally were wary of outsiders. In 1857 the tensions between Mormons and emigrants who were hostile to them and trespassing on their land culminated in the massacre, carried out by Indians led by Mormons, of the Fancher Party, a California-bound wagon train of 120 men, women, and children, at Mountain Meadows near Saint George. A larger war between Mormons and Gentiles was barely prevented by skillful diplomacy. At nearby Orderville an experiment in communal enterprise known as the United Order, which did not prosper in other parts of the territory, thrived from 1875 to about 1886. Kanab, just a short distance to the south, was practically isolated from the outside world until the movie industry discovered that the surrounding scenery was the perfect backdrop for western movies. The choice was at least partly historically justified: Outlaws on the lam abounded in southern Utah.

Geographically, southern Utah comprises two distinct areas: the Great Basin and the Colorado Plateau. The Great Basin, which has no drainage or rivers running to the sea, cuts a diagonal across the southwestern part of the state, today roughly parallel to Route I-15, the main highway between Provo and Saint George. The southeastern part of the state is on the Colorado Plateau, a spectacular area of deep gorges and canyons that is drained by the Colorado River.

An 1898 photograph of the Thomas Potter Family and Smith Shop in Scofield, Utah, a coal mining town south of Manti. PAGES 394–395: *Lake Powell, formed when the Glen Canyon Dam was constructed in 1966.*

Only a few roads connect the two areas, with one cutting far into northern Arizona before emerging again in Utah's southeastern corner. In 1879–1880 Mormon colonists from Holden performed the stupendous engineering feat of cutting a road through and down the canyon wall at Hole-in-the-Rock to reach the Colorado River. The Glen Canyon Dam was built across the border in Arizona in 1966, and the land along the river behind it flooded to form Lake Powell, most of which is in Utah. The region has been preserved as the Glen Canyon National Recreation Area, one of a string of state and national parks that runs across southern Utah.

In prehistoric times southeastern Utah was inhabited by the Anasazi and Fremont people, who left drawings and carvings on cliff and canyon walls before mysteriously disappearing from their pueblos around A.D. 1300. By the time members of Coronado's party arrived in 1540, southern Utah was the land of the Ute Indians. In

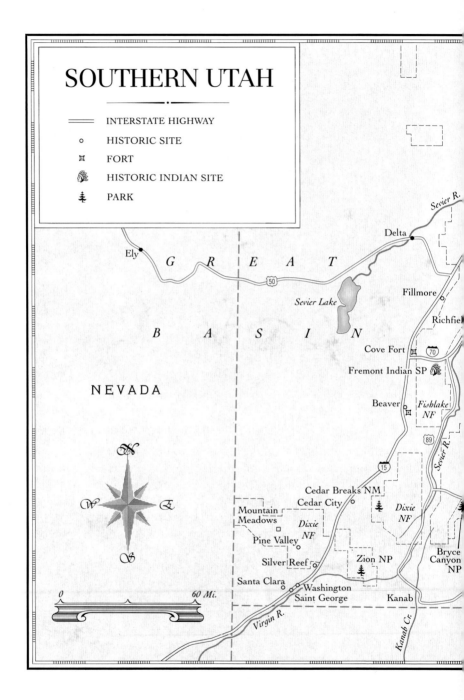

SOUTHERN UTAH

═══ INTERSTATE HIGHWAY

○ HISTORIC SITE

⊟ FORT

🪶 HISTORIC INDIAN SITE

🌲 PARK

Sevier R.

Ely

G R E A T

50

Delta

Fillmore

Sevier Lake

Richfie

B A S I N

Cove Fort ⊟

70

Fremont Indian SP 🪶

NEVADA

Beaver ○ | *Fishlake NF* ⊟

89

Sevier R.

N

W ✦ E

S

15

Cedar Breaks NM

Cedar City ○ 🌲 | *Dixie NF*

Mountain Meadows ⊡

Dixie NF

Pine Valley

Silver Reef ○

Santa Clara ○

Zion NP 🌲

Bryce Canyon NP

Washington

Saint George

Kanab

0   60 Mi.

Virgin R.

Kanab Cr.

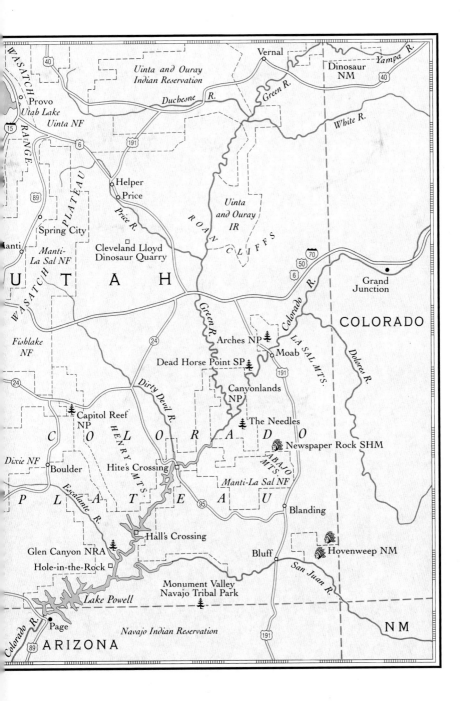

1776 the Franciscan friars Francisco Atanasio Domínguez and Silvestre Vélez de Escalante, seeking a route from Santa Fe to Monterey, California, crossed the Green River near Jensen and penetrated central Utah.

The early Mormon settlers were less than charmed with the prospect of eking out a living in a land that was mostly rock. In 1861 the *Deseret News* described the area as "measurably valueless, excepting for nomadic purposes, hunting grounds for Indians, and to hold the world together." The pioneers can be forgiven for being too concerned with survival to appreciate what was there: the kaleidoscope of colors in the landscape, the fast-flowing rivers, and the unique geological formations of rock eroded into twisted and dramatic shapes.

This chapter begins in Richfield and proceeds northward through Manti to Spring City. It then follows Route I-15 from Fillmore south

The Watchman, a peak in the southern end of Zion National Park, a region of cliffs and canyons named by a Mormon settler after the site of the city of David near Jerusalem.

to Saint George and continues eastward to Kanab. The route continues northward to Capitol Reef and then descends southward to Glen Canyon. The final portion proceeds northward from Monument Valley through Bluff to Moab and concludes in Helper.

FREMONT INDIAN STATE PARK

In 1983 highway construction uncovered the remnants of the largest village of the prehistoric Fremont people yet discovered; to preserve the discovery, the Fremont Indian State Park was established two years later. These people, thought to have lived in ways similar to the Anasazi of Colorado, Arizona, and New Mexico, disappeared over 1,000 years ago. The park's museum building displays examples of their distinctive dull-gray pottery, as well as pictographs, petroglyphs, and the unfired clay figurines peculiar to the Fremont. A pathway leads into Little Dog Canyon, where panels of petroglyphs are engraved with forms that appear to be deer, sheep, and people. There is also a replica of a Fremont pithouse and granary.

> LOCATION: Clear Creek Canyon, just off Route I-70, about 24 miles southwest of Richfield. HOURS: 9–6 Daily. FEE: Yes. TELEPHONE: 801–527–4631.

The year after they came to **Richfield** in 1864, the pioneers built Fort Omni, named for a character in the *Book of Mormon*. There is a campanile at 1st North and 2d West near the site. The adobe **Ralph Ramsay Home** (57 East 2d North, 801–896–6131) was built in 1874 by the woodcarver who created the original eagle for Salt Lake City's Eagle Gate. Ramsay also made furniture for Brigham Young's home.

MANTI

One of Utah's oldest towns, Manti was settled in November 1849 by Mormons who endured a hard winter in dugouts on the hillside or in wagons and tents. Brigham Young visited the settlement the following year and named it after a town in the *Book of Mormon*. Just a few months before he died, Young dedicated the site of the **Manti Temple,** a gleaming oolite limestone structure that took eleven years to complete. Perched above the town, the temple was designed by William Folsom, the self-taught architect of the Council House in Salt Lake City and other Mormon landmarks. Folsom was threat-

ened with arrest for polygamy during much of the construction, and he often appeared on the building site in disguise. Like all Mormon temples, the one at Manti is used for sacred ordinance work and ceremonies and is open only to church members in good standing.

SPRING CITY

Spring City was originally named Allred Settlement after James Allred, one of Joseph Smith's bodyguards, who led the first settlers here in 1852. In the years that followed, the settlement was also called Canal, Little Denmark, and Spring Town until Spring City was adopted in 1870. Once a busy highway and railroad town, Spring City retains many vestiges of a pioneer farming community—irrigation ditches, rows of Lombardy poplars, log and stone farm buildings, stone and picket fences, and many houses built prior to 1920 out of native rock, wood, and locally made bricks and adobe. In recent years many artists and craftspeople have restored Spring City buildings as homes and studios. The **Orson Hyde House** (209 South Main, 801–462–3404) was the Mormon apostle's residence from 1865 until his death in 1878. The oolite structure with its unusual quarter-round windows has springs in the basement, making the house a self-sufficient fortress during Indian attacks. Most of the Hyde outbuildings are also intact. Nearby, **Spring City Ward Chapel** (164 South Main), built between 1902 and 1911 of local quarry-faced ashlar, has a square entrance tower with an octagonal spire. The limestone **Old City Hall** (46 North Main, 801–462–2244) was constructed in 1893 as a school and converted to a city hall in 1900. **Red-Brick Elementary School** (1st East 40 South), built in 1899, served as an elementary school until 1959. Converted to a museum by the Daughters of Utah Pioneers, it displays pioneer artifacts from the community. **Judge Jacob Johnson House** (390 South 100 West), built around 1875, has been restored complete with his law office, carriage house, and orchard. Johnson, a local entrepreneur, was also a circuit judge and district attorney, and in 1902 he was elected to one term as a U.S. congressman. Across the street is the **Jens Peter Carlson House** (355 South 100 West, private). Carlson was a stone-mason who began the polished stone house in 1896 as a showcase for his work. The graves of Orson Hyde and several of his wives, and

OPPOSITE: *The Mormon Temple in Manti is constructed of native oolite limestone, which is easily cut in the quarry but hardens to a granite-like consistency when exposed to air. A block of this limestone was sent by Brigham Young to be included in the Washington Monument.*

The Gothic Revival Spring City Ward Chapel, designed by Richard C. Watkins of Provo, is constructed of oolite limestone quarried just west of the town. The octagonal tower is seventy-five feet high.

of James Allred and members of his family, lie one mile west of town at **Newer City Cemetery,** which dates to 1870. Many early settlers are buried at **Old Pioneer Cemetery** (200 North and 100 East), established in 1857.

FILLMORE

Brigham Young chose Fillmore as the site of the territorial capital in 1851 because it was at the approximate geographic center of the Utah Territory. The town and surrounding Millard County were named for President Millard Fillmore, a Mormon sympathizer. Architect Truman O. Angell's original plans for the statehouse called for an immense structure of four wings topped by a Moorish dome. Only one wing was built, in time for the opening of the territorial legislature in December 1855. In 1856 and 1857, the legislature met in Fillmore, only to adjourn almost immediately and return to Salt Lake City. In 1858 the legislature voted to move the capital back to Salt Lake City. The statehouse was restored and opened as a museum in 1930. Today known as the **Territorial Statehouse State Park** (50 West Capitol Avenue, 801–743–5316), the two-story red-stone building with a Greek Revival cornice is owned by the state and operated by Utah State Parks and Recreation. On display are artifacts and household items such as an early spinning wheel and decorative wax flowers made by pioneer women. Paiute Indian artifacts include a *tikenagen* (baby basket) and pottery. The Paiute chief Kanosh, a Mormon convert, was friendly to the first settlers and married an Indian woman who had been a maid in Brigham Young's household. Among the paintings in the legislative hall are works by Donald Beauregard, an artist born in Fillmore, including his first oil painting, a view of the Fillmore Flour Mill.

COVE FORT

On the day that the transcontinental telegraph line was completed in 1861, Brigham Young ordered a trans-Utah line from Logan to Saint

Old Cove Fort, built in 1867 to guard the Deseret Telegraph Line from Indian attacks.

George. Because of the shortage of materials created by the Civil War, the 500-mile Deseret Telegraph line was not built until 1866–1867. **Cove Fort** (off I-15) was constructed in 1867 at a cost of $20,000 to protect the line from Indians. Eighteen-foot-high walls built of volcanic rock enclose living quarters, a telegraph office, a stage office, and a courtyard 100 feet square. The builders took the precaution of filling the hollow wooden gates with sand to extinguish flaming arrows. The telegraph line was one of the great achievements of the early Mormon settlers. A Western Union employee who supervised the construction later wrote: "Not a man on this line ever worked a telegraph line before, the line was strung and put into operation in the middle of the winter. . . . I think the working of the same almost a miracle."

BEAVER

The Mormons who settled here in 1856 raised sheep and established a large woolen mill. Discovery of minerals in the San Francisco Mountains to the west of Beaver about 1870 drew miners and other non-Mormons into the region. To keep the peace between Mormons and Gentiles and to protect against hostile Indians, federal troops were summoned in 1872. The next year **Fort Cameron** was built to house 250 soldiers at the mouth of Beaver Canyon. Only the **barracks** (one mile east of town on Route 153) still stand. Construction of the **Beaver County Courthouse** (Center Street and 1st East) was begun in 1877 and completed in 1882. The three-story red-brick structure, with stamped-metal and cast-iron trim and a clock tower, was designed by William Stokes, a one-time U.S. marshal of Beaver. The basement is built of black volcanic rock hauled by ox team from the mountains east of Beaver. The clock was shipped from Massachusetts and is original to the building. In the past, citizens of Beaver were assigned hourly turns to use water, and the striking of the courthouse clock proved a useful signal that someone's turn had arrived. The courthouse, which was used as a court for almost 100 years, now houses a Daughters of Utah Pioneers **Pioneer Museum** and an art gallery. Among the many interesting private homes built of black and pink volcanic rock is the **Marcus L. Shepherd Home** (210 East 2d North), erected around 1870. It has been described as "a prime example of a two-story brick Greek Revival structure in Utah." Built by a polygamist, it still has two kitchens.

BRYCE CANYON NATIONAL PARK

Situated on the eastern rim of the high Paunsaugant Plateau, Bryce Canyon ranges in altitude from 6,600 to 9,100 feet. The canyon resulted from sediment deposits 60 million years ago in lakes, rivers, and streams. These sediments were uplifted by a powerful force, creating rock formations on a grand scale. Water, ice, and wind have eroded the soft and hard rocks into decorative forms. Artifacts found at the canyon suggest that the nomadic Paiutes used the region as a hunting ground. Exploration of the area began in the mid-nineteenth century; two early homesteaders, Ebenezer and Mary Bryce, gave the canyon its name. Bryce Canyon was designated a national park in 1928 and encompasses 35,835 acres of vegetation, wildlife, and strange rock formations.

> LOCATION: Route 12, east of Route 89. HOURS: *Visitor Center:* June through October: 8–4:30 Daily; November through May: 8–8 Daily. FEE: Yes. TELEPHONE: 801–834–5322.

ZION NATIONAL PARK

This national park surrounds Zion Canyon, in the middle of the "stairway" between Bryce Canyon and Grand Canyon. All three were formed from sedimentary rocks deposited here 225 to 53 million years ago by vast seas. The walls of Zion Canyon were carved by the Virgin River, cutting its way through the Markagunt Plateau. The Anasazi are thought to be the first to inhabit Zion, around A.D. 750, and remains of a large dwelling were found in the nearby Parunuweap Canyon. The Anasazi farmed in what is now the southern part of the park, and the Fremont worked the northern section. More than 100 miles of trails traverse the 147,000-acre park.

> LOCATION: Off Route 9, east of Route I-15. HOURS: *Visitor Center:* Memorial Day through Labor Day: 8 a.m.–9 p.m. Daily; Labor Day through Memorial Day: 8–5 Daily. FEE: Yes. TELEPHONE: 801–772–3256.

OVERLEAF: *Bryce Canyon's Paiute name means "Red rocks standing like men in a bowl-shaped canyon." Ebenezer Bryce, the Mormon settler for whom it was named, said it was "a hell of a place to lose a cow."*

The ruins of the Rice Bank in Silver Reef, where between 1877 and 1903 more than nine million ounces of silver were removed from the mines.

CEDAR CITY

Brigham Young sent "miners and manufacturers" from Wales, Scotland, and England to settle Cedar City in 1851 and to tap the coal and iron deposits in the region. The so-called Iron Mission eventually failed when the railroad brought cheaper iron to Utah, but the town continued to grow as an agricultural center. A diorama of the original iron foundry is among the exhibits at the **Iron Mission State Park/Museum** (585 North Main Street, 801–586–9290). The museum also displays more than 100 horse-drawn vehicles, including a Stanhope phaeton and a Studebaker white-top wagon, collected by Gronway Parry, one of the Parry brothers of Kanab who brought tourism and the motion picture industry to southern Utah.

The **Mormon First Ward Chapel,** also known as **Old Rock Church,** was built in the 1930s near the corner of Main and Center of local rock—including iron, copper, and gold ore—gathered by church members. The interior is finished in red cedar, also a local product. The **Southern Utah State College,** located on 100 acres in

Rusted ore cars at Silver Reef, which has been a ghost town since the 1940s, when the last company mining there ceased operations due to a drop in silver prices.

the heart of town, was founded in 1897; two of its most notable buildings, **Old Main** (1898) and the **Old Administration Building** (1904), date from this period.

SILVER REEF

After silver was discovered here in 1868, this hillside town, originally known as Bonanza City, quickly grew into the largest settlement in southern Utah, with about 1,500 people. Although the silver boom brought prosperity, the local Mormons resented the rowdy miners (many came from notorious Pioche, Nevada), so when the miners threatened to outnumber—and outvote—the Mormons, apostle Erastus Snow moved the town line a few miles east to take in enough Mormons to retain control. In its heyday the population included a number of Chinese, who, in keeping with their customs, would place food on the graves of their dead. According to legend, the local Paiute, while prowling around at night, developed a taste for Chinese cuisine. All that remains of the town today is the ruins of the **Rice Bank** and the restored **Wells Fargo & Company Express**

Building, which was built with sandstone blocks, arched entrance-ways and metal doors, in 1877.

PINE VALLEY

The forests around this high mountain town produced the lumber used for the organ in the Mormon Tabernacle in Salt Lake City and by many of the early settlements in southern Utah. The **Pine Valley Chapel** was built in 1868 by Ebenezer Bryce, for whom Bryce Canyon National Park is named. Bryce, like so many early Mormon builders, possessed a talent for architecture. A shipwright from Australia, he put together the walls of the two-and-a-half-story meetinghouse on the ground, then hoisted them into position and fastened them with wooden pegs and rawhide.

MOUNTAIN MEADOWS

A **marker** (off Route 18) in this pleasant, grassy valley indicates the location of a bloody incident in 1857, the massacre by Mormons and Indians of the Fancher Party, a group of California-bound emigrants passing through Utah. Some 120 men, women, and older children died in the massacre, which writer Wallace Stegner has called "the capstone to a structure of hatred and misunderstanding that had been building for a long time." The party included a number of rowdy Missourians who shouted insults at the Mormons and named one of their oxen Brigham Young. At the time a federal army was approaching Utah from the east, and the Mormons' hysteria was fueled by the emigrants' threats to return with an armed force once they had reached California.

The Mormons approached the Fancher Party under a flag of truce with an offer to escort the emigrants to safety from an Indian attack that seemed imminent. After the emigrant men had laid down their arms, they were killed by the Mormon militiamen. The Indians, led by the Mormons, then slaughtered the women and children. Only seventeen children, too young to remember details of the massacre, were spared. Afterwards the local community closed ranks, and it took the federal government twenty years to obtain a single conviction in the affair. After his first trial ended in a hung jury, John D. Lee, the Mormon in charge of Indian affairs in southern Utah, was convicted and sentenced to death. Before he was executed at Mountain Meadows on March 23, 1877, Lee accused Young of betrayal and wrote: "Young has sacrificed me through his lust for power." The Mountain Meadows massacre also added to the Mormon reputation for zealotry and fanaticism, leading the San Francisco *Bulletin* to call for "a crusade . . . against Utah which will crush out this beastly heresy forever."

SANTA CLARA

Jacob Hamblin, a Mormon missionary renowned for his success in keeping peace with the Indians, settled here in 1859. As described by the explorer Major J. W. Powell, Hamblin was "a silent, reserved man, and when he speaks, it is in a slow, quiet way that inspires great awe. . . . When he finishes a measured sentence, the chief repeats it, and they all give a solemn grunt." Hamblin died in 1886 while in hiding to avoid prosecution for practicing polygamy. The red-sandstone **Jacob Hamblin House** (Route 91, 801–673–2161) was built solidly in 1863 to withstand Indian attacks. It is a prime example of frontier construction, with chimneys at each end and an

The dining table in the Jacob Hamblin House is set in traditional Mormon pioneer fashion. Plates were stored upside down on the table between meals, and chairs were placed facing out, so that family members could kneel in front of them while saying prayers before each meal.

overhanging shingle roof supported by four ground-to-roof posts; the floor of the second-story balcony is slanted so drying fruits and herbs would receive more sun. There is a large room upstairs that was used for sleeping, domestic chores, and social occasions, and the house is furnished with simple pioneer pieces.

SAINT GEORGE

Although the Saint George region is called Utah's Dixie because of its mild winters, the first contingent of 309 families, sent there by Brigham Young in 1861, complained vigorously of the sand, wind, and heat. "I believe we were close to hell, for Dixie is the hottest place I ever was in," a visitor wrote a few years later. Brigham Young wanted the Mormon state to be completely self-sufficient, so the colonists were instructed to grow not only cotton but also "sugar, grapes, tobacco, figs, almonds, olive oil, and such other useful articles as the Lord has given us." The cotton-growing enterprise was successful (fifty tons of seed in 1862) through the end of the Civil War, when the Utah product could no longer compete in the marketplace. In recent years Saint George has grown rapidly, but the center of town still contains many homes and public buildings of architectural and historic interest.

Saint George Temple

At the ground-breaking on November 9, 1871, Brigham Young and the Mormon apostle Erastus Snow, leader of the Saint George community, raised their right hands and shouted: "Hosanna! Hosanna! Hosanna! To God and the Lamb. Amen! Amen!" The temple, Utah's first, took six years to complete. To establish a solid bedrock in the swampy ground for the structure, the builders pounded down volcanic rock with a huge pile driver devised from an old cannon filled with lead. When the cannon bounced three times, the crew knew it had hit bedrock. In 1874 Young and Snow placed a box containing a bottle of Dixie wine and other items in the building's southeast corner. The temple was dedicated on April 6, 1877.

The Saint George Temple cost nearly $1 million to build. Mormons from all over the territory were called on forty-day missions to work on the construction; local men gave one day out of ten

OPPOSITE: *The Saint George Temple, the first Mormon temple in the west, was completed in April 1877, just four months before the death of Brigham Young.*

to the job. Oxen teams hauled 17,000 tons of hand-quarried rock—black volcanic and sandstone—to the site; lumber came from Mount Trumbull eighty miles away. The eminent Mormon architect Truman O. Angell designed the gleaming white stuccoed building, which covers nearly an acre. The height of the 141-foot-long structure is 84 feet to the top of the parapet and 175 to the top of the weathervane on the tower. With its buttresses, crenelated roofline, and fortresslike appearance, the building was an obvious symbol of stability to the settlers who were still struggling to survive in this harsh land. Like all Mormon temples, Saint George's is closed to non-Mormons, but there is a visitor center with guided tours of the grounds and exhibits on the building and its construction.

LOCATION: 250 East 400 South. TELEPHONE: 801–673–3533.

Saint George Tabernacle

This handsome vermilion-sandstone meetinghouse is everything that Brigham Young wanted it to be: "a good, substantial, commodious well furnished meeting house, one large enough to comfortably seat at least 2,000 persons, . . . an ornament to your city, and a credit to your energy and enterprise." The cornerstones of the building were laid on June 1, 1863; work was completed thirteen years later. In appearance much like a New England church, the building has a steeple 140 feet high, an inside gallery, and two self-supporting interior staircases. Payment for most of the work and materials was made in commodities such as grain or molasses from the local tithing office. The installation of a clock and bell in the square tower in 1872 brought a new regularity to life in Saint George. Zaidee Walker Miles wrote: "From now on people were born by the Clock; they died by the Clock. . . . We went to Church on time, came home on time, opened and closed parties by its time. Our night ramblings were stopped by the pointing hand of the Clock and the clear ring of the Bell."

LOCATION: Main and Tabernacle streets. HOURS: 11–4 Daily. FEE: None. TELEPHONE: 801–673–5181.

Brigham Young Winter Home

During his frequent visits to Saint George, Brigham Young discovered that the temperate climate of Southern Utah relieved his rheumatism, and he began to spend more time there, planning and supervising the construction of the temple and conducting other business. He purchased a house in 1870 and installed one of his wives, Lucy Bigelow, as hostess to receive his many visitors. When her health began to fail he built the present, unpretentious adobe "winter home" and moved in with a younger, childless wife, Amelia Folsom, to act as official hostess, in December 1873. "Mother's heart twisted with sorrow," Lucy's daughter wrote, "at the thought of her dear husband coming down to spend his winters in another woman's home. [After all] she was human—she was a woman."

The back of the two-story dwelling was built in 1869; the large front section with a wooden porch and balcony adorned with Victorian fretwork was added later. A one-story white adobe building on the north end was built in 1876 as Young's office.

LOCATION: 89 West 200 North Street. HOURS: 9–9 Daily. FEE: None. TELEPHONE: 801–673–2517.

The two-story brick **Washington County Pioneer Courthouse** (97 East Saint George Boulevard, 801–673–8824) has a classical portico and a foundation of basalt lava rock. The building was constructed between 1867 and the early 1870s. A scaffolding and trapdoor designed for hangings were built into the cupola. Today the building houses the chamber of commerce and other town offices. To the rear of the courthouse, the **Daughters of Utah Pioneers Museum** (133 North 1st Street East, 801–628–7274) displays a diverse collection of items from the early days of the community, including an exhibit on silk manufacturing in the Mormon Dixie, a foot-operated dentist's drill, and an organ from the home of Erastus Snow, the leader of the first Mormon community.

Northeast of Saint George in **Washington** is the well-restored **Washington Cotton Factory** (375 West Telegraph Street, 801–673–0375). The long two-and-a-half-story building, with peaked dormer windows in the center of the east and west sides of the roof, was built in 1865–1866. Although it is now used for private receptions and community events, it is worth seeing as a vestige of the cotton industry in Utah's Dixie.

KANAB

After the Tom Mix film *Deadwood Coach* was filmed here in 1924, this small, isolated Mormon community rapidly grew into the movie-making capital of Utah. Here producers found breathtaking desert scenery as well as horses and extras, some of whom became accomplished stuntmen. Much of the credit for attracting Hollywood film crews goes to the Parry brothers—Chauncey, Gronway, and Whit—who opened a small motel in 1931 and, as business increased, let it grow into the Colonial-style **Parry Lodge** (89 East Center Street). Photographs of John Wayne, Glenn Ford, Charlton Heston, Barbara Stanwyck, Ava Gardner, and other stars who stayed here line the dining room wall. According to one chronicler, in the late 1930s and 1940s, "Kanab had the hectic air of one of Hollywood's busiest backlots, hardly owning up to its seeming environmentally imposed destiny as a quiet Utah border town." More than 300 films were made in Kanab. In 1912 Zane Grey came to Kanab to research his book, *Riders of the Purple Sage.*

There are a number of historic houses in town. The **Heritage House Museum** (100 South Main Street) was built out of red rock and brick in 1894 by Henry Bowman, one of Kanab's original settlers. The house contains furniture and artifacts from the community. The Mormons built a fort in Kanab in 1867–1868.

About fifteen miles east of town on Route 89 a historic marker indicates the location of **Paria,** meaning "muddy water," the first settlement (1865) in the area. An unimproved road behind the turnout for the marker leads to a Hollywood ghost town, a Western street of false-front buildings that looks as if its inhabitants had just vacated. It was used to film episodes of the "Gunsmoke" television series.

BOULDER

This 1889 settlement takes its name from the volcanic boulders found on the side of Boulder Mountain. Until a highway was built in 1935, Boulder was accessible only by pack train from Escalante, thirty-five miles to the southwest.

OPPOSITE: *Sandstone formations in Capitol Reef National Park, in prehistoric times a tidal flat, resemble waves that have hardened into stone.*

Anasazi State Park

This state park is on the site of a large frontier community of Anasazi who occupied for about 150 years from in A.D. 1050 to A.D. 1200. The community disappeared about the same time other Anasazi settlements were abandoned. The village was excavated from 1958 to 1959 and later reburied for protection. At the state park is a replica of a six-room Anasazi dwelling and a museum displaying many of the artifacts found here as well as exhibits about the site. Some of the ruins have been stabilized, and a self-guided tour leads through the site.

> LOCATION: Route 12. HOURS: Mid-May through mid-September: 8–6 Daily; mid-September through mid-May: 9–5 Daily. FEE: Yes. TELE-PHONE: 801–335–7308.

CAPITOL REEF NATIONAL PARK

This national park of rock eroded to fantastic forms and colors takes its name from a high reef (or barrier) shaped like the dome on the

Burr Trail, a series of narrow switchbacks, provides access to the top of Waterpocket Fold in Capitol Reef National Park. It was originally used to move cattle to summer grazing areas on Boulder Mountain.

U.S. Capitol. Fremont Indians lived along the Fremont River for about 400 years, and their petroglyphs depicting bighorn sheep and human forms can be seen carved in the rocks along the river. The Fremont people stored corn and beans in bins made from wood and rock, and these structures, preserved by their protected locations, are visible along some trails. In 1872 a surveying party belonging to the John Wesley Powell expedition named the Fremont River after John Charles Frémont, who had crossed its headwaters twenty years earlier, and later the ancient peoples were given the same name by archaeologists. Only some southern Paiute were living in the region when the Mormons arrived in the 1800s and founded the town of **Fruita,** now within the confines of the park. The Mormons planted orchards here and supplied travelers until the village was acquired by the National Park Service in the 1960s. The **Fruita Schoolhouse,** a one-room log structure built in 1897, still stands. Capitol Reef was made a national monument in 1937 and a national park in 1971, when a large section known as the **Waterpocket Fold** was added to the preserve.

LOCATION: Route 24; Visitor Center and Headquarters at Fruita.
HOURS: *Visitor Center:* Memorial Day through Labor Day: 8–7 Daily; Labor Day through Memorial Day: 8–4:30 Daily. *Park:* Always open. FEE: Yes. TELEPHONE: 801–425–3791.

GLEN CANYON
NATIONAL RECREATION AREA

Although the headquarters of the Glen Canyon region is at Page, Arizona, almost all of Lake Powell, the magnificent body of water with fingerlike branches reaching up its tributaries, lies within Utah. The 200-mile-long artificial lake twists its way north from Glen Canyon Dam, with a shoreline ten times its length, or almost 2,000 miles. The lake was created when the Colorado River was dammed in the late 1950s, and its waters cover a network of spectacularly scenic canyons and untold remnants of prehistoric cultures.

The harsh region was inhabited until about A.D. 1300 by the Pueblo cultures of the Anasazi and Fremont Indians. The Domínguez–Escalante party, the first European-Americans in Utah, forded the river at the **Crossing of the Fathers.** In 1869 a Mormon militiaman eloquently described the area: "It is rock around, rocks above, rocks beneath, rocks in chasms, rocks in towers, rocks in ridges, rocks everywhere; it is, in fact, all rock; what little sand there may be is decomposed rock." Glen Canyon was also the site of an epic of Mormon colonization, the perilous crossing through Hole-in-the-Rock by Mormon settlers in 1879. That year 230 Mormons from southwestern Utah were "called" to cross the state and settle in the vicinity of the San Juan River. The pioneers chose a direct but unexplored route and, when they reached the Colorado River, found themselves at the abyss of Glen Canyon. By then it was too late in the season to turn back, so they blasted a notch through a fifty-foot cliff and built a perilously steep road down to the Colorado River, a drop of 1,800 feet in three-quarters of a mile. The party's eighty wagons were lowered with their rear wheels locked and a dozen or more men hanging on to chains and ropes attached to a wagon to slow it down. After a hazardous crossing of the Colorado on rafts they had made, the pioneers struggled on to the site of Bluff, on the San Juan River. **Hole-in-the-Rock** can be reached by a dirt road from Route 12, although the

Old wagons at Goulding's Trading Post, a Monument Valley institution established by Harry Goulding, who came to the valley to raise sheep, in 1923.

lower part is submerged beneath the surface of Lake Powell. Travelers continued to use Hole-in-the-Rock and also **Halls Crossing,** now the site of a marina farther upstream, until a far better crossing point, **Hites Crossing,** still farther north, was discovered. It was named after Cass Hite, a prospector who built a rock shelter here in the 1880s. Reports of Hite's gold strikes sparked a major gold rush in 1893, and when these reports turned out to be false Hite was forced to hide from vengeful miners for two years. There is now a marina at Hites Crossing where Route 95 crosses the Colorado River.

MONUMENT VALLEY NAVAJO TRIBAL PARK

Perched on the Arizona/Utah line within the Navajo Indian Reservation, Monument Valley has been a Navajo tribal park since 1959. This 29,816-acre expanse of mesas, buttes, cliffs, gullies, and canyons is so arid that it can barely sustain a few sheepherders, but its beauty has drawn tourists and filmmakers, most notably the director John Ford, who made several westerns here, beginning with *Stagecoach* in 1938. Guided tours leave from the visitor center, and a seventeen-mile drive along unpaved roads passes such geological phenomena as **Elephant Butte, John Ford's Point, North Window,** and **The Thumb.** The well-known **Goulding's Trading Post,** established in 1923, is located just west of the park. The founder, Harry Goulding, persuaded John Ford to bring his film crew to the valley.

> LOCATION: *Visitor Center:* 4 miles southeast of Route 163; junction 20 miles south of Mexican Hat, 28 miles north of Kayenta. HOURS: May through September: 7 AM–8 PM Daily; October through April: 8–5 Daily. FEE: Yes. TELEPHONE: 801–727–3287.

BLUFF

Bluff was founded in 1880 by Mormon pioneers who made the epic descent of Hole-in-the-Rock and crossing of the Colorado. They came to convert the Indians and to establish a Mormon foothold in southeast Utah. "The net result of that unbelievably toilsome trip," wrote Wallace Stegner in *Mormon Country,* "was one pin on the map of empire; one settlement, Bluff . . . one struggling constantly-unsuccessful colony from which the colonists asked more than once to be

released." There are a number of distinctive pioneer buildings to be seen by driving through town and a **pioneer cemetery** off Route 191.

HOVENWEEP NATIONAL MONUMENT

This small but archaeologically and historically rich national monument is located on the Utah-Colorado line. The best and most accessible of the six groups of masonry towers and pueblos, **Square Tower Ruin**, is in Utah. *Hovenweep* is a Ute word meaning "deserted valley." Although Cajon Mesa, on which Hovenweep is located, was probably visited by nomadic hunters as far back as 14,000 years ago, the Anasazi in about A.D. 500 were the first prehistoric people to settle in villages and grow crops. The Anasazi stayed until the year 1300; why they left and what happened to them remain a mystery. After 1150 the population concentrated at the heads of the many canyons in the area, where they built massive masonry pueblos around canyon rims and tall and square, D-shaped, or circular towers that, even in ruins, are the architectural wonders of the monument. The sturdy construction, their beauty, and their reasons for being have caused intrigued experts to speculate that the towers were used for food storage, ceremonies, defense, communication, astronomical observation, or a combination of many functions.

There is a small visitor and ranger center at the Square Tower Ruin. This group includes the well-preserved **Hovenweep Castle,** consisting of two wings, several towers, and ceremonial kivas. Others in the group are **Hovenweep House, Square Tower,** and **Talus Pueblo.** Trails lead to the other groups—**Cajon Ruins,** also in Utah, and in Colorado, **Holly Ruins, Hackberry Canyon, Cutthroat Castle,** and **Goodman Point.**

> LOCATION: Route 262 to Hatch Trading Post, then 16 miles of graded dirt road to the monument. HOURS: 8–4:30 Daily. FEE: None. TELEPHONE: 303–529–4461.

BLANDING

An irrigation project bringing water from the Abajo Mountains brought the first settlers to Blanding in 1905. The town was named

OPPOSITE: Hovenweep House, the ruin of a large semicircular structure that may have sheltered some fifty families during the period of Anasazi occupation, now a part of the Square Tower Ruin group in Hovenweep National Monument.

Grayson until an eastern millionaire, Thomas Bicknell, offered a library to any town in Utah that would take his name. Both Grayson and the town of Thurber accepted the offer. Thurber got Bicknell's name, Grayson became Blanding (Mrs. Bicknell's maiden name), and both towns got half a library. The last Indian war in the nation started in Blanding in 1923 when the Ute chief "Old Posey" helped two Indian cattle thieves to escape. The conflict consisted of several clashes between the Indians and a posse during which one of the escapees was killed and Posey mortally wounded.

Edge of the Cedars State Park

The first white settlers discovered the remains of this Anasazi village, inhabited from A.D. 750 to 1200, in 1905. From 1969 to 1972 archaeologists from Weber State College in Ogden excavated and stabilized the site. The six habitations and ceremonial complexes include the remains of a great kiva, which was used as a community center and for ceremonies. Its large size indicates that Edge of the Cedars might have been a ceremonial center for a larger area. The museum, built of native stone, opened in 1978. Among the well-displayed exhibits is a remarkable collection of Anasazi pottery produced over 700 years. It includes storage and ceremonial objects; kitchen vessels, including ollas, or water jars, with concave bottoms so they could easily be carried on the head; duck pots and bird effigies probably used for ceremonies; and an assortment of corrugated pottery for cooking that was produced by pinching the coils as they were laid down. Excavations and stabilization of the site are ongoing.

> LOCATION: 660 West 400 North. HOURS: Mid-May through mid-September: 9–6 Daily; mid-September through mid-May: 9–5 Daily. FEE: Yes. TELEPHONE: 801–678–2238.

En route to the area of Canyonlands known as Needles, Route 211 passes a remarkable collection of rock carvings at **Newspaper Rock State Historical Monument.** More than 350 tantalizing and mysterious petroglyphs are crammed together on the smooth rock face

OPPOSITE: *The Five Faces in Davis Canyon, one of three groups of Fremont pictographs using the face motif in the Canyonlands National Park.* OVERLEAF: *Anasazi ruins in a cave within Canyonlands National Park. Evidence of Anasazi habitation is found throughout the southeastern section of the park.*

under a protective overhang. Scholars believe that the images were produced over a period of 3,000 years by the prehistoric Archaic, Basket Maker, Anasazi, and Fremont peoples; by the Ute and Navajo; and even by white settlers. In Navajo the panel is called Tse' Hane', or "rock that tells a story."

CANYONLANDS NATIONAL PARK

This spectacularly scenic 337,570-acre park is divided into three districts by the Green and Colorado rivers. John Wesley Powell, one of the first white men to navigate the rivers, first in 1869 and then in 1871, wrote: "Wherever we look there is but a wilderness of rocks; deep gorges where the rivers are lost below cliffs and towers and pinnacles; and ten thousand strangely carved forms in every direction; and beyond them, mountains blending with the clouds."

The Fremont and the Anasazi peoples, hunted and farmed along the rivers from about A.D. 1000 to 1250. The walls of the park's **Horseshoe Canyon** contain superb examples of rock art, probably carved by the Fremont Indians but possibly by the earlier Barrier Canyon people. There are ruins of Anasazi pueblos and granaries at **Salt Creek.** The first known trapper in the region was Denis Julien, who signed his name and the date—1836—on the river canyons. In 1859 explorer Captain John Macomb traveled overland through the area. His journal keeper described the geologically unique area of pointed rock spires known as **Needles**: "battlemented towers of colossal but often beautiful proportions, closely resembling elaborate structures of art."

After ranchers began to graze cattle along the rivers in the 1870s, the confusing geography of the canyonlands made natural hideouts for rustlers and other outlaws. Butch Cassidy and his Wild Bunch hid out in the 1880s and 1890s at Robber's Roost, a large area west of the park, and a horse thief named Cap Brown used the area to corral his stolen mounts as early as 1874. Unconfirmed reports that loot hidden by the Wild Bunch is still buried in Robber's Roost continue to draw treasure seekers. Canyonlands became a national park in 1964 due to the efforts of Stewart Udall, secretary of the interior under Presidents John Kennedy and Lyndon Johnson.

LOCATION: *Visitor Center:* 125 West 200 South in Moab. HOURS: *Park:* Always open; *Visitor Center:* 8–4:30 Monday–Friday. FEE: Yes. TELEPHONE: 801–259–7164.

MOAB

Near the trail of the Escalante expedition of 1776, and at one of the best crossings of the Colorado River, Moab was first settled in 1855 by Mormon missionaries who were driven away by Indian raids. The Mormons returned in the late 1870s. Tucked in an oasislike setting with acres of fruit trees right in the center of town, Moab takes its name from a biblical kingdom east of the Dead Sea known for its remoteness. The settlers' problems with Indians continued until late in the century. In 1881 a band of renegade Indians who had killed a rancher in Colorado ambushed a pursuing posse near Moab. The mass grave of the eight white men who were killed is today marked by a headstone at the **Pinhook Battleground,** a national landmark located off the La Sal Road in the **Manti–La Sal National Forest.**

In the 1950s Moab quadrupled in size after it became the center of an intense but short-lived uranium boom. Although prospec-

Three stuntmen seemingly fall to certain death into the middle of a buffalo stampede, during the filming of How the West was Won *in 1962. This publicity still is now in the collection of the Hollywood Stuntmen's Hall of Fame in Moab.*

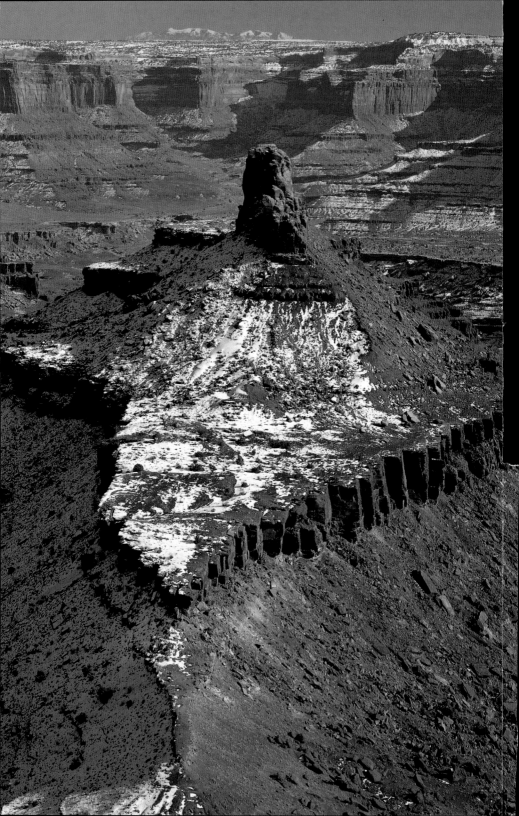

tors had been looking for uranium since about the turn of the century, the bonanza did not begin until 1952 when a young and virtually destitute geologist named Charles Steen staked several unpromising claims and purchased a dilapidated drilling rig in a desperate attempt to mine them. On the day his equipment gave out on his Mi Vida claim, Steen happened to test that day's cores with a Geiger counter and found them loaded with uranium. The discovery set off a uranium rush and a period of intense stock speculation. By 1956, however, the rush was over, although uranium mining in the Moab area continues. Steen became a benefactor of Moab, and he was given to grand gestures such as throwing parties for the entire town. The modern **Charles A. Steen House** (North Highway 191), known as **Mivida,** is located high on a hill with a splendid view of the valley and the Colorado River. It is now a restaurant. Steen and his wife lived in the house for about ten years. Many of Moab's other historic buildings have been adapted to commercial use. The **Arthur Taylor House** (North Highway 191), also a restaurant, was built in 1896 by Taylor, who brought sheep and cattle into the region in the late 1800s. The two-story home, with its sandstone block foundation, was built with local clay. In the center of town, Moab's oldest commercial building, the **Old Hammond Store Building** (11 East 100 North), was built in 1887 by merchants and later served as the town post office. In February 1989 the building burned, leaving only the adobe shell. The **Old Courthouse and Jail** (103 North Main), built in 1892, also did duty as a post office and stagecoach headquarters. The **Dan O'Laurie Museum** (East Center Street, 801–259–7985) has exhibits on the early explorers, trappers, and missionaries and a display about transportation in the region from early settlement to the present. One exhibit re-creates a 1907 kitchen from a Moab home. The museum is named for its chief benefactor, an associate of Charles Steen in the uranium mining business.

The 1925 **Old LDS Church** has been converted into Moab's latest tourist attraction and museum, the **Hollywood Stuntmen's Hall of Fame** (111 East 100 North, 801–259–6100), housing photographs, costumes, special equipment, and a series of dioramas explaining how certain stunts are performed and special effects

OPPOSITE: *Dead Horse Point State Park, east of Canyonlands National Park, preserves a promontory rising 2,000 feet above a large bend in the Colorado River.*

achieved. There is a screening room where action films are shown, and stuntmen from the Moab area, where many westerns have been filmed, put on live demonstrations.

Moab is also the headquarters for two national parks: Arches National Park and Canyonlands National Park. **Dead Horse Point State Park** (Route 313, west of Route 163, 801–259–6511), an area with splendid views of the Colorado River and Plateau, is reached by crossing a narrow neck flanked by gorges more than 1,000 feet deep. The park's name recalls a herd of wild horses that were once driven onto the point. After the best few were captured, the remaining horses were left to find their way back to the open range. Confused by the terrain, the horses wandered in circles until they died of thirst on the bluffs high above the Colorado River.

ARCHES NATIONAL PARK

This 73,379-acre park contains the largest number of natural stone arches in the country—more than 966 arches standing with a light opening of three feet or larger—as well as a number of other scenic wonders. The arches were formed by erosion in the rock layers of sandstone that were deposited 140 to 230 million years ago. There is evidence that the prehistoric Fremont Indians used the park as a seasonal hunting ground, and the rock art was probably carved and drawn by the Pueblo people before A.D. 1200. Within the boundaries of the park at **Wolfe Ranch** is a cabin built in the late 1880s with a root cellar and corral. This is all that is left of the ranch established by John Wesley Wolfe, a disabled Civil War veteran, and his son. Arches became a national monument in 1929 and, after several major additions, a national park in 1971.

LOCATION: Route 191, 5 miles north of Moab. HOURS: *Visitor Center:* Mid-March through mid-October: 8–6 Daily; mid-October through mid-March: 8–4:40 Daily. FEE: Yes. TELEPHONE: 801–259–8161.

PRICE

The first settlers near the Price River were Mormon farmers in the late 1870s, but the discovery of coal early in the next decade and the completion of the railroad between Colorado and Salt Lake

OPPOSITE: *Turret Arch, seen through the South Window, two of the nearly 1,000 natural stone arches preserved in Arches National Park.*

City in 1883 brought in large numbers of non-Mormons of various racial and ethnic backgrounds. Coal mining created wealth, which attracted outlaws such as Butch Cassidy and his Wild Bunch. Price was on the Outlaw Trail and served as a supply point for these men. The only local holdup was that of the Pleasant Valley Coal Company payroll at Castle Gate on April 21, 1897, by Butch Cassidy and Elzy Lay, who were assisted by Joe Walker. Walker was followed by a posse to the upper Green River and killed on Moonwater Point on May 8, 1898. His body was brought back to Price for burial.

The **Price Municipal Building** (200 East Main Street) was constructed by the WPA in 1938–1939. A mural on the lobby wall depicts the pioneer history of Carbon County. Painted by the prominent Utah artist Lynn Fausett, the mural includes eighty-two life-size portraits of actual settlers. The international complexion of the community is reflected in two churches: The Byzantine **Hellenic Orthodox Church** (61 South 200 East) is noted for its icons and stained glass. Hanging from the center of the church's dome is a large brass and crystal chandelier. The **Notre Dame de Lourdes Catholic Church** (200 North Carbon Avenue) was built from 1919 to 1923 by an Italian priest, Father Alfredo F. Giovannoni. A Prairie-style building with a peaked roof, the church has a large rosette window over the entrance. Giovannoni was sent to Price to minister to the large Italian population. However, a number of French and French Basques contributed generously to the church's construction, and it was named in honor of their mother church in France.

A highlight of the varied collection at the **College of Eastern Utah Prehistoric Museum** (off 2d East, 801–637–5060) is four complete dinosaur skeletons, including the magnificent *Allosaurus* nicknamed Al, that were unearthed at the nearby Cleveland-Lloyd Dinosaur Quarry. There is also an outstanding collection of prehistoric Indian art and artifacts from the region, including a large mural of pictographs from Canyonlands National Park and the Pilling Figurines, eleven small unbaked Fremont clay figurines that probably date from the eleventh century.

The **Cleveland-Lloyd Dinosaur Quarry** (30 miles south of Price off Route 155, 801–637–4584) is a dinosaur graveyard run by the

Bureau of Land Management that has been open to the public since the 1960s. More than twenty-five dinosaurs in museums around the world have been reconstructed with bones from this quarry. Exhibits at the visitor center explain the ongoing excavations at the site.

HELPER

Although this town was first settled in 1870 by a Mormon, Teancum Pratt, who lived in a dugout with his two wives and prospected for coal, the combination of railroading and coal mining, and the diverse sort of workers those industries attract, made it one of the most defiantly non-Mormon towns in the state. Even today, with most of the mines closed and railroading greatly diminished, the town is proud of its one-time reputation as Utah's Little Las Vegas. Helper also claims to be the only town in the country named after a locomotive, the engine that helped the coal train ascend to Soldier's Summit.

The town's main attraction is the excellent, somewhat eccentric **Mining and Railroad Museum** (296 South Main Street, 801–472–3009), housed in a hotel owned by the railroad from 1942 to 1982. Gleaming railroad and mining equipment is displayed in the lot next door, including a 1918 caboose and a Sullivan Shortwall Machine used to undercut coal prior to blasting. Inside is an extensive model train set that took fifty years to build, old mining photographs and equipment, a 1930s dentist's office, oil paintings made during the late 1930s by WPA artists, and the wooden steps on which Butch Cassidy stood when he robbed a local mining company in 1897. Two rooms of the museum are devoted to two local mining disasters: the Winter Quarters disaster on May 1, 1900, in which 200 men and boys were killed, and the 1924 Castle Gate No. 2 mine disaster, which killed 171 miners and one rescuer. Many of those killed in both disasters were immigrants.

Historic markers on Route 6 just north of Helper indicate the locations of the town of **Castle Gate,** now gone, where the Butch Cassidy robbery—"one of the most daring daylight robberies"—took place, and also of the Castle Gate mine disaster.

NOTES ON ARCHITECTURE

SPANISH COLONIAL

SAN MIGUEL MISSION, NM

Spanish mission churches in the Southwest were provincial adaptations of Baroque forms transformed further by the use of local materials and labor. The style of New Mexico missions was greatly influenced by the building techniques of the indigenous Indians, and features massive, plain, windowless adobe walls, flat roofs with timbers supported on brackets, and clerestory windows lighting the altar, which is frequently made of polychromed wood.

GREEK REVIVAL

UTAH TERRITORIAL STATE HOUSE, UT

The Greek Revival manifested itself in severe, stripped, rectilinear proportions, occasionally a set of columns or pilasters, and even in a few instances Greek-temple form. It combined Greek and Roman forms—low pitched pediments, simple moldings, rounded arches, and shallow domes, and was used in public buildings and many private houses.

GOTHIC REVIVAL

SALT LAKE CITY ASSEMBLY HALL, UT

The Gothic Revival brought darker colors, asymmetry, broken skylines, verticality, and the pointed arch to American buildings. New machinery produced carved and pierced trim along the eaves. Roofs became steep and gabled; "porches" or "piazzas" became more spacious. Oriel and bay windows became common and there was a greater use of stained glass.

ITALIANATE

LAKE MANSION, NV

The Italianate style began to appear in the 1840s, both in a formal, balanced "palazzo" style and in a picturesque "villa" style. Both versions of the style had round-headed windows and arcaded porches. Commercial structures were frequently made of cast iron, with a ground floor of large arcaded windows and smaller windows on each successive rising story.

QUEEN ANNE

DEVEREAUX HOUSE, UT

The Queen Anne style emphasized contrasts of form, texture, and color. Large encircling verandahs, tall chimneys, turrets, towers, and a multitude of textures are typical of the style. The ground floor might be of stone or brick, the upper floors of stucco, shingle, or clapboard. Specially shaped bricks and plaques were used for decoration. Panels of stained glass outlined or filled the windows. The steep roofs were gabled or hipped, and other elements, such as pediments, Venetian windows, and front and corner bay windows, were typical.

RICHARDSONIAN ROMANESQUE

CITY COUNTY BUILDING, UT

Richardsonian Romanesque made use of the massive forms and ornamental details of the Romanesque: rounded arches, towers, stone and brick facing. The solidity and gravity of masses were accentuated by deep recesses for windows and entrances, by rough stone masonry, stubby columns, strong horizontals, rounded towers with conical caps, and repetitive ornament based on botanical models.

RENAISSANCE REVIVAL OR BEAUX ARTS

GOVENOR'S MANSION, UT

In the 1880s and 1890s, American architects who had studied at the Ecole des Beaux Arts in Paris brought a new Renaissance Revival to the United States. Sometimes used in urban mansions, but generally reserved for public and academic buildings, it borrowed from three centuries of Renaissance detail—much of it French—and put together picturesque combinations from widely differing periods. The Beaux Arts style gave rise to the "City Beautiful" movement, whose most complete expression was found in the late nineteenth– and early–twentieth century world's fairs in Chicago and San Francisco.

PUEBLO REVIVAL

SANTA FE MUSEUM OF FINE ARTS, NM

The Pueblo Revival features walls made of adobe, or made to look like adobe, and flat roofs with vigas (wooden beams that project beyond the exterior wall). Second and third stories are frequently set back, to resemble the pueblos that give this style its name. Beginning in the early years of the twentieth century in California, this style was frequently utilized during the 1910s and 1920s in New Mexico and Arizona in houses, school buildings, hotels, and public buildings in cities with a Hispanic past.

SPANISH COLONIAL REVIVAL

PIMA COUNTY COURTHOUSE, AZ

Inspired by Bertram Grosvenor Goodhue's designs for the 1915 Panama-California Exposition in San Diego, the Spanish Colonial Revival style relied on forms close to Spanish sources, including low pitched tile roofs, plastered walls, decorative iron grillwork, French doors leading to terraces and pergolas, and cast concrete or terra-cotta ornament. During the 1920s and 1930s, its greatest period of popularity, it was used throughout the Southwest, California, and Florida for houses and public buildings.

I N D E X

The editors gratefully acknowledge the assistance of Ann J. Campbell, Rita Campon, Didi Charney, Elizabeth Corra, Moira Duggan, Fonda Duvanel, Julia Ehrhardt, Max Evans, Ann ffolliott, Carol McKeown Healy, Ron James, Andy Mascih, Brigid A. Mast, Kathy Rosenbloom, Robert Torrez, Linda Venator, and Patricia Woodruff.

Composed in Basilia Haas and ITC New Baskerville by Graphic Arts Composition, Inc., Philadelphia, Pennsylvania. Printed and bound by Toppan Printing Company, Ltd., Tokyo, Japan.